Advance Praise for *A Few Bad Men*

"Among the many impressive military men and women I've met while producing such films as *American Sniper* and *Flags of Our Fathers*, Fred Galvin stands out as one of the most remarkable. Intelligent, honorable, and with an extraordinary list of accomplishments as a Marine, he is the real deal. His dramatic retelling of his experience as commander of Fox Company reads like a thriller— full of twists and turns—filled with unassuming heroes and deceitful villains. In dogged pursuit of justice for his Marines, Fred Galvin exemplifies the very essence of leadership and Corps Values."

—Rob Lorenz, Producer and Director for films
including *Letters from Iwo Jima*, *American Sniper*,
Flags of Our Fathers, *Mystic River*, *Trouble With
The Curve*, *The Marksman*, and *Gran Torino*

"Fred Galvin's story is a page turner that reads like the fanciful plot of an A-list Hollywood movie. It's an extraordinary cliffhanger that deserves attention, and shows just how dangerous 'fake news' can be, when no one is willing to stand up for the truth. This is a cautionary tale that should be read by all who are interested in politics, war stories, courtroom drama, and international affairs as this new world we're living in, where simple lies are being propagated as the truth, is sadly not one that is going away anytime soon."

—David Jung, Screenwriter and Director
of films including *Roam*, *The Possession
of Michael King* and *Genre Summit*

"*A Few Bad Men* reveals how the U.S. military, desperate to protect its public image at all costs, sometimes sacrifices the honor of men in combat. The country's first Marine special operations unit was falsely accused of killing Afghan civilians, then subjected to years of lies and deceit by top generals. The unit and its commander, retired Maj. Fred Galvin, were ultimately cleared of any wrongdoing, but not before their careers were ruined and their honor stained."

—David Zucchino, Journalist covering the 2008 MARSOC Court of Inquiry for the *Los Angeles Times*

"This book is a must read for every American who wants to know why, after *twenty* long years in Afghanistan, we did not win. This is a story how a small group of U.S. Marines counter-attacked multiple teams of deadly Taliban fighters during a complex enemy attack. These Marines were unfairly tried by a government-led prosecution who imposed a gag order and barred the press from most of the trial involving a deadly gun battle against a ruthless enemy. It's abundantly clear that good Marines were expediently sacrificed to advance the careers of senior officers. In these conditions, as their own top brass turned against them, what incentive was there for the best trained warriors in the world to win?"

—Jessie Jane Duff, retired U.S. Marine Gunnery Sergeant, Combat Veteran, and Political Analyst for *CNN* and *FOX News*

"We take for granted that our American heroes will be supported by their own country when sent off to war. In *A Few Bad Men*, Maj. Fred Galvin, USMC (Ret.), and Sal Manna detail the painful story of these seven heroes who, when their honor and freedom were on the line, found themselves abandoned by those they counted on most. It reads like a Hollywood blockbuster but, as Galvin tells in personal detail, it was sadly true. It's a story I was proud to report for local news in Los Angeles, and it's now a story every American should read for themselves."

—Jory Rand, Television Anchor with ABC7 in Los Angeles where he covered the MARSOC 7

"Pennsylvania Avenue is 'paved in politics' from Capitol Hill to The White House. But Fred Galvin has written a real page turner, that demonstrates how politics permeates The Pentagon and posts abroad...even for Marines who come under hostile fire on the battlefield—and off. I highly recommend this book."

—J.D. Hayworth, former Member of the U.S. House of Representatives for Arizona's 5th District, Television and Radio Show Host

"When Marine Special Operations Commander Maj. Fred Galvin went to Afghanistan, he knew, in his own words, that the fighting there was, 'violent, uncertain, complex, and ambiguous.' In 2007, when he and his company survived a massive Taliban ambush, Galvin felt successful. But a day later a Taliban-orchestrated disinformation campaign alleging war crimes—swallowed hook, line, and sinker by Galvin's Marine superiors—resulted in an abuse of the military justice system that lasted until Galvin and his Marines were vindicated in 2019. *A Few Bad Men* is a must-read story of valor, betrayal, and keeping the Marines' honor clean."

—Jed Babbin, former U.S. Air Force Staff Judge Advocate, former Deputy Under Secretary of Defense for Acquisition Planning; former Editor of *Human Events*; Commentator and Contributing

"I appreciate the initiative when Patriots write about our military heroes. This book is an incredible account and history of the fighting spirit of the 'Marine Raiders' under fire and the relentless fourteen-year campaign by their leader to clear their names and, 'keep their honor clean.' Many thanks to Fred Galvin for enlightening us!"
—Major General Paul Vallely, U.S. Army (Ret.), former Deputy Commander of the U.S. Pacific Command

"Major Fred Galvin has written an incredible account of how our front-line leadership overcame insurmountable odds. A must read for all leaders."
—Lieutenant General Thomas McInerney, U.S. Air Force (Ret.), former Assistant Vice Chief of Staff—Headquarters U.S. Air Force

"Simply put, *A Few Bad Men* captures the difficult nature of raising young men to fight our complex wars—from diverse backgrounds, cultures, and political beliefs—while expecting perfection and good decision making, while under fire, in such a short time. *A Few Bad Men* additionally illustrates the importance of proper training, leadership, and complete trust in the men and women on the ground fighting on the front lines. This book also shows us how big of a mistake it is to allow politics to get involved during investigations while some are chasing careers at any cost, and that there should be a separation between politics and war fighters to keep those actions that are distinctly different apart, and allow both sides to properly and honestly conduct their jobs. Major Galvin captures this well and explores the thoughts behind

rushed judgments, politics, and those on the ground simply doing their jobs the best they can."
—Sergeant Major Tom Satterly, U.S. Army (Ret.),
former Command Sergeant Major of a Joint
Special Operations Unit, Combat Veteran, Author,
Co-founder and Co-CEO of All Secure Foundation

"*A Few Bad Men* is a journey into the mindscape of the warfighter, fought first on the battlefield, then in the court of opinion, where politicians and Monday morning quarterbacks rule. I believe that 'the use of force produces many effects, not all of which can be foreseen.' This book is a powerful depiction of combat and a battle for justice and vindication. A must-read."
—Jason Van Camp, former U.S. Army Special
Forces Operational Detachment A-Team
leader, Combat Veteran, Executive Director—
Warrior Rising, Bestselling Author

"Major Galvin epitomizes 'no better friend, no worse enemy.' This book should be required reading for the next generation of leaders who want a real-world lesson in honor, courage, and commitment from the first commander in modern Marine Raider history."
—Nick Coffman, Journalist covering the MARSOC 7
case for Special Operations Forces Report (SOFREP);
served in the Marine Corps in Iraq as a Sergeant

"When America sends her Marines to war, we expect that our country will be as faithful to us as we are to our country; that our political and military leaders— those responsible for sending us to war—will have our backs; that we will always receive the benefit of doubt, especially in a war that we have been fighting for more than twenty years now—a war our political and military leaders seem unwilling to win, yet unable to leave. We sleep safely in our beds at night only because rough men stand ready to visit violence on those who would harm us. Major Fred Galvin is, and always will be, a Marine's Marine; driven, focused, and totally committed to mission and his Marines. Someone our political and military leaders should be humbled by, or at the very least faithful to—always."

—Perry Puccetti, retired Marine Corps
AH-1W Cobra Attack Helicopter Pilot,
current Executive Director of VMLY&R

"*A Few Bad Men* is a blistering, top-to-bottom critique of how senior Marine Corps leaders (and the institution itself) completely mishandled a situation in which members of a Marine Raider unit were falsely accused of war crimes. I found myself unconsciously squirming in my chair as I read Galvin's litany of shocking examples of failed leadership and unethical behavior by senior officers that illustrate the undeniable fact that he and his men were not only abandoned by the Marine Corps, but were subjected to a politically expedient 'witch hunt' that in some ways, continues to this day. I am hopeful that current Marine Corps leaders will publicly acknowledge the innocence of the MARSOC 7, and apologize for the grave injustices these brave Marines had to endure."

—Michael Ettore, retired Marine Corps
Infantryman, Drill Instructor, Infantry Officer, Combat
Veteran, Author, and retired from Kforce, Inc.

A
FEW
BAD
MEN

THE TRUE STORY *of* U.S. MARINES
AMBUSHED *in* AFGHANISTAN
and BETRAYED *in* AMERICA

A FEW BAD MEN

THE TRUE STORY *of* U.S. MARINES
AMBUSHED *in* AFGHANISTAN
and BETRAYED *in* AMERICA

MAJ. FRED GALVIN, USMC (RET.)
with SAL MANNA

A POST HILL PRESS BOOK

ISBN: 978-1-63758-413-2
ISBN (eBook): 978-1-63758-414-9

A Few Bad Men:
The True Story of U.S. Marines Ambushed in Afghanistan and Betrayed in America
© 2022 by Maj. Fred Galvin, USMC (Ret.) with Sal Manna
All Rights Reserved

Cover design by Cody Corcoran
Cover photo: Col. Paul D. Montanus receives a Legion of Merit award from Gen. James F. Amos, commandant of the Marine Corps, for his achievements while commanding Marine Barracks Washington during a change of command ceremony June 21, 2012. (Released by the United States Marine Corp with the ID 120621-M-OU625-002)

This is a true story. Some names have been changed to respect the privacy and security of the individual. Only unclassified or declassified information is contained within.

Post Hill
PRESS

Post Hill Press
New York • Nashville
posthillpress.com

Published in the United States of America
1 2 3 4 5 6 7 8 9 10

Dedicated to the late Congressman Walter Beaman Jones Jr. of North Carolina for relentlessly defending the MARSOC 7

"The essence of war is a violent struggle between two hostile, independent, and irreconcilable wills, each trying to impose itself upon the other."

—*Warfighting*, U.S. Marine Corps Doctrinal Publication MCDP-1, 1997

Contents

Foreword

by Lt. Col. Steve Morgan, USMC (Ret.)

Independence Day 2021
Sarasota, Florida

As I write this, almost twenty years have passed since the surprise attack of 11 September 2001. I was there, at the beginning, to see the start of this national heartbreak. I was assigned to Headquarters, United States Marine Corps (HQMC) at the Navy Annex. The Annex was designated Building One on the Pentagon Reservation and sat on a hill above the Pentagon and adjacent to Arlington National Cemetery. Our rally point, in case of an emergency evacuation, was the cemetery. Arlington National Cemetery is where I stood and watched the Pentagon burn. And I braced for war. Again. But this time, I doubted it would end in four days.

For the next two and a half years, I helped plan for war and ongoing operations as combat developed. Eventually, the opportunity came to return to combat operations. I'm a Marine. Duty called. Off I went. To Afghanistan, perhaps the most hauntingly beautiful place I've ever been. Beauty, horror, and heartbreak. Where, to paraphrase Tom Ricks, "combat diminished my soul." A story for another time.

When I was there, the Rules of Engagement (ROE) were not nearly so restrictive as they later became. As time went on, the ROE became ever more inhibiting, to the point that my friends/peers returning from the war started to question why we were even bothering to continue. The bad guys had an edge, gifted by United States Government policy. No matter. Now, let's do Counterinsurgency (COIN). And the ROE became tighter. Genius! Well, that worked. Didn't it?

And here we are. Approaching fifty years since Air America helicopters lifted the last evacuees off rooftops in Vietnam. Never again, we were told. As you read this story, my advice would be to remember that many of the flag officers of this war are the sons of flag officers of the Vietnam War. Never again? Oh, okay.

Before I cast too many stones, let me clarify and fully acknowledge I am an imperfect officer. Anyone that knows or served with me can surely affirm my imperfections. When I was a young captain, and field artillery battery commander, my first sergeant counseled me that I should try to be less controversial. He allowed that I spoke too freely, drank too much, had too many girlfriends, and permitted my subordinate officers to raise "too much hell." Guilty! I didn't and don't fit the mold of a career Marine Officer. But. I NEVER betrayed my soldiers, sailors, airmen, Marines, and allied troops I was privileged to command over the years.

This is a story of betrayal. Were it not for their own misperceived self-interest, the villains of this story could have been heroes and saved their integrity. They failed mightily, though they continue to walk this earth smugly continuing to earn a living based on their military resume.

Oddly, I was present at the beginning of the betrayal. I was in the room at HQMC where the root of the betrayal was planted. The core general staff officer leadership (at the three-star level) were meeting to discuss the implementation of what became the United States Marine Corps Special Operations Command (MARSOC) as directed by the late Secretary of Defense, Donald Rumsfeld and the high general Commandant of the Marine Corps (CMC), General James Jones. The gist of the meeting was, "this is a bad idea, and we need to find a way to get out of it." Some might find it curious, but nothing was said about not needing another "elite within an elite." It was a practical matter. This is going to cost money and manpower. Never mind that CMC said to get it done. Mind you, I was very much a backbencher in the room, but I was stunned. Within the Marine Corps, CMC has something of a godlike stature. I had never seen CMC openly defied and haven't since. Because of the decisions taken during that and subsequent meetings, the betrayal was assured. As MARSOC was initially implemented, money, manpower, internal/external, and most importantly moral support were withheld by the powers that were within the Marine Corps, petty stinginess without thought to the rifleman who bears the brunt.

I would ask the reader to bear in mind that although Kafkaesque in nature, this story is true. Aside from the author's autobiographical comments, this is a tale based on official documents and courtroom testimony. I was a panel member on the Court of Inquiry (COI) described herein. As it pertains to the COI, I am familiar with these official documents and sat through every second of courtroom testimony. I also asked a lot of questions of the witnesses. Nothing the author offers up is outside the bounds of truth. This story exemplifies the sort of venality and narcissism that has been allowed to infect our officer corps. I have been quoted in official Office of the Secretary of the Navy correspondence that this was a case of, "a perfect storm of toxic leadership." How did we get here? Is this "never again"?

So. Here we are, almost twenty years after the 11 September 2001 surprise attack. Was it really that long ago? Too often, I find myself again in Arlington National Cemetery. You know, visiting friends. I never fail to look back on that nightmare Tuesday and recall that this sacred ground is where the war started for me. Is the loss of life, limb, and mind in vain? I say no. Because we died, suffered, and continue to suffer for an ideal we believe in the United States of America and the Constitution. Was the enterprise itself worth it? I say no. Our leadership, civil and especially military, failed us. Again. Just like your fathers failed ours, you failed us. The game is up. We don't trust you anymore. And we don't like you. You lack proper moral hygiene and are in want of a shower. Don't you dare say "never again." You bastards!

This is a hard story to read. Because it happened as told, I'm proud to claim the Marines of Fox Company as friends and brother Marines. I'm always here for you.

Over the years, Fred Galvin and I have become close friends. During Christmas 2018 Fred spent the day with my family and me in central Pennsylvania and shared a meal fit for Vikings. The following day we toured Valley Forge National Historical Park. It was a stonking cold Pennsylvania's winter day and we were cloaked in modern-day fleece and technical outdoor gear. That battlefield walk was a stark physical reminder of what our earliest military predecessors, many clad in the thinnest of garments, lived through during a very tough winter. A memorable day completed with a beer and a burger at a nearby American Legion Post. We've walked the halls of Congress together, floated/fly-fished down the Bighorn River in Montana with the Bar X Project, and have talked countless hours on the phone. Fred is a classic combination of type A and type D personality, mission-focused and people-centric. For those familiar with General Lejeune's guidance on leadership and caring for the welfare and development of subordinates, Fred Galvin should come to mind. Fred has been called a cowboy. Well now, if that's the truth, then giddyap!

Fred Galvin is a God-fearing, truly decent human being, a good son, and one hell of a United States Marine.

Key Military Leaders 2006-2008

President George H.W. Bush Jr.	Commander-in-Chief
Doctor Donald Rumsfeld	Secretary of Defense
General Peter Pace, USMC	Chairman of the Joint Chiefs of Staff
General Doug Brown, US Army	Commander, Special Operations Command
Secretary Gordon England	Secretary of the Navy
General Michael Hagee, USMC	33rd Commandant of the Marine Corps
General James Conway, USMC	34th Commandant of the Marine Corps
General James Mattis, USMC	Commander, Marine Central Command (MARCENT)
Major General Dennis Hejlik, USMC	Commander, Marine Special Operations Command (MARSOC)
Colonel Pete Petronzio, USMC	Operations Officer, MARSOC
Lieutenant Colonel Paul Montanus, USMC	Commanding Officer, 2nd Marine Special Operations Battalion (2nd MSOB)

Major Scott Ukeiley, USMC	Executive Officer, 2nd Marine Special Operations Battalion (2nd MSOB)/ MARSOC LNO to the CJSOTF-A
Major Fred Galvin, USMC	Commanding Officer, Foxtrot, 2nd MSOB, MARSOC, one of the MARSOC 7
Colonel Christopher Haas, US Army	Commander, Combined Joint Special Operations Task Force – Afghanistan (CJSOTF-A)
Major General David Rodriguez, US Army	Commanding General, Regional Command - East
Colonel John Nicholson, US Army	Commanding Officer, 3rd Brigade/10th Mountain Division, RC-East
Master Sergeant David Young, USMC	Operations Chief/Senior Enlisted Advisor, Foxtrot Company, 2nd MSOB, MARSOC
Captain Sid East, USMC	Direct Action/Special Reconnaissance Platoon Commander, Foxtrot Company, 2nd MSOB, MARSOC – one of the MARSOC 7
Gunnery Sergeant Mike Clarke, USMC	Direct Action/Special Reconnaissance Platoon Sergeant, Foxtrot Company, 2nd MSOB, MARSOC, one of the MARSOC 7
Major General Francis Kearney, US Army	Commander, Special Operations Command Central (SOCCENT)
Colonel Patrick Pihana, US Air Force	Chief of Staff, SOCCENT and Preliminary Investigating Officer of the MARSOC 7 case
Colonel Mark Porter, USMC	MARSOC Court of Inquiry, President of the Panel
Colonel Eric Daniels, USMC	MARSOC Court of Inquiry Panel Member

Lieutenant Colonel Steve Morgan, USMC	MARSOC Court of Inquiry Panel Member
Sergeant Jack Lester, USMC	Turret Gunner in Vehicle One, one of the MARSOC 7
Sergeant John Klein, USMC	Turret Gunner in Vehicle Two, one of the MARSOC 7
Corporal Jeff Walker, USMC	Light Machine Gunner in Vehicle Two, one of the MARSOC 7
Sergeant Bill Pratt, USMC	Turret Gunner in Vehicle Six, one of the MARSOC 7
Staff Sergeant Marvin Milton, USMC	Counterintelligence Specialist, Foxtrot Company, 2nd MSOB
Haji Liwani Qomandan	Tribal Elder of the Shinwari tribe, Bati Kot, Afghanistan
Lieutenant Colonel Scott Jack, USMC	Military Defense Counsel for Major Galvin
Mark Waple	Civilian Defense Counsel for Major Galvin
Major Scott Woodard, USMC	Military Defense Counsel for Captain East
Knox Nunnally Sr.	Civilian Defense Counsel for Captain East
Major Kurt Sanger, USMC	U.S. Government Prosecuting Attorney – Court of Inquiry
Major Philip Sanchez, USMC	U.S. Government Prosecuting Attorney – Court of Inquiry
Congressman Walter B. Jones	Member, House Armed Services Committee

Acronyms and Terms

AO	Area of Operations
AOR	Area of Responsibility
CAS	Close Air Support (air to ground attack aircraft)
CENTCOM	Central Command (Middle East Region)
CJSOTF-A	Combined Joint Special Operations Task Force – Afghanistan (typically commanded by a colonel in Afghanistan)
CMC	Commandant of the Marine Corps
COC	Command Operations Center
COI	Court of Inquiry
CQB	Close Quarters Battle
DA	Direct Action (Raids)
DASR	Direct Action Special Reconnaissance (1st Platoon of Foxtrot Company)
HQMC	Headquarters Marine Corps
HMMWV	High Mobility Multi-Wheeled Vehicle
DOD	Department of Defense
ISAF	International Security Assistance Force (ISAF – highest level command in Afghanistan)
JAF	Jalalabad Air Field
JBAB	Jalalabad

JOC	Joint Operations Center
JTAC	Joint Terminal Attack Controller (controls aviation assets)
M-249	Light Machine Gun
M-4	Carbine Rifle
MARCENT	Marine Central Command (Marine Operations in the Middle East)
MARSOC	Marine Special Operations Command
MEU	Marine Expeditionary Unit (Foxtrot Company deployed with the 26th MEU aboard the *USS Bataan*)
MSOB	Marine Special Operations Battalion
MSOC	Marine Special Operations Company
NCIS	Naval Criminal Investigative Service
RC-E	Regional Command – East (Eastern Region of Afghanistan)
ROC	Reconnaissance Operations Center
SF	Special Forces (US Army Special Forces – Green Berets)
SFG	Special Forces Group (Commanded by an Army SF colonel)
SOCOM	Special Operations Command
SOTF	Special Operations Task Force (typically commanded by a lieutenant colonel or major in Afghanistan)
UCMJ	Uniform Code of Military Justice

Military Rank Structure of Personnel Mentioned in this Book

Officer Ranks (Abbrev. USAF, USMC, USA)	Service	Pay Grade
General (Gen/GEN)	USAF, USMC, USA	0-10
Lieutenant General (LtGen/LTG)	USAF, USMC, USA	0-9
Major General (MajGen/MG)	USAF, USMC, USA	0-8
Brigadier General (BrigGen/BG)	USAF, USMC, USA	0-7
Colonel (Col/COL)	USAF, USMC, USA	0-6
Lieutenant Colonel (LtCol/LTC)	USAF, USMC, USA	0-5
Major (Maj/MAJ)	USAF, USMC, USA	0-4
Captain (Capt/CPT)	USAF, USMC, USA	0-3
1st Lieutenant (1stLt/1LT)	USAF, USMC, USA	0-2

Enlisted Ranks (Abbrev. USMC, USA, USN)	Service	Pay Grade
Sergeant Major (SgtMaj/SGM)	USMC, USA	E-9

Master Sergeant (MSgt/MSG)	USMC, USA	E-8
Gunnery Sergeant (GySgt/Gunny)	USMC	E-7
Sergeant First Class (SFC)	USA	E-7
Chief Petty Officer (CPO)	USN	E-7
Staff Sergeant (SSgt/SSG)	USMC/USA	E-6
1st Class Petty Officer (PO1)	USN	E-6
2nd Class Petty Officer (PO2)	USN	E-5
Sergeant (Sgt/SGT)	USMC/USA	E-5
Corporal (Cpl/CPL)	USMC/USA	E-4
Specialist (SPC)	USA	E-4
Lance Corporal (LCpl)	USMC	E-3

Introduction

One reason I wrote this book was so that every American citizen would know how U.S.—led coalition forces had won a decisive victory against terrorists in Afghanistan by 2005 and yet lost the war, ignominiously bugging out in August 2021.

The frontline foot soldiers of the U.S. and coalition forces did not let us down. Rather, it was the words and inactions of senior military leaders who restrained and hamstrung tactical units, while repeatedly falsely testifying to Congress and the international press that the training of the Afghan National Army would lead to an effective exit strategy. This senior military officer mantra was reinforced with their repeated pleas to stay the course for just ten years, then twelve, then fourteen, until their "forever war" finally ended. In fact, the effort in Afghanistan lacked the ability to ever succeed in the way U.S. forces guided peace and democracy in Germany, Japan, or South Korea—and our senior military and Department of State leaders were fully aware of that. Yet they prevented the American people from knowing the on-the-ground truth.

Unfortunately, there will not be any accountability in this life for those leaders who squandered nearly twenty years, lost 2,325 service members Killed In Action, suffered 20,705 service members Wounded In Action, and spent more than one trillion dollars in Afghanistan—and only made the international terrorist threat worse. Unrestrained senior military officers unrepentantly used censure, threats of imprisonment, and professional devastation of their own forces to guide tactical units to play nice, ride out the deployment clock, and cooperate and graduate, so everyone would receive a "successful combat deployment" and end up getting promoted. All while losing a war.

With America threatened today by rival states and both internal and external non-state parties, our national defense is more important than ever. The twenty years that the Pentagon focused on the Middle East accelerated China and Russia's strategy to revitalize their military technologies and aim their 21st century information warfare directly at the United States with the intention of creating a "Divided States of America." The health of our national defense partly depends upon comprehensive policy changes to prevent the promotion and retention of military leaders who advocate and benefit from unwinnable strategies that needlessly sacrifice those who have served, are currently serving, and will serve.

Our military leaders must be accountable to us, the citizens. After all, our national defense is paid for in our blood and our dollars. We, the people, have been passed down an inheritance of freedom from our Founding Fathers that we should not and must not squander. When those leaders err, they should answer to us for their grievous mistakes.

I also wrote this book to aid the future of those who sacrificed so much. Much was paid and lost, which is irrecoverable. It is important for all of us who have endured dark valleys which were seemingly impossible to survive to assist our brothers and sisters by encouraging and supporting them in their trials. I am utterly humbled to have served beside the most dedicated warriors in the world. To them, I cannot express enough my gratitude; your faithful service will always be remembered. And to the parents of the one percent of Americans who answered their country's call, and especially to our nation's Gold Star families who paid the ultimate price of losing a son or daughter, without your support of their call of duty, America would cease to have the freedoms we enjoy. May God always bless you.

Yet perhaps the most important reason I wrote this book is you. Just as I have, every reader has or will eventually encounter your own life's crucible, whether difficulties in personal or professional relationships, health challenges or tragic accidents. In the end, this is a book about unflagging perseverance in the face of seemingly unconquerable odds and crushing adversity. I hope you will find reading my story will help you tackle the struggles in your own life.

Surely good shall overcome a few bad men.

—Maj. Fred Galvin, USMC (Ret.)

Condemned

7 January 2008
Camp Lejeune, North Carolina

As I walked toward the courtroom, I did my best to look calm and confident. A reporter's camera flashed in my eyes while news accounts of my "crimes" rang in my ears.

I wasn't surprised the media was present for the trial. Headlines around the world had already damned me as a poster child for American war crimes in Afghanistan. But with my future hanging in the balance, I wasn't about to show any weakness. I marched forward in my camouflage uniform, unmoved and resolute.

I had faced fear many times—in Iraq, Afghanistan and other war zones. Before battle, I prepared for fear and could set it aside. But on this day I faced a very different sort of battle, and inside I was gripped with a new kind of fear—fear of an enemy who wore the same uniform as I did.

I had been the commander of Fox Company, the first Marine Special Operations Company (MARSOC) in the Corps' 230-year history. I had led my men on what was supposed to be just another day and another routine mission. But on that day, Fox Company was ambushed. We found ourselves blown up by a suicide bomber and then under deadly fire from a coordinated, premeditated attack. We returned fire at our well-armed assailants, kept our heads on straight, and made it back inside the wire. I knew exactly what had happened that day on the road in Bati Kot.

But the media told a different story. According to news reports, we were mass murderers, shooting to death at least sixteen men, women and children as we rushed down the road. Some witnesses said we were drunk and had gone door-to-door to execute innocent people in revenge. The "Shinwar Massacre" allegedly claimed the highest number of civilian deaths and casualties due to direct fire by American forces in the entire Afghan war. Within a week, I was publicly humiliated and relieved of command, and my company was tossed out of the country, the first Marine unit ever booted from a combat zone.

I was thirty-eight years old, engaged to a woman I loved, and in the prime of my career. I was a major in the United States Marine Corps, a band of brothers I had joined right after high school. And now I was disgraced, about to face a military court.

United States v. Maj. Fred Galvin and Capt. Sid East would be only the second Court of Inquiry (COI) for the Marine Corps in more than fifty years. If the COI's three-member panel recommended us for court-martial and we were convicted, the penalty could range from a dishonorable discharge to prison time to death. And if we went down, so too would the rest of the MARSOC 7.

Officially, the COI was supposed to be just a fact-finding exercise. In reality, nearly everyone in power had already decided we were guilty. We had been condemned by a preliminary investigation, by the press, by politicians, and by some of the most powerful men in the U.S. military establishment.

Only two months after the ambush, while a criminal investigation was still ongoing, Army Col. John W. Nicholson said to a group of Afghan leaders, and later to the Pentagon press corps: "I stand before you today, deeply, deeply ashamed and terribly sorry that Americans have killed and wounded innocent Afghan people. We are filled with grief and sadness at the death of any Afghan, but the death and wounding of innocent Afghans at the hand of Americans is a stain on our honor and on the memory of the many Americans who have died defending Afghanistan and the Afghan people. This was a terrible, terrible mistake. And my nation grieves with you for your loss and suffering. We humbly and respectfully ask for your forgiveness."

Colonel John Nicholson, Commanding Officer 3rd Brigade, 10th Mountain Division, U.S. Army, Afghanistan 2006-2007 (Courtesy of 10th Mountain Public Affairs Officer)

The two highest-ranking Marines had also proclaimed us guilty, either of negligent homicide or dereliction of duty. Marine Gen. Peter Pace, chairman of the Joint Chiefs of Staff, called it "a nick on Marine pride, for sure." He said he had discussed the incident with the Marine Commandant, Gen. James Conway, and Conway was "clearly disappointed in the performance of those Marines." The Commanding General for all U.S. Marines in the Middle East, Lt. Gen. James Mattis, had ordered the COI to take place.

A few politicians piled on. Rep. Adam Smith (D-Wash.), chairman of the House of Representatives panel that oversaw Special Operations forces, told *The Washington Post* that there was "more than sufficient evidence of wrongdoing" and "at a minimum this was excessive force" by the Marines.

We were front page news. As journalists say, "If it bleeds, it leads."

3

16 Civilians Die as U.S. Troops Open Fire in Afghanistan

The New York Times
By Carlotta Gall

KABUL, Afghanistan, March 4 (2007) – American troops opened fire on a highway filled with civilian cars and bystanders today, American and Afghan officials said, in an incident that the Americans said left 16 civilians dead and 24 wounded as they fled the scene of a suicide car bombing in eastern Afghanistan...

"They were firing everywhere, and they even opened fire on 14 to 15 vehicles passing on the highway," said Tur Gul, 38, who was standing on the roadside by a gas station and was shot twice in his right hand. "They opened fire on everybody, the ones inside the vehicles and the ones on foot."

Six weeks later, the same reporter followed up in gory detail:

Marines' Actions in Afghanistan Called Excessive

The New York Times
By Carlotta Gall

KABUL, Afghanistan, April 14 (2007) — American marines reacted to a bomb ambush with excessive force in eastern Afghanistan last month, hitting groups of bystanders and vehicles with machine-gun fire in a rampage that covered 10 miles of highway and left 12 civilians dead, including an infant and

4

three elderly men, according to a report
published by an Afghan human rights commission on Saturday.

Families of the victims said this week
that they had demanded justice from the
American military and the Afghan government,
and they described the aftermath of the
marines' shooting, in Nangarhar Province.
One 16-year-old newly married girl was cut
down while she was carrying a bundle of grass
to her family's farmhouse. A 75-year-old
man walking to his shop was hit by so many
bullets that his son did not recognize the
body when he came to the scene…

"They committed a great cruelty; they
should be punished," said Ghor Ghashta, 65,
whose daughter-in-law was killed at the door
of their farmhouse compound, several hundred yards from the road and the scene of
the blast. The American troops were firing
from the road and raked the river bed where
workers were digging a ditch and the surrounding fields with gunfire, he and other
witnesses said.

The Associated Press, Washington Post, BBC, FOX News, and other media outlets around the world carried similar accounts.

This was not going to be a fair fight.

Entering the building and heading for the courtroom that Monday, I glanced into a large room on the left. A group of Marines was vigorously at work, writing notes beside names and photographs on whiteboards hanging on the walls, much as I had done when targeting terrorists we wanted to capture or kill. But the names and photographs were of me and my men in Fox Company.

Just like a battle. You try to game plan against the enemy. And, in this case, I was the enemy. It would be some time before I understood why.

As I sat stone-faced in that stark military courtroom in Camp Lejeune, North Carolina, a stoic Marine with a high and tight haircut, hardened by combat and the Corps during two decades in uniform, I steeled myself for what was to come.

I thought to myself, "I don't stand a chance."

Contact!

4 March 2007
Bati Kot District, Afghanistan

The sun was barely rising at 0600 on the rainy, windy Sunday morning of March 4th as we set out from our Camp Raider base at the Jalalabad airfield. We were headed toward Torkham Gate, thirty miles to the east, in Nangarhar Province just on the Afghan side of the border with Pakistan.

An Afghan National Army soldier trained by Fox Company
with the backdrop of the Tora Bora Mountains

Our mission was to scout the area for possible routes into the Tora Bora area of the White Mountains. Hopefully, with the snow melting, we could uncover trails from the flat, desolate, moonlike desert floor to the higher elevations that we could use to insert reconnaissance teams in the future.

Sid East, the platoon commander, looked like Captain America—in his late twenties, blonde-haired and blue-eyed—and led the patrol. As a major, I was expected to stay at the company's command center to oversee any operation, but this day I felt I needed to "leave the wire," venture outside the base, to put my eyes on the ground before I sent my men there. I wanted to see for myself the terrain, the avenues of approach, and areas of cover and concealment. I wanted to know the lay of the land firsthand.

Best known for being the hideout of Osama bin Laden following the attacks of September 11, Tora Bora was what a Marine major would call "a very complex threat environment" and what a civilian would call "one helluva bad neighborhood." Though no one believed Osama was still in Tora Bora, Torkham Gate was nevertheless a significant pile of dust in the desert. The primary border crossing for American supply convoys and the second busiest border crossing in all of Afghanistan, Torkham Gate was also a major entry point for jihadists entering the country from their training sanctuaries in Pakistan, thanks to a paved highway built by the U.S.

Considered the most dangerous road in the world, Highway 1 was rightly nicknamed Hell's Highway. The only direct route between the capital cities of Kabul in Afghanistan and Islamabad in Pakistan, the road was plagued by armed robberies, kidnappings, and extortion shakedowns, along with militant attacks on U.S. convoys carrying fuel, food, and supplies.

Controlling that corridor was essential for Al-Qaeda, the Taliban, and their sympathizers. Border guards and tax collectors were bought off, and the elders of villages along Hell's Highway were paid generous bribes to allow access, or they succumbed to brutal coercion and intimidation.

A beheading here or there had a way of encouraging cooperation.

To dissuade coalition forces from interfering, the militants used suicide bombers and Improvised Explosive Devices (IEDs) to sow fear among our troops. Commanders grew hesitant to venture outside the wire because of the danger to their soldiers as well as civilians.

As a result, Al-Qaeda and the Taliban could avoid the treacherously steep snow-covered passes of the White Mountains, with its summits of more than fourteen thousand feet, which they crossed on foot or horseback to smuggle poppy into Pakistan or jihadists into Afghanistan. They could simply drive their cars and trucks on Hell's Highway.

Bati Kot, the first village inside Afghanistan as you crossed the border on Hell's Highway, was a strategic logistical hub for the Taliban. They owned Bati Kot, and surrounding villages such as Spin Pul, having fully established a shadow government through the area's tribal elders. Foreign fighters flowed through the border control point, and then their Taliban handlers would coordinate their missions across Afghanistan.

Three weeks earlier, just after we had arrived in Afghanistan, intelligence assets had informed us that four men recently radicalized and sworn to be suicide bombers had entered the area from Pakistan. We knew who they were and where they were—they were in Bati Kot.

But we could not go after them on March 4. That day we were a Level Zero mission—we were supposed to do little or, better yet, nothing except show our faces to the populace.

Level Zero meant there was no coordination needed with adjacent troops, which would have been Level One, and certainly no expectation of kinetic or direct action, such as killing or capturing any enemy, which was Level Two. A Level Zero was so inconsequential that if the command did not object to the Concept of Operations (CONOP) we submitted beforehand, we were good to go.

My commander, Army Col. Christopher Haas, Combined Joint Special Operations Task Force – Afghanistan (CJSOTF-A), warned me that he didn't want a repeat of Operation Red Wings when a four-man Navy SEAL team was ambushed in June 2005 in the province to the north.

Three were killed in action, leaving seriously wounded Marcus Luttrell the lone survivor (his book about the incident would be published two years later). The tragedy became even worse when the helicopter sent to rescue them was shot down, killing the eight-man crew and eight more SEALs.

The imposing, broad-shouldered Haas said he didn't want another such debacle under his watch and insisted that we stay out of trouble.

Back on the hardball road of Hell's Highway, our convoy of six Humvees carried twenty-seven Marines, most of them experienced combat veterans from the elite 2nd Force Reconnaissance Company, plus two Navy corpsmen and an Afghan interpreter. We moved uneventfully through the Mar Koh bazaar, a cluster of small shops and market stands, outside Bati Kot. A couple of hundred villagers, young and old, men and women, as well as children, strolled through the busy bazaar alongside the road as we passed. Unlike the boys and girls happily running around and waving at us, most of the adults paid little attention.

Just another day on Hell's Highway.

I sat behind the platoon sergeant, Gunnery Sgt. Mike Clarke, a hard-nosed veteran of Iraq, Somalia, and Yemen, who was in the passenger seat in Vehicle Six. From my position, I could bird-dog the mission, viewing all the "chariots" in front of me, each 150 to 200 feet apart.

At 0645, we arrived at the coalition base at Torkham Gate, where I had arranged to meet Lt. Chelsea Gabel, the platoon commander for the Army's 66th Military Police. Gabel had been stationed there for about a year and presumably had information that could be valuable to us newcomers. Communicating by voice or email was not enough for me. I wanted to interact face-to-face.

I didn't like what I saw. As we exited our vehicles, we were stunned to watch her troops rehearsing for a mission later that morning. We were stunned because the base was on low ground, in plain sight of any daytime observer in the surrounding mountains. Her troops were clearly telegraphing their intention to move onto Hell's Highway.

Surprise turned to dismay when we saw what they were rehearsing. Whenever her sergeant yelled "Contact front!" or "Contact right!" or "Contact left!" the turret gunner, encased in a big bubble helmet and wearing an explosive-resistant suit, dropped down into his vehicle out of sight. They were training to duck and run! Their slogan should have been "death before dismount." Apparently, they didn't realize they were also training the enemy, emboldening them to attack because there was no fear that the Americans would fire back.

Gabel, disheveled, her dark hair a wild mess and her boots unlaced, as if she had just rolled out of the bag, briefed us about the local warlords and the opium trade funding the jihadists. This area was the second most important for the cultivation of poppy in the country, behind only Helmand Province. But that was it. She didn't say anything about nearby terror cells, including the one our other intelligence sources had identified.

She seemed satisfied for her troops to patrol rather than probe.

I shook my head in disappointment.

Unlike Gabel, I believed in total commitment to the mission. In Iraq, I had earned the unflattering nickname Filthy Fred because I was so busy doing pre-mission planning, executing missions, and creating post-mission reports that I rarely showered.

"Man, what's that smell?" one of my fellow captains once asked, sniffing the air. He looked at me. "Geez, it's you!"

My mom wouldn't have liked the name, but I took a perverse pride in being Filthy Fred. There was no time for a shower, not when the bad guys were shooting at us and placing bombs on the roads, in the desert, in cars, on motorcycles, and even in animals, to blow us up and burn us to bits. In the hierarchy of what-needs-to-be-done-right-now, personal hygiene was low on my list.

Leaving Torkham Gate at about 0800, with the rain stopped and the wind having died down, we conducted our visual reconnaissance south into the foothills for about an hour, checking out trails that were growing increasingly muddy from the recent snowmelt.

Heading north on dirt roads, we then passed through a series of very small villages. At the first one, the people seemed friendly, smiling and waving at us. At the second, closer to Hell's Highway, the people briefly glanced at us but then turned away. At the third, the people saw us and quickly pulled whoever was with them back into their houses. That was odd—and ominous.

We hung a left and returned to Hell's Highway, driving west past large, walled compounds we were told were home to Afghan warlords. There was a lot more traffic than earlier, with some drivers playing cat and mouse with us, seeing how we would react when they would drive toward us.

When a large white bus accelerated and sped directly towards the convoy, Sgt. Alberto Ruiz, the gunner on top of Vehicle Three, tensed and gently laid his finger on the trigger of his medium machine gun. If the bus posed a threat, Ruiz was ready to fire.

But that would be the last resort. The military had recently adopted a new Escalation of Force (EOF) doctrine as part of our Rules of Engagement (ROE).

When confronted by a vehicle, we were supposed to first go through a series of nonlethal actions, beginning with yelling and waving our arms to motion them away. If that didn't get the driver to pull off to the side and stop, sometimes the turret gunners would launch a small pen-sized flare or throw a water bottle or a rock. Though they were neither approved nor condoned, rocks were stored in ammo boxes for just such cases. Denting a hood or cracking a windshield usually persuaded a driver.

If the driver still didn't yield, only then could we fire into the ground in front of the vehicle or shoot into the engine to disable the vehicle.

Last on the list?

Shoot through the windshield to kill the driver.

As Ruiz, a street-smart thirty-something from Puerto Rico, targeted the bus through his gunsight, Sgt. Jack Lester, the cool-handed twenty-three-year-old from Boston who was the turret gunner in Vehicle One, threw a rock that smashed one of its front windows. The bus pulled off the road and stopped.

Ruiz raised his finger off the trigger. A rock was better than a bullet, he figured.

Presumably, the bus driver agreed.

On our way back to Jalalabad, we again approached Bati Kot, where I hoped for a meet and greet with key tribal elders. They probably wouldn't tell us much, but perhaps we'd at least get a sense of what was going on in the town. We would drink some *chai* and maybe make some personal connections that could help our intelligence gathering in the weeks ahead.

This wasn't our first "get to know you" mission.

A few days earlier, we had traveled to a small village near Khogyani, where we'd set up a forward operating base for Fox Company, to suss out the elders in that area.

Along with Staff Sergeant Marvin Milton, who was part of our intelligence team, I hatched a scheme to try to get as much useful and reliable information from them as possible: I allowed him to pose as the commanding officer.

With the elders focused on Milton as the leader, perhaps they or other villagers would let their guard down a bit with the rest of us. Also, rather than being tied up with the hospitality of a tea ceremony, which the chitchatty Milton was far better at than I, tight-lipped Fred could move around more freely and take the temperature of the village.

I knew that tribal elders were just that—the eldest of the tribe. The true power, the muscle, was the Al-Qaeda and Taliban shadow government, which would never sit down to sip *chai* with the Americans. They would try hiding in the crowd around the edges of our meet and greet so they could do the same thing I was—gauge the strengths and weaknesses of the enemy. We were engaged in a strange dance, *mujahideen* and Marines, each of us thinking we were leading.

I could tell who the warlords and fighters were not only because their harsh experiences were written on their tough leathery faces but because the faces of the ordinary villagers registered fear when they approached. The heads of those villagers were in the hands of the militants behind the scenes.

The elders were their pawns, helping the insurgents sniff out the new boys in town. Recognizing that we wore different uniforms than the Army, they were very curious as to who the Marines were in the grand scheme of the American military. They asked what we were doing in their neck of the desert since, as the elders told us point blank, "There are no Taliban here."

That was interesting because simultaneously our teams of linguists were picking up chatter that the elders were assessing us on behalf of the

Taliban! But, as with most Level Zero missions, the visit went off without incident, and we departed as peacefully and pleasantly as we had come.

Now as we neared Bati Kot, I was gripped with an uneasy feeling. This wasn't a vague sense of foreboding; an actual shiver went up my spine.

Road in the vicinity of Bati Kot—near the ambush site

As we drove down the highway, something didn't look right.

Unlike earlier that morning, the shrouded women and barefoot children on the road leading to the Mar Koh bazaar were gone. As we entered the village of Spin Pul in the Shinwar District, we saw only males, dozens of them, mostly of military age, lined up on each side of Hell's Highway, all facing the road as though they were waiting for a parade to begin.

Or maybe a funeral.

My pulse raced like it had before every battle in Iraq.

Suddenly, without saying a word to each other, everyone in the convoy was on high alert. They sensed the danger too.

We scanned the bazaar, the alleys, the rooftops, the vehicles approaching and passing, and the hands of the Afghan men, looking for any unnatural bulges pushing against their *shalwar kameez*, the overcoats baggy enough to conceal weapons or explosives.

The time was exactly 0903.

"WATCH OUT!"

The instant those words erupted from my mouth, I heard a BOOM! and a WHOOSH!

A shock wave rushed through space and hammered me in the chest, knocking the breath from my lungs.

Ahead of me, a massive yellow and orange fireball shot a couple hundred feet into the sky, scorching the branches of nearby trees and sending thick black smoke in all directions.

It was an enormous explosion, the largest any of us had ever experienced. The force of the blast could be felt three football fields away.

As jagged bits of scorched metal fell like rain on our windshield, Vehicle Two vanished from my sight, swallowed by the dark cloud billowing outward in waves from the explosion. I suspected it had been hit by a Suicide Vehicle Borne Improvised Explosive Device, i.e., a car bomb, or perhaps synchronized IEDs from both sides of the road.

I radioed Vehicle Two, but there was no response.

I had surely lost men, probably every one of the five Marines in that chariot—Sgt. Miguel "Miggy" Ortega, the driver; Sgt. John Klein, the turret gunner; Cpl. Jeff Walker, the radioman; Sgt. Beau Harley, our attack controller coordinating the ground mission; and Staff Sgt. Joey Doyle, one of East's team leaders. No one could have lived through a blast that ferocious.

Looking ahead from Vehicle Three, Milton told East sitting in front of him, "Vehicle Two is gone."

He later recalled that "(we) went from an easy-going, standard day to 'Are we all going to make it home tonight?'"

Sgt. Ron Reece in Vehicle One heard the deafening explosion and said "the bomb was close enough that I could feel its heat. I thought I was dead. I thought there was no way I'd make it through this and everybody in our vehicle would be killed also."

My heart leaped into my throat. I had never before lost a man under my command—and now I had failed in my duty to these Marines, these brothers-in-arms, with whom I had trained shoulder to shoulder for more than a year.

Together, we had reached the highest level of combat arms in the Marines. We were the best of the best, the first Marines in special operations. Every one of my Marines was doing the job he wanted to do, the job he was proud to have been given the chance to do.

After the explosion, it flashed across my mind that, for the first time, I would bring home Marines, my Marines, in body bags.

Thousands of Bullets

22 January 2008
Jalalabad, Afghanistan
Camp Lejeune, North Carolina

"I swear by the name of Allah and I swear to the Koran that whatever I say is going to be the one hundred percent truth."

So said Haji Liwani Qomandan, an elder of the Shinwari tribe, and the star witness for the prosecution at the COI. His story, and the photo of his shot to pieces car, had appeared on the front page of every major newspaper in the world the day after the ambush.

Overweight, with a gray beard, about forty-five years old, wearing traditional Afghan garb—including the *pakol*, the round-topped hat—he testified via a live video feed from an office at the Jalalabad airfield. As I stared at him on the screen from my chair in the Camp Lejeune courtroom, almost a year after March 4, my back went rigid.

Qomandan related that during the Afghan war against the Russians, he had joined the jihad against the occupiers, becoming a *mujahideen*.

"I do not have any actual military training; but, yes, I was involved in jihad," he said through an interpreter.

His name was also a clue to his past. Haji meant he had done his pilgrimage to Mecca. Liwani meant "crazy." Qomandan translated as "commander."

He said he'd joined the resistance "because the Russians occupied Afghanistan by force.... I was a group leader.... There were anywhere to a hundred people, sometimes less and more.... They were just a tribe, you know, villagers, and they were not registered soldiers because we were not paying them." In that conflict, he lost the lower part of his left leg and part of his right foot. "I stopped fighting when the Russians left the country," he said.

With the Taliban assuming power, Qomandan said he moved with his family across the border to Pakistan. "There were civil war in the country and Pakistan was safer," he explained. They returned to Afghanistan, to Nangarhar Province, with the rise of the new government, and Qomandan opened a number of businesses. He became a relatively wealthy man and was currently residing in a large compound.

On the morning of March 4, Qomandan recounted that he was driving his blue Toyota Prado SUV near Highway 1 with his father and a twelve-year-old nephew. Normally, he would have one of his eight sons do the driving, because of his war injuries. But that day he was in the driver's seat heading to the Mar Koh bazaar to purchase fertilizer for his cattle ranch before going on to Jalalabad to pay for fuel he had obtained earlier for the gas stations he also owned. Stuffed in five packets in the dashboard glove compartment were 500,000 Afghanis, the equivalent of 10,000 U.S. dollars.

He said he stopped his Prado on a dirt road as he neared Hell's Highway, so he could let pass a bulldozer, used in a construction project in the riverbed, which had pulled out in front of him.

Then the Marines started shooting.

Though *The New York Times* quoted him saying, "I heard the blast. I stopped the car," at the COI he insisted he never heard an explosion. In either case, he said he did not see the convoy until the Marines began firing.

"They were just shooting to everyone. That is all they were doing," he told the court. "When they started heading to my vehicle...my first window broke down... Then my father got hit, my nephew got hit, and I got hit and I knew right away that I was in danger."

Shot twice between his shoulder and lower back, with blood soaking his clothes, he said he dropped to the floorboard, opened the door, and scrambled out to hide behind a mound of sand.

After the shooting stopped, "they brought my father dead body and my nephew dead body to my home and they moved me to a small hospital or clinic in Mar Koh and they put some bandages on my back to help me out."

By 2 p.m., his father, Zarpadshah, and nephew, Farid Gul, were buried in the family cemetery in the village of Spin Pul.

"Why were they buried so quickly, sir, if you don't mind my asking?" asked the court's legal advisor, Marine Col. Dan Lecce, a pit bull of a lawyer who still looked like the stumpy muscled college wrestler he had been. As the legal advisor, his role was to perform many of the same functions as an impartial judge and also be an unbiased questioner.

"Because they were hit by thousand(s) of bullets from you guys," answered an irritated Qomandan. "And their bodies were just in small pieces, so we couldn't wait longer."

Islamic law also required that the dead be buried before sunset, and with the head pointed toward Mecca.

"Other than your father and nephew, I know were killed," Lecce continued, "did you know anyone else in the immediate area who was killed or wounded?"

Qomandan threw his hands up and spoke rapidly.

"I was absolutely in a very, very panic state and I was shocked because, you know, my clothing was like all bloody. And I couldn't think or see anyone at this time because I was just thinking about myself at that moment."

Lecce nodded in agreement.

"And, sir, did you learn of any women or children being wounded or killed on the 4th of March?"

Qomandan also nodded.

"Because this is a very important highway, there are some people even from other provinces from all over the country that were either wounded or killed. Among those, I heard that three women were killed and some children were killed as well and wounded as well."

He was an innocent man, he said, merely a bystander.

Lecce asked, "Did you or anyone in your vehicle intend to attack U.S. forces on the 4th of March?"

"No," Qomandan said adamantly. "We never had intention on the 4th of March, not before that, and not now, and not ever because this is something we don't do."

"Do you own any weapons?" Lecce asked.

"No, I do not have any weapons because I do not need to have any weapon."

That seemed a little flippant, so Lecce probed further: "It is still a dangerous area. Why don't you need them?"

Qomandan smiled just a little.

"Where I live it is very safe and secure and there is nothing happen wrong."

He was pressed again, but he held his ground.

"If I had weapon in my vehicle then where have that weapon gone? Either you guys could let me have it or the Afghan police have it. I have no weapon. It was me, my father, and my nephew. They were killed and I was injured and I had no weapon in my vehicle. We did not attack the coalition."

Lecce expanded his question: "Did you see *any* anti-coalition force or personnel attacking the U.S. convoy?"

"No, sir," Qomandan said with a strong voice. "I have not seen anyone to attack your American convoy because, you know, earlier, today, at the beginning, I swear to Koran and Allah, and I would never lie to you."

Scrunching up his lips and briefly closing his eyes, the brawny Lecce was nearly in tears.

"Thank you. And I express my condolences," he said, his voice cracking, "for the loss of your father and your nephew and the pain in your community."

Fight Your Way Out of a Fight

4 March 2007
Bati Kot District, Afghanistan

Minutes before the explosion, Lester, in Vehicle One leading the convoy, had waved off the road a couple of cars who drew near us in Spin Pul. But a Toyota HiAce light commercial van did not heed his hand gestures. Passengers in a taxi behind the van wondered why it was not pulling over and stopping. The driver must be crazy, they thought.

The oncoming van maneuvered to the right of Vehicle One and Reece caught a glimpse of the driver—a middle-aged man with a big white beard.

Suddenly, the van accelerated and made a sharp left. Its tires squealing, the HiAce screeched to a stop—about fifteen feet in front of Vehicle Two.

The driver may have then said a quick prayer of martyrdom before he pushed a button, or connected two wires, that detonated what was inside the back of the van—an IED composed of fuel oil, ammonium nitrate (a fertilizer), and mortars. We will never know exactly what he said or did because he was instantly blown to kingdom come.

Rocked by the explosion, Vehicle Two swerved into the fireball and disappeared.

East ordered Cpl. Jon Hackett, his driver in Vehicle Three, to back up a little to give them room to protect and defend. In front of Vehicle

Two, Vehicle One stopped while the four behind Vehicle Two spread out in a herringbone formation, turning to position themselves left and right at 45-degree angles to each other.

For a few excruciating seconds, we waited, wondering what was next.

And, shoving painful thoughts of the loss of five Marines to the back of my brain, I went to work trying to get the rest of us out of there alive.

I sent voice and text transmissions to our operations center at Jalalabad and Special Operations headquarters at Bagram:

"Troops in contact! Troops in contact!"

Then, as the smoke slowly began to clear, coming into focus through the dusty haze—I saw Vehicle Two, still on its wheels!

Miraculously, it appeared to be intact. But was anyone inside alive? Klein the turret gunner, a big strappin' hoss of a twenty-five-year-old from Mississippi, was nowhere to be seen, and I could not raise anyone on the chariot's radio.

In front of Vehicle Two was the incinerated van, grotesquely twisted and smoldering metal. The bomber? His body parts were splattered onto the Humvee that had been his target.

Deet deet deet...deet deet deet...deet deet deet...

I heard the distinct sound of AK-47s fill the air. Vehicle Two was now taking automatic weapons fire.

This was not a simple suicide bombing. We were being ambushed.

And we were pinned down in a kill zone.

4 March 2007, Bati Kot Ambush site overview

But we were not about to hit the gas and run. We were Marines. Trained to fight our way out of a fight.

From a dirt side road near a dry riverbed, a blue Toyota Prado SUV sped perpendicularly toward the convoy. Was the driver hurtling towards us with death and destruction in his heart and mind? Was this another suicide bomber, another "martyr" from the terror cell that had been identified in Bati Kot?

As the driver sped closer, three men leaned out the windows, their AK-47s bursts flames sputtered from the muzzles as they fired at our patrol.

A helmet popped up in Vehicle Two's turret.

Klein!

He pulled himself up into the turret. He was alive, but he was on fire.

Knocked down to the floor of the Humvee by the blast, hot shrapnel had ignited his body armor. After beating his chest with his hands to put out the flames, and with the whiz and crack of rounds flying over his head, he grabbed hold of his turret-mounted M240B machine gun and fingered the trigger.

Klein's voice thundered, "Contact left!" and he fired.

He did not "spray and pray." "Aim small, miss small" had been our mantra in training. His flurry of bullets punched through the SUV's thin aluminum skin, shredding the attackers and bringing the vehicle to an abrupt halt.

The driver leaped into a ditch. The dead bodies of his passengers lay slumped where they had sat.

Then there was silence.

I saw Klein wave his left arm in a circle above his head, in a big 'O,' as a combat diver would after surfacing to indicate he was okay.

Fortunately, the explosion had not only gone off prematurely but upwards, through the van's roof, rather than horizontally to impact Vehicle Two. The blast took out the vehicle's radio communications, but a few hasty hand and arm signals got the message across: Everyone in Vehicle Two was okay, and they were good to go.

I did not have time to be grateful. We needed to get out of the kill zone.

To my amazement, Vehicle Two's engine kicked in and rumbled.

With the chariot inching forward under its own power, the convoy reformed and moved ahead. The bomber's apparent plan to destroy Vehicle Two and separate the others so the attackers could swarm us with superior numbers—a classic tactic of divide and conquer—had failed.

At least so far.

Klein shouted again, this time, "Contact right!"

We were receiving a fresh onslaught of small arms fire, from the north, the right side of the road. Bullets ricocheted off tree trunks and cut down branches that fell across the road. I could hear the *ping ping ping* of bullets glancing off our vehicles.

Half a dozen or more of the attackers ran single file against a wall, maneuvering in concert, some shooting while others advanced closer to us by using prepared positions where they had cover. This was their turf and they knew what to do and where to go.

They had been expecting us. Our attackers were not angry goat herders taking potshots at the invaders with rusty Soviet bolt-action rifles. These were men with the fearlessness of religious zealots engaged in a coordinated assault.

Suddenly, a figure stood up in Vehicle Two's rear unroofed crew compartment. It was Walker!

The boyish twenty-year-old from Georgia hefted his M-249 light machine gun to his shoulder and let fly at the attackers. He then ducked behind the side armor protection of the vehicle to avoid the return fire.

Meanwhile, Harley helped Klein reload by handing him a second can of 7.62mm linked ammunition. Swinging his machine gun to the right, Klein let loose holy hell. After a few added bursts from Lester, the outgunned attackers broke contact and dispersed across the riverbed, away from us.

Again, except for the sound of our engines, there was silence outside our chariots.

East asked for ACE reports—Ammo, Casualty, and Equipment—from each of our vehicles. We needed to know the damage done and what was available in case we were attacked again, which seemed likely.

Meanwhile, I texted Jalalabad: "VBIED SAF RETURNED FIRE BROKE CONTACT NO CASUALTY REPORT NO VISIBLE BDA CONTACT FROM ENEMY WAS FROM BOTH SIDES OF THE ROAD." (SAF was Small Arms Fire, BDA was Battle Damage Assessment.)

The Jalalabad watch officer forwarded the message to Maj. Scott Ukeiley, our MARSOC liaison officer in Bagram, via secure email. But he received no response from the major.

He then called Ukeiley on a secure phone line. Still, no response.

Eventually reaching him on Ukeiley's personal mobile phone, the major said he had not been at his desk because he was in the break room. Since Ukeiley was on an unsecure phone, the watch officer could only tell him to log onto his classified internet account. Back at his desk, Ukeiley checked his email and finally learned that Fox Company had come in contact with the enemy. He forwarded my message up the chain of command. He also used his unsecure phone to call Master Sgt. Dave Young, my senior enlisted advisor in the operations center in Jalalabad, to ask for more information about the attack.

"Gunny answered and I said, 'Who is that?'" Big Dave remembered at the COI.

"'It's Maj. Ukeiley,'" he was told.

"I told him to 'get off that phone,'" Young bellowed in an impossibly deep voice befitting a six-foot, five, 270-pounder. "'We will not talk about that stuff on that phone. Tell him he will get the information when we are able to give it to him. I'm not going to beat up the men who are out there in contact and add to the confusion. He (Galvin/East) has enough things going on, worrying about his men and enemy and everything else.'"

Following Capt. East in Vehicle Three, Vehicle Four rolled past the bomb site. The latter's Sgt. Imran Khan, a New York City native born of Egyptian parents, later spoke about the horrific damage caused by the explosion.

"I observed what appeared to be a taxicab on the left-hand side of the road with a group of people... There was one male on the road side of the vehicle with his hands up, and to signify to us that he didn't have any weapons on him. Behind him in the rear...I saw what appeared to be a woman...

on the dirt... I observed three (other) personnel there. Two of them were men. The first man appeared to be fine. The second male (he) appeared that he didn't have a face. It was covered in complete blood, and then that last one I didn't really get a good look at."

He took a deep breath, trying not to show any emotion.

Just the facts, the brutal facts.

"They were yelling. They were screaming."

After Vehicle Five moved through, my Vehicle Six made its way past the large black scorch mark left on the pavement from the car bomb. The van's charred skeleton rested nearby, the metal still smoking from the intense heat.

Remnants of the suicide car bomb that detonated on Fox Company (Courtesy of *Associated Press*)

Nearing the shot-up Prado, I saw its three bloody bodies, including one slumped through the window of the rear right passenger seat, the man's AK-47 on the ground outside the door. Sgt. Bill Pratt, my turret gunner, a wiry kid with reddish-blonde hair who hailed from Mississippi like Klein, also saw something else—someone crouching in the ditch next to the Prado.

The man was holding an AK-47 and aiming it at our vehicle. Just as the Afghan fired, Pratt fired too.

I saw the man fall backward into the ditch but I didn't know if he'd been hit or perhaps killed.

Many months later, I would see Haji Liwani Qomandan again and tell Pratt how disappointed I was with him. Failing to kill Qomandan was poor marksmanship.

The immediate threat was eliminated, but the fight wasn't over. Drivers in other vehicles attempted to weave in and out of our convoy as we proceeded on Hell's Highway. Trying to deter any threats posed by them, Klein fired rounds into the pavement and into the engine blocks of approaching cars that did not heed his hand signals to pull to the side of the road.

Sgt. Russell Wallace, the turret gunner in Vehicle Four, faced the same situation when a white four-door sedan sped beak to beak toward him. He grabbed a rock, about to throw it at the car. But his team leader, Khan, was taking no chances. He yelled, "Fire!"

Wallace fired a burst from his machine gun into the pavement in front of the sedan.

The driver was unfazed and kept coming.

Wallace then laid rounds into the vehicle's engine block, disabling shots aimed at the radiator, and the car rolled into a gully, smoke, and steam pouring from beneath the hood.

As we continued chugging ahead at some forty miles per hour, we were in a heightened state of alert, aware of anything that moved.

We saw a small black pickup truck emerge from a gas station at the bottom of a hill and dash ahead of us and to the right alongside Hell's Highway. The truck then pulled onto the road and did a U-turn—driving head-on at Vehicle One. Lester shot at the engine, and the truck pulled over at another gas station farther down the road. Had that been another suicide bomber?

"Watch that hill," East cautioned over the radio.

Almost on cue, Wallace and others in the convoy spotted puffs of smoke and muzzle flashes, 450 to 500 feet away, behind the first gas station. Wallace also saw black dots in the distance, perhaps men, maneuvering on the hillside. He fired in their direction—and there were no more muzzle flashes.

When our lead vehicles crossed the Spin Pul bridge, they again took fire, from the ground and elevated sniper positions. Nearing an orchard, Sgt. Luke Davenport, the driver of Vehicle One, heard "snaps and pops" from small arms. But the fire came from the front, not the sides.

They were trying to stop us.

A large mob, maybe forty men, had formed on the road ahead. Having dragged or driven a white car across the road to block us, they were not going to let us continue to our base.

Standing around the car, they were extremely agitated, gesturing and shouting, as Vehicle One drove toward them.

We had trained to deal with dozens of scenarios, but we never had any training about how to deal with an angry mob. But I was sure of one thing: If we stopped, we would be easy prey for other suicide bombers and the jihadists shooting at us.

Once upon a time, Marines were known to never fire warning shots, bragging that every shot was a lethal shot. Marines would be punished for firing warning shots! But times had changed, fortunately for the men in that mob.

They were within foul language distance when Lester fired.

His were warning shots, aimed over their heads.

Like the Red Sea parting for Moses, the crowd split in two and the men ran off the road as fast as they could. We drove around the blockade and plowed ahead.

Over the radio, which was again operational, East told everyone to ceasefire.

"I felt it was important for the men to hear my voice in a calm manner to tell them to calm down," he said, "to tell them that no one was seriously wounded, and that we were getting closer to JAF."

After confronting deadly threats over a distance of about a mile and a half, somewhere between five and eight minutes, we had escaped the Taliban trap.

I aborted the original mission. It did not make sense to dismount and have a so-called "tribal leader engagement" with people who had just tried to kill us after spouting their well-rehearsed song and dance that "there are no Taliban here." We had defended ourselves and aggressively counterattacked. Maybe the next group of American troops venturing around Bati Kot would have a safer trip, maybe even sit down to share a pot of *chai* with the elders. But we would not do that today.

During the fifteen-minute return to Jalalabad, Klein, suffering pain in his right bicep from being hit by shrapnel from the explosion, could not continue in his turret. He yelled down into his vehicle, asking to be replaced. Harley took his position, wielding only his M-4 rifle. We remained vigilant but no one needed to fire another shot.

Once safely behind the wire in Jalalabad, we enjoyed a well-deserved moment of satisfaction. We had driven through a hornet's nest and lived to tell about it. Facing what we had, at least some of us should have been dead.

I agree with Winston Churchill: "Nothing is so exhilarating in life as to be shot at with no result." But we were an experienced bunch who had been well trained and seen war up close and personal before. There were excited high fives and bear hugs, but none of us was hootin' and hollerin'.

One of our Navy corpsmen, Chief Petty Officer Matt Stevenson, took Klein to the aid station. The patrol's other Marines downloaded their weapons, replenished spent ammunition, and took the vehicles to the fueling area to be topped off. That was standard operating procedure. You never knew what you might be asked to do at a second's notice. You had to be prepared.

While inspecting Vehicle Two, we saw bullet impacts on the front headlights, windshield, turret, and right side of the Humvee. Two impacts appeared to be from a Dragunov, a Russian-made sniper rifle, and the tip of an AK-47 round was lodged in the turret.

I checked in on Klein. His right arm was swollen, and he was hurting, but we both smiled.

"It felt like I was hit with a baseball bat," he said in his Southern drawl.

I let him know what a great job he had done and handed him a satellite phone. I told him to not discuss anything about the mission but to call his wife directly to assure her that he was okay and not to worry. Otherwise, the Marines at Camp Lejeune might contact her as next of kin and freak her out. He made the happy call before being helicoptered to Asadabad for X-rays and further treatment.

I headed for the room we often used as a chapel for the post-mission debrief with the platoon. Everyone was there except for the injured Klein; the corpsmen, who had more pressing duties; our interpreter Ali, whose security clearance did not allow his presence; and intelligence officer, Milton. I thought Milton's absence was strange but did not think much of it at the time.

As I was about to enter, our operations center watch chief came up, with deep concern etched on his face. He told me that the incident, which had taken place not much more than thirty minutes earlier, was already being reported on radio and the internet—and that we had reportedly massacred innocent men, women, and children!

"What?" I was so surprised that I couldn't utter another word.

Vehicle Four's Sgt. Khan, a Muslim who had been in more than two dozen firefights in Iraq while in Force Recon, and was seriously wounded in Fallujah, saw the news reports too.

"Once we got done looking at the vehicle, I went inside to our team room and jumped on the computer," he remembered. "I was going to check my email, and lo and behold, the Associated Press already had the incident, and said something like we killed some astronomical number of women and children."

He was shocked. So were all of my Marines.

"It made us feel pretty disappointed and angry," Khan said. "We were all happy and amped up about how the situation went due to the fact that we train so long and so hard. When we were tested, we did exactly what we were trained (to do)."

I was proud of how my men had performed. We had acted coolly and professionally. We were warriors but humble warriors.

Yet, a chagrined Khan said, "here we are, we look like murderers in front of the world."

Fair and Impartial

The launch of a preliminary investigation by Special Operations Command–Central was announced the afternoon of the March 4 ambush and began four days later. Following on its heels was a more extensive probe ordered by the Marine Corps Central Command (MARCENT), commanded by Lt. Gen. Mattis, and conducted by NCIS, the criminal investigative branch for the Marines. Over the next month, NCIS grilled my Marines in Afghanistan and Kuwait, where we had been banished. Two months later, the investigators finally put their boots on the ground in Bati Kot. When the men of Fox Company returned to the U.S., NCIS interrogated many of them again. In total, they took 160 statements from witnesses of the March 4th bombing and its aftermath.

Meanwhile, we were being hammered by the media and even senior brass at the Pentagon, prompting me to enlist the services of Marine Lt. Col. Scott Jack, a military defense attorney. But I felt certain we would never find ourselves in a courtroom. Not because of any whitewash by some of our own that would quickly absolve us of any crime, rather because we hadn't been bloodthirsty American troops on a rampage. We hadn't killed any civilian—not a man, not a woman, and not a child.

Still, considering the severity of the potential accusations, Jack was doing his job when he informed me that he could try to seek immunity for me. In exchange for testifying against others of the MARSOC 7—East;

Lester, the gunner in Vehicle One; Klein, the gunner in Vehicle Two; Walker, the gunner in the back of Vehicle Two; Clarke, East's platoon sergeant; and Pratt, the gunner in Vehicle Six—I could escape the possibility of criminal prosecution and prison.

Secretary of Defense Mattis meets with Maj. Gen. Haas, ISAF J-3 Operations Officer in Afghanistan (Courtesy of *Stars and Stripes*)

I declined, emphatically.

If my men were going to go down, then I was going to go down with them.

The pressure was intense for me and my men, particularly Ortega, the driver in Vehicle Two, and Ruiz, the turret gunner in East's Vehicle Three. Investigators felt they might have leverage on them because of their Hispanic heritage.

I admired Ortega. He had heart and guts. Short and slight, probably weighing no more than 135 pounds, he would carry loads of 120 pounds, sweat pouring off his face in training, and never complain. Born in Guadalajara, Mexico, he legally immigrated with his family to the U.S. seeking a better life. As a teenager in troubled East Los Angeles, he was raised by his mom before joining the Marines.

**1st Platoon, Fox Company completion of Close
Quarters Battle Course, Camp Lejeune, NC**

During one interview, the NCIS agent was accompanied by two unnamed men in civilian clothes who occasionally took over the questioning. The strangers never told Ortega who they were, and he assumed they were also NCIS.

Ortega told them he heard incoming fire and saw puffs of smoke on a hilltop when the convoy moved past the blast site and over the bridge. He said he heard a lot of shooting during the ambush, but the only person he saw shoot was Klein since they were in the same Humvee. He said the turret gunner shot to the left, stopped, and then fired to the right.

When he hesitated about whether Lester in Vehicle One fired, the NCIS agent pounced.

"It felt like he was, like, saying certain things to try to back me into a corner," Ortega later testified at the COI. "They were like, well, 'What do you think he (Lester) was shooting at?' I was like, well, I can only assume he was shooting."

After two hours of intense questioning by the three men, they ordered Ortega to write a statement about what he saw on March 4. That it was an order, not a request, made Ortega suspicious of the "impartial" motives of the investigators.

"I don't even have to be here if I don't want to," he told them. "I don't have to do anything if I don't want to. But now you are telling me that I have to."

So they threatened to have U.S. Immigration and Customs Enforcement deport his mom back to Mexico that night if he did not cooperate. "It would be a shame if she went away," they said, sounding like mob guys in a movie!

In truth, they could not have returned her to Mexico. She was a naturalized American citizen. But an immigrant's fear of sudden and arbitrary expulsion never completely goes away. His interrogators sweated him until an uncertain Ortega felt he had to choose between his family and his brothers-in-arms. Though he never wrote a statement, he signed one dictated by them, which left open the possibility that Fox Company had murdered innocent civilians on March 4.

Ruiz was strong-armed in the same way. In Kuwait, he was stashed in a hotel room and examined twice, for five hours each time, by NCIS. In North Carolina, there were four or five additional interviews. He said he was questioned for twenty-one or twenty-two hours in total.

"I kept getting drilled, drilled, drilled," he testified at the COI.

But Ruiz, older than Ortega, stood fast. Besides, they could not frighten him with threats of deporting anyone in his family, including his wife and kids—since they were from Puerto Rico. They were Americans by birth.

The prosecutors did, however, ask him to submit to a polygraph test. Fortunately, Jack had cautioned him that the results of polygraphs taken by non-native English speakers can be flawed. Ruiz was a fast-talking Marine with a heavy accent who had difficulty with the English language. Hooked up to a polygraph machine, trying to translate the questions in his mind could come across as deception. Recalling Jack's advice, Ruiz refused. The investigators said they could order him to submit to the polygraph, but they did not, knowing full well that doing so would be illegal given the constitutional right against self-incrimination.

When Ruiz held his ground, they offered him immunity from prosecution in exchange for his cooperation.

He refused.

"(I) told them they could keep their immunity because I have nothing to hide," he said.

But the investigators were relentless, often visiting him at his house as he was trying to enjoy time with his family. Finally, to get them off his back and out of his house, Ruiz accepted the offer. Immunity made his life easier.

Ortega and Ruiz were not the only ones who received special attention—so did Khan. Because his parents were Egyptian, and he was a Muslim, perhaps the investigators felt he might be more amenable to the Afghans' version of events. Interrogated numerous times by the same three men in civilian clothes, all presumably NCIS agents, he was granted immunity as well.

Buoyed by two Marine witnesses with immunity, a signed statement by another, a scathing yet to be revealed charges by yet another of my Marines, as well as sworn testimony by several Afghans, including the aggrieved Qomandan, the odds were completely stacked against us. The prosecutors told us on Friday, October 19, that Mattis ordered a Court of Inquiry and that the two officers from Fox Company, East and I, would stand trial in ten days.

While we were the only named parties, trials and punishment could come later for the rest of the MARSOC 7. Their fates were tied to ours.

Purportedly an examination of facts, a COI is a peculiar undertaking. In a court-martial, just like civilian trials, speculation and hearsay must be supported by a preponderance of evidence. But a COI is more of a free-for-all, with very loose rules of evidence. For example, testimony could be presented before the three-member panel without any basis of fact, i.e., without any proof or corroboration.

Col. Pete Petronzio, MARSOC's assistant chief of staff for operations when I joined, told me to be wary of a COI.

"Watch out, Fred," he said. "They can say anything. They can bring up anything."

Armed with information gained in the COI, convicting the MARSOC 7 of wrongdoing in a court-martial would be a lot easier, just as it was the last time it was invoked by the Marines—more than fifty years earlier.

In 1956, a Marine drill instructor, Staff Sergeant Matthew McKeon, led his platoon of recruits at Parris Island, South Carolina into a swamp at Ribbon Creek during a midnight march. Six recruits drowned. Even before all of the bodies were recovered, a COI was convened the following day and McKeon was recommended to be court-martialed for the oppression of recruits and manslaughter by culpable negligence. The rush to judgment only slowed thanks to McKeon's high-profile lawyers, who proved at the court-martial that McKeon was not the brutal, drunk Marine the COI had painted him. McKeon was eventually convicted of the much lesser charge of simple manslaughter. The incident and trial were a national sensation, prompting both a Congressional investigation and a movie, 1957's *The D.I.*

On October 19, East and I were informed that our COI would begin on November 1. We had two weeks to prepare.

And we could not tell anyone in the media what was going on. The defendants and all the attorneys, both military and civilian, were put under a "protective order" (a gag order), which held that under no circumstances could any of us communicate with any member of the media. If our civilian attorneys disobeyed, they could be disbarred. If the defendants or military attorneys disobeyed, we could face military discipline.

The action was touted as a means to ensure a "fair and impartial" proceeding. With the order in place, the only information the press would hear would be what they heard in court. Of course, controlling *when* the press would be in the courtroom was the COI's media liaison, Lt. Col. Sean Gibson, the public affairs officer for Lt. Gen. Sam Helland, the new MARCENT commanding general.

Gibson flew up to North Carolina from MARCENT headquarters in Tampa, Florida solely for a job usually performed by a locally based lieutenant or captain, not a lieutenant colonel. Working for those who ordered us prosecuted, he would be in a position to tip the scales of blindfolded Lady Justice in their favor.

Gibson's first press release to the media made it obvious that was his intention.

Dutifully, he noted that the purpose of the COI was to "examine facts and evidence concerning an incident on March 4, 2007 in which a U.S. Marine Corps special operations unit conducting a movement by convoy in Nangarhar Province, Afghanistan allegedly fired on and killed Afghan civilians."

But there was more: insinuations that rules were broken every step of the way and led to March 4, "The Court of Inquiry will inquire into issues concerning the conduct of the convoy, fire discipline, adherence to Operations Orders and Rules of Engagement, reporting and documentation of the incident, and the command climate in Marine Special Operations Company-F (MSOC-F)."

Then he divulged not only our names but our ranks and ages. Before that press release, not even our names had appeared in the media, not in *The New York Times*, not in *The Washington Post*.

Because of potential physical harm and harassment from enemies foreign and domestic, it was customary to conceal the identity of a special operator unless perhaps he was the subject of a court-martial. Guarding his privacy helped protect the service member and his family as well as future operations. (In this book, the true name of every special operator below the rank of colonel has been changed except for those who have agreed to be identified.)

I was concerned not only for myself and my family, particularly my mother, but for the wives, children, and families of the other members of Fox Company. My worry grew when, as the COI went on, the hometowns of East and myself were also somehow revealed.

NCIS followed up by dumping binders holding more than 12,000 pages of testimony and evidence on us. What we read was not encouraging. Among the first emails we saw was a conversation between two of the lead agents in which they called our case "akin to Haditha."

Less than a year and a half earlier, a roadside IED in Haditha targeted a squad from the 3rd Battalion, 1st Marines, and Lance Corporal Miguel Terrazas was killed on the spot. Two other Marines were wounded. Soon after, five Iraqi men were shot dead in the street by Marines and, after reporting they were taking small arms fire, Marines entered three houses and killed nineteen more Iraqis, including women and children. What happened was repulsive, and the news reports astonishing—from the shooting at close range of unarmed civilians attempting to surrender to urinating on one of the dead bodies.

Being compared in any way to Haditha was not good for us. Worse, the tone of the email implied that convicting us might help the careers of the prosecutors. Winning a high-profile legal effort like this could mean promotions for the prosecutors and those at NCIS.

As I went through the binders each night, I became more and more aware of what East and I were up against. The NCIS investigation had been insidious and invasive. It was also personal.

I expected agents to look at emails from our civilian accounts, but why only those involving family members such as my mother and my girlfriend Holly?

They knew it was a long shot that there would be anything incriminating in them, but perhaps in the emails between Holly and me, something titillating or embarrassing. If not, they had at least demonstrated their reach and the ruthlessness of their "fact finding."

I had thought of the Marines as my family. Now I felt as if that family had turned against me.

Family

Many, if not most, sons want to be like their father. I never wanted to be like mine. Robert Galvin was a bully, an alcoholic, a womanizer, and a wifebeater. A short balding man with a bit of a belly and a constant scowl, he was selfish and irresponsible. I was the second son, the fifth of six children, and maybe a family of that size was too much pressure for him. But there can be no excuses for what he did.

I was three years old when I saw him slap my mom Toni, viciously choke her and rip handfuls of hair from her head in our kitchen. He was stinking drunk, smashing glasses and plates, and yelling that he was not happy being with her, unlike the women he met at a local bar. My mom was crying uncontrollably and screaming in pain, both physical and emotional.

Witnessing a scene like that lasts a lifetime. To this day, I find it very hard to talk about it. What he did broke the bond of trust between a father and a son. And when that is broken, it is never restored.

My father was unrepentant. Though he moved out of our Kansas City, Missouri home a year later, he would come around and brag about his other women. I could smell the booze on his breath. He drank to get drunk and occasionally ended up in jail as a result. Nevertheless, my mother stayed legally married to him for years after. We were Catholics and, at least back in the '70s, divorce was not a respectable option.

He abandoned us. Desperate to try to support our large family, my mother went to work for a travel agency and had a delivery route for a local newspaper. All the kids would help fold and bag the newspapers each morning before throwing them out the window as she drove the car. She also gave piano lessons three nights a week, arranging for a neighbor lady to cook dinner for us on the weekdays she would come home late. She tithed our family income so we could attend St. Thomas More, a Catholic elementary school, where I was taught about faith, principles, believing in things greater than ourselves, and always giving your very best.

My brother and four sisters and I shared most material possessions. If I wanted anything special, I had to earn the money to buy it. I did any odd job a kid could do.

When I was about thirteen, my father showed up at the house and, for a reason I no longer remember, began threatening me. He became physical, pushing me.

I had enough. Since I was five years old, I had studied martial arts, where I was taught to never start a fight. But if there was going to be one, said the *sensei*, then you fight with all you have.

"I'll kick your ass!" my father shouted.

"Then let's fight," I answered.

I was taller and bigger than him, even at that age. I might have been stronger too. Though not a bodybuilder, I had become a physical fitness addict.

My father was no match for me, and he probably knew it. He backed down and walked out of the house. I was glad that he never again came around or threatened me or my mother. My mom finally divorced him that year—soon after she came home one day after work and found that he put a For Sale sign on the front lawn of our house, which he still owned.

Some children who have parents with deep character flaws follow in their footsteps. Others, like me, head in the opposite direction. I have my father to thank for being a bad example and instilling in me the conviction to never tolerate the abuse of the defenseless, to never stop fighting with all my God-given abilities for those who cannot stand up to the evil giants dominating their lives.

But looking past my upcoming graduation from Rockhurst High School, an all-boys Jesuit Catholic school, I truly didn't know what I wanted to do with my life. I was not geared up for any particular career. Though I hoped to be successful, I also wanted to do something that would fulfill me emotionally and spiritually.

A friend told me about the Marines and how, when it came to the military, they were the best of the best. That appealed to me, and I soon decided that I wanted to be a Marine. I was a recruiter's dream, ready to go.

One problem: No one in my family had ever been in the military. I was born in 1969, at the height of the country's disdain for the Vietnam conflict. No one in my family was receptive to me joining the military, particularly my mom, who wanted me to go to college.

Only seventeen years old, I needed her permission to enlist. She was not about to give it. But when a Marine recruiter came to our house, he told her that, if she signed off, I would be able to get a scholarship and enroll in college. He was somewhat vague about having to join the Marines first. Anyway, she gave her permission, and the next day I enlisted.

When I told her I was going to boot camp, she freaked out. That was not what she thought she was allowing me to do. She complained to the recruiting office, and a senior enlisted recruiter and his sergeant major came to our house to resolve the situation.

She finally realized that I genuinely wanted to be a Marine and that when I turned eighteen in a few weeks, I would enlist with or without her permission. So she agreed to let me go right after graduation.

I stepped off the bus and put my feet on the yellow footprints painted on the pavement outside the Marine Corps Recruit Depot in San Diego, California. The square-jawed drill instructor shouted to us, as a D.I. does to all recruits their first night, pertinent articles of the Uniform Code of Military Justice, including:

"Article 15, nonjudicial punishment, that means your commanding officer can punish you at his discretion! Article 31, compulsory self-incrimination prohibited! This is the Marine Corps version of your Miranda Rights! Article 92, failure to obey an order! That means if you don't do what we say, when we say it, and how we say it, you can be charged under the Uniform Code of Military Justice! Article 134, general article! Anything you do against good order and discipline, that brings discredit upon the Marines, you will be charged under the Uniform Code of Military Justice!"

The D.I. scared the daylights out of most of us. But not me. Honor, courage, and commitment were the core values of the Marines, and they were the values I wanted to represent too, having seen little of them from my father.

I actually enjoyed boot camp! I embraced the intensity and relished the physical activity at Camp Pendleton. I was never homesick. Having come from the flat prairies of the Midwest, I reveled in the beauty of the rolling hills and seaside of southern California. Even today, when I return to Camp Pendleton and inhale the licorice smell of the fennel growing there, I think "home" and "happy."

Most of my fellow enlistees knew that training to be a Marine was going to be tough, probably tougher than the other services—and they wanted that. They joined the Marines, not for the long-term health, education, or retirement benefits; not to learn a skill; not for the prestige or the uniform. They joined for the country, yes, a call of duty to serve our nation, but also to be part of a family they could count on, no matter what, a family they could wholly commit to and was wholly committed to them.

That's why I became a Marine too.

Bring My Husband Home Alive

I was a twenty-one-year-old corporal in a tank battalion the day Iraq, led by Saddam Hussein, invaded Kuwait in August 1990. When the *USS Tarawa* reached Hawaii on our way to the Middle East, it was the first time I set foot outside continental America. After we landed in the Philippines, that was the first time I saw an officer slip a condom onto a dummy tank round to demonstrate how to protect ourselves from venereal diseases spread by the local bar girls.

As the air war began, we off-loaded in Saudi Arabia, where the American ground forces were building for an invasion. Assigned as a machine gunner on top of a gun truck, I was ready for whatever I was called to do. But our company didn't see action. While other Marines entered Kuwait City, we stopped short. Within a few days, the war was over. Within a few months, so too was my enlistment, which I ended as a sergeant.

But I didn't want to leave the Marines. I had found a home there.

I decided to try to earn a commission and become an officer. I joined an active reserve unit training one weekend a month and two weeks during the summer. I also worked part-time jobs to pay for courses at San Diego colleges, soon graduating with majors in history and social science. Finally, I had all the credentials I needed to apply for Officer Candidates School (OCS).

Along the way, I fell in love with a beautiful blonde I met in class—and she wanted nothing to do with the military. She insisted that I give up the idea of rejoining the Corps.

I remained a civilian, took a job selling stocks at a small brokerage firm, and we married.

That was a mistake.

Only a month after tying the knot, a friend told me he saw her dancing with other men at a nightclub. When I confronted her, she fumed that I wasn't paying her enough attention.

"This is wrong," I said. She had been the person I had allowed to get closest to my heart, and now I felt as if I'd been knifed in the back. "We're married," I said, pleading for an apology.

She was not ready for what that meant, the meaning of that commitment. Once again, a bond of trust in my life was shattered. We separated and I went back to Kansas City, where I found a job with a major brokerage, Smith Barney. But I kept in touch with my Marine buddies on the west coast. When they talked about what they were doing, I desperately wished I was there with them.

In San Diego to finalize the divorce, I stopped for a haircut at the Camp Pendleton barbershop. Of all people, who should I bump into but the recruiter for OCS I had talked to prior to getting married.

A light bulb went on over my head. This was my chance to get back on track, to go where I belonged. But this time I wanted to be more than just an officer. I wanted to be an officer in Force Reconnaissance.

I did not know a single soul in Force Recon. I had only seen Force Recon Marines in person from afar as they did their morning runs around Camp Pendleton.

I was fascinated by what I heard they did on the battlefield, though the details were classified. They went further than even Recon Marines, who were trained for "green" operations such as long-range reconnaissance, intelligence, and surveillance. Force Recon Marines were also trained for beyond the battlefield "black" operations such as clandestine missions and direct action as well as deep reconnaissance and unconventional warfare. They were the only Marines who performed both high-altitude parachute and underwater infiltration operations, the only Marines who moved far behind enemy lines for close-quarter battle. The Recon motto said it all: *Celer, Silens, Mortalis* (Swift, Silent, Deadly).

Force Recon Marines were the equivalent of the Navy SEALs—and there were far fewer of them. In 2006, Force Recon totaled 364 Marines; the SEALs had more than 7,000 sailors. The few? The proud? These were the fewest of the few, and the proudest of the proud.

I discovered too that most Marines who joined Force Recon seemed to come from broken homes. They were not raised in privilege or had families that supported and encouraged them as they grew up. Maybe they were latchkey kids, left alone much of the time by a single parent. Maybe they had a parent who was abusive and/or addicted to drugs or alcohol. If the image of the SEAL was of the All-American boy, the image of the Force Recon Marine was of the Everyman who wanted something he never had before—a sense of family, a feeling of brotherhood. Each man was willing to give everything he had not only for the mission but also for the Marine beside him.

Because of that dedication, very few in Force Recon were married, and those who were often found their marriages short-lived. Husbands were so focused on training and were away from home for such lengthy periods that few wives hung around for long. The nickname "Divorce Recon" was well-earned.

I also noticed that they tended to be on the straight and narrow, especially while on the job. They had to be. If they screwed up, they would be taken out of their unit. No longer being part of the family that you trained and worked with, no longer being with your brothers-in-arms, was the worst punishment they could imagine. So they did their jobs and did them the right way.

I wanted to be one of them, one of those very few.

At the time, the only avenue to becoming an officer in Force Recon was through the infantry. I drove to OCS at Quantico, Virginia, and after completing the necessary schools, was selected for the Infantry Officer Course.

That experience was a gut check, physically and psychologically. Yes, I was taught knife fighting, but more significantly I learned that, as an instructor put it, "If you get into a knife fight, you are going to bleed." Yes, the instructors broke out boxing gloves and lots of Marines beat on you to toughen you up, but what was truly taught was that "if you get into a fight, sometimes the enemy does not play fair."

I would vividly recall both lessons in the midst of the COI.

Commissioned as a lieutenant, my first tour as an infantry platoon commander was with the 1st Light Armored Recon Battalion. After training for desert warfare and amphibious operations for a year at Camp Pendleton, in early 1998 the Marine Expeditionary Unit (MEU) we would deploy withheld a celebratory officers' mess night. Every Marine was in dress blues and those who had significant others brought them along to the swanky Friday night party in the U.S. Grant Hotel's ballroom in the downtown Gaslamp Quarter of San Diego. I was alone but I was happy.

Suddenly, the commanding officer ordered the doors closed.

Standing before us with a deadly serious look, he announced:

"Gentlemen, recall all of your Marines right now. We're leaving on Monday."

Saddam Hussein was continuing to block the activity of United Nations weapons inspectors and another conflict with Iraq was looming. As part of the military build-up, our MEU was being sent to Kuwait.

That Monday, preparing to board our ship, the families of our Marines were allowed dockside to see their men embark. In the crowd, I spotted the wife of one of my sergeants.

She looked terrified.

I could read what was on her mind: "You bring my husband home alive."

Without a word, with only a look, I promised that I would do everything in my power to not fail her.

To this day, I have never forgotten her face, or what she saw as my duty, my responsibility—to take care of the sons, brothers, husbands, and fathers of America.

Screams in Iraq

From Kuwait, we pushed to the Iraqi border. But there we stopped, as diplomacy, airstrikes, and sanctions took center stage. I didn't see any action as an infantry officer. When we returned to the States, I was due to be promoted to captain and shuffled off to an executive office desk job.

If I were selected for Force Recon, however, which was my goal all along, I could be saved from such a dismal fate.

But first I needed to take an "indoc," short for indoctrination, to Force Recon. On the third Thursday of every month at Camp Pendleton, any Marine, enlisted or officer, could show up outside the 1st Force Recon compound in the pitch-black of 0500 and be tested. During the one-day ordeal, the Force Recon leaders evaluated more than your physical fitness. They examined your grit, your heart. They wanted men who would not quit.

Part of the Recon creed read: "Conquering all obstacles, both large and small, I shall never quit. To quit, to surrender, to give up is to fail. To be a Recon Marine is to surpass failure; To overcome, to adapt and to do whatever it takes to complete the mission."

The indoc began with a Kim's Game, a "keep in memory" exercise. An indoc leader pulled a poncho off a sand table, a sandbox used to plan missions, and the twenty or so other Marines and I had ten seconds to take a mental picture of the setup with its toy vehicles and soldiers. At the end of the day, we would be asked to recall what we saw.

We then went through the basic Marine physical fitness test, but they wanted to see near perfection—twenty dead hang pull-ups, running three miles in less than eighteen minutes, and one hundred sit-ups. We followed with ten exercises of two minutes each (pushups, flutter kicks, mountain climbers, leg lifts, etc.).

Then we dove into the pool wearing our full uniform, swam nearly five hundred meters, and performed a series of rescues towing another Marine. Then we tread water for fifty minutes.

Water aerobics was next. For thirty minutes, we repeatedly dove into the pool and swam distances using a different stroke each time. Then we did more push-ups. Rinse and repeat.

Changing into dry camo uniforms, we exited the building and ran the outdoor obstacle course not once but twice. There was a maximum time they considered a passing grade, but they did not tell you what that was. You had to go all out. Were we done yet? Hardly.

We were ordered to sprint back to the compound, stuff a fifty-pound sandbag into a rucksack and strap it to our backs. We then endured a twelve-mile recon shuffle, faster than a walk but slower than a run, up and down the hills of the camp. During the final three miles on the thick beach sand, several Marines stopped. They had enough.

I was the first to finish, which thankfully allowed me some rest until the last man stumbled in. When he dropped his rucksack, we were immediately sent into the icy cold surf to fight the waves as we swam three hundred meters into the ocean before returning to shore—which we did over and over. My legs cramped up but I continued, even through the next twenty minutes of flutter kicks in the shallow water.

With most of the candidates unceremoniously carted off in Humvees, only three of us remained—and the indoc leader took off running! We didn't know where he was going, but we followed him at a full gallop. After two and a half miles, we approached the compound where we began the day and, relieved, I figured I was finally done. I had survived.

But he ran past the compound.

For one of the remaining three, that was the final psychological straw, and he quit.

The indoc leader ran only a little beyond the compound before turning back toward the building and ending the run. His feint had been another test of perseverance.

I was smoked, but the day was not over. Inside the building, a group of Force Recon officers tested the two of us still standing on military knowledge. The final question?

"What was on the sand table?"

I passed the indoc and was selected for Force Recon. But there would be no opening for a captain at 1st Force Recon for a year. If I was willing to go to 5th Force Recon in Okinawa, Japan, however, I could join right away.

There were always slots available because not many Marines wanted to be stationed on the island called "The Rock." There was little to do on Okinawa, and the locals weren't very friendly to Americans.

I flew to Okinawa and was sent to a RIP, a Recon Indoc Platoon.

"If you think this job is about being cool or touching the magic," the cadre chief explained, "you stood in the wrong line. Listen up, ladies, as a Force Recon Marine you will experience PMS—Pain, Misery, and Suffering—not once a month but every day. You're tired, hungry, cold, and wet? Embrace the pain, misery, and suffering."

In RIP, you were issued a piece of sling rope you wore around your neck and down your back. A portion of a static line used to rappel down steep terrain identified you as a "roper," the lowest form of life. A roper had to run everywhere, from the chow hall to the classroom to wherever, and any Force Recon Marine could stop you and say, "Hey, roper, give me twenty-five and five," which meant twenty-five push-ups and then five more.

The training lasted two months, including a brutal "beach week," basically six days of living in the sand and water, with barely two hours of sleep a night. If you were weak, physically or mentally, you were either counseled to improve and brought back into the fold or you were removed from the program.

I wanted the training to be as difficult as possible. I wanted the Marines next to me to be men I could depend on.

Upon graduation, I took the rope off my neck, stashed it with my gear, and deployed the very next day with my command, 2nd Platoon, 5th Force Recon, to South Korea for cold-weather training. I had decided to sign us up for as many different exercises in as many exotic locations across the Pacific as possible, from Thailand to Korea, Australia to the Philippines.

When I told Big Dave, who was my gunnery sergeant and platoon sergeant, he shouted, "Hell yeah! Roger that, sir!"

After three years on the Rock, the Corps informed me that I had to move on, and the choice given for my next stop was either the Pentagon or the Marine Corps Air Station in Yuma, Arizona.

The choice was between getting coffee for general officers in D.C. or learning how to coordinate air power using attack helicopters and fixed-wing aircraft at the Marine Corps version of the Air Force's Red Flag or Navy's Top Gun school. For me, that was an easy decision.

I arrived in Yuma in the summer of 2001, completed the course at the top of my class, and immediately became an instructor. One morning that September, I walked out of the gym and started my car to drive to the chow hall. The radio was on, and I heard that a plane had flown into one of the World Trade Center towers in New York City. I had a feeling that was not an accident. I walked back into the gym, where there was a television. By then, the second plane had slammed into the other tower and we knew the United States had suffered a terrorist attack.

There were no expressions of anger. Instead, there was resolve. We had been provoked. Retribution would come.

But while many of my Force Recon buddies began to head to Afghanistan, I was stuck in Yuma—until a tragic accident changed the course of my life.

After a young Marine was killed during training, his platoon commander was replaced by an officer from 1st Force Recon. I was the only captain available with the necessary experience to fill that officer's spot. Granted early parole from my instructor duties in Yuma, off I went to lead 4th Platoon, 1st Force Recon, stationed at Camp Pendleton.

Yet the fight in Afghanistan appeared to be over within months. Al-Qaeda and the Taliban were routed in cities across the country and their fighters either went into hiding or escaped to Pakistan. Even as an insurgency was beginning to surface, Afghanistan was relegated to the back pages. My platoon never left the States.

Another war with Iraq, however, was soon on the docket. In March 2003, I watched the "shock and awe" air bombardment of Baghdad on television. I chomped at the bit and begged for my platoon to be flown into southern Iraq, where Marine units were doing combat patrols.

Instead, we were assigned to maritime interdiction duty around the Arabian Peninsula. We were to stop any vessel in international waters suspected of smuggling fighters, weapons, or drugs used to finance terrorism.

Typically, these interdictions were done by sliding down ropes from helicopters and boarding what was usually a small wooden *dhow*. Rather than assault a ship from the top down, I thought, why not attack from the bottom up, from the sea rather than the air?

Our task force carried rigid hull inflatable boats (RHIBs) featuring deck-mounted machine guns and high-powered engines made for the high seas. I suggested that we motor alongside a suspect ship in an RHIB, attach a grappling hook at the end of a telescopic painter's pole to the deck and use a cable ladder to climb aboard.

It was not smooth sailing. The targeted ship was often being tossed around like a rag doll in rough seas as ten to twelve Marines, each weighed down with body armor and weapons, tried to get on deck. Scrambling up the ladder, we would be slammed against the hull. We would get seasick too. I imagined surveillance aircraft and satellites transmitting video of us puking and laughter breaking out in intelligence centers worldwide!

But in three months, we racked up an extraordinary number of interdictions, taking down thirty-six ships at sea. Inside bags of vegetables, we found aluminum foil packages containing black tar heroin. Beneath fresh fish on a layer of ice, we uncovered AK-47s. Sometimes we were instructed to handcuff and blindfold a *dhow* passenger, put the bad dude in a litter, and raise him into a helicopter flying to one of our ships for interrogation.

Ironically, given what later happened to Fox Company, we were finally sent into Iraq to take over for a Marine infantry company that was sidelined after being accused of firing at civilians. Flown into a camp at the southern end of the Al-Faw peninsula, near the Iranian border, I was called into the tent of the MEU commanding officer.

"Here's the problem, Fred," said the colonel. "They were doing a patrol in a village and got spooked and started shooting. We're taking them out and putting you in."

That seemed reasonable, except that I knew the captain of that company and he was not the sort to get "spooked," an insult to any Marine infantry officer.

"What's the deal?" I later asked the captain.

"There was an element in the village firing at us," he said, "and another element was maneuvering to flank us. We were decisively engaged. This was no joke."

"Did you tell that to the colonel?"

"He never asked," he said, bewildered. "They just pulled us out and we're sitting around waiting to see what happens next."

The colonel told me he talked to the tribal elders but he had no interest in talking to his officers to get their side of the story. I was shocked by his indifference to his men. Weren't they as important, even more important, than those of the tribal leaders? His reaction, however, foreshadowed the experience of Fox Company.

Later that day, I inserted with my Force Recon platoon via a light-armored company and we traveled to that village to discuss the incident with the elders. As we arrived, the light-armored company commander removed his body armor and told us to do the same.

"We're just going to have some tea," he said matter-of-factly.

"We're not taking off our body armor," I said sharply. "I don't trust these people." I kept an open mind, but I was not about to take a foolish chance with the lives of my men.

Not happy with me when we stepped into the meet-and-greet, he gave me a condescending look of "I told you so" when the elders assured us they were peaceful and had no weapons, and that there was no enemy activity in their village.

As they continued talking with the company commander, I was called to the side by my radio communicator. He had received a message from the

Cobra attack helicopters above us that there was a suspicious movement of people to the east.

I motioned to the light-armored company commander and, with his unit at our side, we walked to the area pinpointed—and uncovered a huge weapons cache. The men spotted by the helicopters had been retrieving weapons in anticipation of attacking us.

Now, the Cobra pilots told us, the insurgents were moving farther east, to a tiny island in the Shatt al-Arab, a river that bordered Iraq and Iran. Leaving the light-armored company behind, I decided my platoon would follow the insurgents.

We linked up with a British Army officer who had access to an RHIB and used the boat to ferry our twenty-five guys onto the island. But as we moved through dense vegetation, the Cobras, running low on fuel, had to leave the scene. Worried that we were being lured into a trap, out of range of our mortars and artillery on the river bank, and now without air support, I pulled my platoon back to the shore.

The RHIB had gone elsewhere but I called for troop lift helicopters that were available.

They refused to pick us up.

Their Marine helicopter commander said we were too close to Iran. A helicopter landing on their territory would be politically explosive, he said. Only when the full bird colonel at Al-Faw gave his permission did helicopters fly in to get us out of there.

When I saw him in person, I laid into that helicopter captain.

"You knew we were vulnerable, but you refused to give us the support you're trained to provide because it *might* ruffle feathers. Your concern was for your career, not for us." I did not mince words. "To me, you're a coward. Don't you ever again even think about leaving Marines behind."

I am pretty sure I rattled him. At least I hope I did.

Following that deployment, the 4th Platoon returned to San Diego, but not for long. We were back in Iraq in 2005, this time in Al-Anbar Province. This was the wild, wild west, a part of the country not even Saddam could control when he was in power, with hotbeds of resistance in cities such as Ramadi, Fallujah, and Haditha. The Marines were the smallest element in the U.S. armed forces, but we were tasked with policing the country's largest and most violent province.

The insurgency there was organized and well-armed. Plundering the Iraqi Army's ordnance supplies, they were using armor-piercing ammunition that sliced through our Humvees like Swiss cheese and rocket-propelled grenades in volumes of volley fire. All across Al-Anbar, the enemy was winning and the coalition was losing.

We were first sent to the Syrian border town of Al-Qa'im, the Dodge City of Iraq. A recently deployed Marine infantry battalion had been attacked there by two suicide bombers in rapid succession, one blowing himself up at the front gate to the base and the other detonating himself inside the wire.

Since then, the battalion had hunkered down and Islamists who wanted to get their jihad on were freely streaming across the porous border into Iraq.

The insurgents had learned that if they hit hard after a new unit arrived, they could instill such fear that even a twelve hundred man battalion outfitted with armored vehicles would stay inside the wire. They fed that fear with IEDs that combined artillery rounds with a propane tank, causing a frightful fireball and inflicting grotesquely disfiguring burn injuries. Threat briefs I received when I was in Iraq warned that Islamists also defecated on rounds before firing them, resulting in heinous infections from shrapnel wounds.

If Al-Qa'im was Dodge City, then Husaybah next door was Tombstone. That's where I came under enemy fire for the first time.

Our mission was to take over the biggest compound in town, a place we called the Mansion. The idea was to house our task force there for five days to demonstrate to the general staff that we could operate from the center of a *mujahideen*-controlled town.

Lt. Col. George Smith Jr., the commanding officer of 1st Force Recon, planned to send our vehicles down the only road in town and surround the Mansion. Smith was genuinely intelligent, having been the lead planner for the I Marine Expeditionary Force for the invasion of Iraq. But Sammy, my interpreter, a former Kurdish special forces soldier, shook his head during the briefing and whispered to me, "Bad call." I agreed. The insurgents would see us coming from a long way off, meaning not only would we lose the element of surprise but the convoy could be easily targeted.

I figured there had to be a less risky way of getting into Husaybah than rumbling in with heavy armor, smashing through doors with an explosive charge or the steel bumper of a Humvee, and shooting up a town. Inciting a gunfight was a good way to get my guys killed. The Force Recon platoon that deployed in the area before us had twenty-two casualties among twenty-four men.

I remembered the face of that sergeant's wife: "Bring my husband home alive."

But Smith was my commanding officer. His plan was *the* plan.

With F/A-18 Hornet attack jets cruising above us out of audible range and AH-1 Cobra attack helicopters circling in a holding pattern far behind us, we mounted up after midnight, with my platoon in front. I was in the lead vehicle. I was saying to my men, "Follow me!"

And as soon as we crossed the bridge into Husaybah, we were hit with a massive barrage of rocket-propelled grenades.

Then their medium machine guns erupted on us.

We were getting dumped on.

Our choice was fight, freeze, or flight. We chose to fight.

Our turret gunners fired back, giving the enemy the good news, full auto. We gave it as tough as we were taking it.

The communicator in my Humvee saw an RPG headed for one of our vehicles and yelled over the radio, "Vehicle Six is taking FIIIRRRRE!"

I clicked the headset and acknowledged the information by responding, "400," my call sign as the 4th Platoon's commander. The excited communicator later told me he was struck by how calm I was. But as Force Recon leaders, we were trained to visualize beforehand what might happen, including deaths and injuries. When you go into a battle where you might get killed, you cannot have any hesitancy. You need complete dedication to the mission, no matter the cost.

The helicopters with the red crosses on them flying around were constant reminders of someone having been killed or injured. Yet I was never anxious or nervous, never asked myself, "Am I going to die today?" Because it was not about me. It was about my men. I needed to be composed to give them the best chance for survival.

As the RPGs rained down, my forward air controller ordered the Hornets to come in "guns hot" for a 20mm cannon strafing run and the Cobras to engage with their Hellfire laser-guided missiles. The devastation they unleashed leveled the buildings shielding the enemy, and allowed us to reach the Mansion.

As soon as we arrived, I heard a burst of gunfire and was told we had taken casualties. I hustled out of my vehicle to investigate and found a Marine who had been shot in the leg with a heavy machine gun round while in his Humvee. The turret gunner in another Humvee was also hit in his left triceps when a round ripped through his chariot, with the shrapnel tearing up the right cheek of the master sergeant who was sitting next to, of all people, Smith the CO!

"Where'd that fire come from?" I asked my sergeant as I surveyed the street and readied to have my Marines target the insurgent gun emplacement.

But, without saying a word, he strangely shrugged.

"Sergeant!"

"It was a mistake," he said.

Reluctantly, he explained that one of our turret gunners saw two vehicles down a side alley, did not recognize them as friendlies, and went trigger down with .50 caliber armor-piercing rounds.

"One of our own guys?" I said in disbelief. Luckily, the wounds turned out to be relatively minor. But someone could have been killed.

Like the Big Bad Wolf, except with explosive charges, we huffed and puffed and blew the Mansion's doors down. Those that huddled inside were swiftly policed up. They were also given papers telling them where they could go to be compensated by the U.S. government for any damages and the inconvenience of their displacement.

No one during the entire mission was killed or injured by an Iraqi. But three Marines were hit by another Marine.

I reported to Smith in the Humvee: "Sir, the Marines wounded tonight were shot by one of our own men."

He angrily bit down on his lip and, unexpectedly, the first words out of his mouth were: "Those men will get the Purple Heart!"

He did not say that out of pride but rather frustration and embarrassment. Friendly fire was a mortal sin, particularly in a highly trained Force Recon unit, and he and I as commanders were responsible for what our men did. Awarding Purple Hearts was the least he could do in face of our failure.

Throughout the night, we went into nearby homes, those within small arms range, and had Sammy tell the families they had to leave. They too would be paid and, when we were gone in a few days, they could come back.

Meeting those families was my first contact with Iraqi children. I was not Godzilla, but I was six foot three, pretty tall compared to most Iraqis, and a very honed 225 pounds, and here I was storming into their home wearing a monocle night vision goggle and body armor, and wielding a high-tech weapon, unlike any rifle they had seen. I knew they were scared and could see some of them shaking. Some were too frightened to speak. Some would yell and scream. Their lives and families were being disrupted by war and, even if their daddy was a bad guy, they had not done anything wrong. I truly felt for those kids.

Sammy was not so sympathetic. Every time we entered a house, he acted like he was exorcising a demon. His entire family, actually their entire Kurdish village in northern Iraq, had been wiped out in a gas attack ordered by Saddam. He had no love for Iraqi Shias.

In one house, while identifying the occupants, I asked, "Sammy, do we need to take anyone with us?" If there were terror suspects, we could detain them.

"No," he said. "Kill them all!"

"We can't do that," I told him.

"Kill them all!" he repeated.

He stepped into one of the other rooms and in a minute came back out holding up a poster of Saddam. For him, that was evidence enough that everyone in the house deserved death then and there.

Throughout history, Marines have often been accused of being too aggressive. Some have only half-jokingly referred to us as "throat slitters."

But even in total war, there are rules. We flex-cuffed three of the Iraqis and took them with us for further interrogation.

Only once did a member of my platoon shoot and kill someone in their home. In Haditha, while I was on the first floor, a Marine entered a second-floor room and encountered a man with a rifle in his hand. The Marine shot him twice in the center of his chest and once in the head, just like he had been taught. He then did a dead check, thumping his hand across his eyes to see if there was a response. There was not.

As we made our way out, the man's family swarmed into the room and saw their loved one. The women started moaning and wailing. Their bone-chilling cries do not haunt me, but I surely remember them. To me, more than explosions or gunfire, those are the sounds of war.

After the Mansion mission, Smith targeted another village for similar treatment. Once more, we would drive in and surround a compound with Humvees. This time I objected—and in front of his other officers at the confirmation brief.

"Sir, if we go into that town tonight..." I raised my voice. "We were lucky in Husaybah. If we go in like that again, we are going to have Marines die." I was not rude or disrespectful, but the situation in my opinion called for me to be, well, forceful.

Smith, however, felt I was challenging his authority, and raised his voice too.

"You are not in charge, Captain!" His face grew red. "I want to see you in my office right now!"

Once behind closed doors, I began to lay out an alternative: Rather than travel in an easy-to-follow desert convoy that would drive directly to 'X' on the map, I proposed flying in by helicopter or driving to a point nearby, dismounting, and entering on foot. It would take hours longer than a bull rush assault. But the enemy would never know we were coming and the advantage of surprise would limit our casualties.

He raised a hand to stop me.

"Don't ever push it like that again with my Marines in the room," he said sternly. "If you do, I'll send you home. Is that understood, Captain?"

"I had an obligation to speak up, sir," I said and braced for the blowback.

Smith waited a few moments and his anger subsided.

"If you have any 'suggestions,'" he said, "come and see me in private. Is that understood, Captain?"

"Aye, aye, sir."

"Now, tell me again what you have in mind."

I did, and Smith scrapped his plan in favor of mine.

I also convinced him to stop using explosives to breach houses during raids to capture terror suspects unless we absolutely had no choice. They made too much noise. Instead, we built wooden ladders to climb up and over the outer walls of compounds, whose gates would often be chained.

Under the cover of darkness, we would then methodically move from room to room and, before our jackpot knew it, we were waking him up in his bed with a rifle in his face, flipping him over, flex-cuffing his hands behind his back, blindfolding him and spiriting him away.

None of the villagers would hear or see us, and we would dust our trails clean so they would not even know where we came from. Yet the suspect would disappear. Sammy told me some villagers credited aliens from outer space for the abductions!

We were swift, silent, and violent without being deadly. It would certainly have surprised those who later painted me like an out-of-control cowboy in Afghanistan to learn that other Marine units in Iraq insinuated I was afraid to get into a gunfight. As Sun Tzu said, "The supreme art of war is to subdue the enemy without fighting."

Sometimes though, killing was the only option.

Roadside IEDs targeting coalition forces were a plague throughout Al-Anbar. Triple stacked with anti-tank mines, an IED could mangle an armored vehicle, create a hole six feet deep, and end several lives. We were in their backyard and they knew how to sneak up to military-only dirt roads using *wadis*, what we would call gullies, to hide their movements even from our satellites and plant the bombs. Marines across western Iraq were taking a bloody beating.

The enemy was clever, well-financed, and brutal. Insurgents would pay one local to ride his motorbike to the road at night and dig a hole. A different local would be paid to drive there on another night and drop artillery round into the hole. And a third local would be paid to go to that spot on yet another night and wire up the explosive. Since none of them could be labeled a "combatant" for our Rules of Engagement—just digging a hole, just found an artillery round, just carrying a bunch of wires—we were not permitted to target them. Each had plausible deniability.

Then our ROE changed.

The new rules were clear. If someone on that desert road had a shovel, we could kill him. If he had ammunition on him, we could kill him. If he had wires on him, we could kill him.

Tasked with conducting sniper ambush missions, my platoon was inserted on hills overlooking one of those roads. Underneath hides covered in desert camouflage netting, we waited.

You do not fight wars forever; you fight to win wars—and that requires men and women who are willing to do the job of killing. Not everyone can do that. Everyone wants to be a lion until it is time to do what lions do. We were a pride of lions, and we were on a hunt.

One night, we spotted two insurgents drive their car to the road. Confident they were shrouded in darkness, the passenger opened his door, lifted an artillery round from a burlap bag, and deposited it in a waiting hole.

In the vast emptiness of the desert, we did not bother with sniper rifles. We opened up on the two men with our medium machine gun.

We trekked down the hill, dragged their bodies to the side of the road, took the fuel can from their car, poured gas on their vehicle, and set it on fire. To those seeing the flames that night, and the bodies and the car's burned-out hulk in the days after, we had sent a message: If you try to blow us up, there will be payback.

Filthy Fred picked up another nickname that night—Fightin' Fred.

After seven rough days in those hills, we returned to our base, where the battalion commander happily commented, "We haven't had any of our people killed since you went out there." Then he added, "I'm sure some of those people you killed may not have been bad guys but...."

I looked him straight in the eyes and nipped that thought in the bud.

"Sir, every person we killed was a bad guy who either had already killed some of your Marines or was in the act of trying to do so. I say with 100 percent certainty that we did not fire on anyone who did not meet the Rules of Engagement for us to shoot and kill. We did not kill anyone who did not deserve it."

He wanted to absolve himself, just in case there was a problem with our understanding of the ROE. He wanted to be able to say in an investigation, "Well, I told them..."

The regimental commander, Col. Stephen W. Davis, was quite different. Instead of always looking for a way to shield himself from controversy or criticism, he unequivocally supported those under him. He was a warrior's warrior.

"Fred, I want you to get back up there on top of those cliffs," the colonel said in his gritty voice as we looked at a map in his office. He was about to launch a regimental sweep on the north side of the Euphrates River near the Syrian border, and he wanted Force Recon to help provide cover.

"If you see the *muj* on the move," he said, getting right to the point, "I want you to call in air strikes and kill every one of them. Any questions?"

"No, sir."

Eggbeater helicopters dropped us into the desert at night and we patrolled up into the cliffs. We thought we arrived unannounced, but the insurgents had heard our helicopters. Intelligence told us our location was compromised—and the *muj* were sending hit squads to track us down.

Only two days earlier, a pair of three-man Marine sniper teams on the outskirts of Haditha had been attacked and overrun by insurgents. Five Marines were killed and most had their throats cut. The sixth was wounded and captured. He was handcuffed and paraded through the streets before he too was killed. We knew all the gory details.

Immediately, we shifted from the summit to entrenching ourselves into the vertical cliff face a couple hundred feet off the desert floor. If they found us, we were determined to make ourselves tough to kill.

From our posts, we saw the Marines in the distance drive their AAVs across the Euphrates River from the south and push along the north bank. For two days, we sat in our holes, watched, reported, and sweated our balls off as the regiment moved closer.

On the third day, in bright sunlight, with elements of the regiment almost below us, I heard a BOOM!

About three-quarters of a mile away, one of the AAVs burst into flames.

The blast, probably from hitting a mine, penetrated the bottom of the vehicle, and the high-explosive grenades and machine-gun rounds inside the AAV began cooking off.

BANG! BANG! BANG!

I could hear screams too, and my entire body shuddered.

I will never forget the grisly cries of those men, sixteen of them, as they writhed in pain and desperately tried to get out of their vehicle. The sounds grown men make when they are burning alive are unholy and unnatural. Even as far away as they were from us, they pierced the air.

As their hell unfolded in front of me, I knew there was nothing those men could have done any differently. Fifteen of the sixteen perished. Their time had come. It was a sobering, humbling moment, a moment when I thanked God for protecting me. I knew that there but for the grace of God go I.

Sitting in my hole on that cliff face, I didn't consider seeking vengeance.

I've had close friends, great Americans, killed in war zones. Maj. Jay Aubin, known as Sweet Pea, died in an accident while flying a helicopter in Kuwait on the first day of the Iraq war in 2003. Maj. Ray Mendoza stepped on an IED in Iraq in 2005. I went to their funerals and saw their wives weep and heard their children speak about them. Their deaths touched a nerve deep in my soul.

But one of the roles of an officer is to regulate the violence. It was no coincidence that there was no senior officer on-site at Haditha (William

Calley of the My Lai massacre in Vietnam was a second lieutenant). Only by keeping your emotions in check can you remain focused on the mission.

During that seven-month deployment, we went on more than one hundred direct action raids and more than forty recons and sniper ambushes. We accomplished more missions in a deployment than any Force Recon platoon in history, including during the Vietnam War—and none of my men was killed.

Back at Camp Pendleton, I was awarded a Bronze Star with valor. Soon after, I was promoted to major. A good day? No, a depressing day. Once you were a major, your career as a gunfighter was over. I could no longer serve shoulder to shoulder with the men whom I'd fought beside for years. I was being moved up and out.

When Smith asked if I wanted any friends or family to be at my promotion ceremony, I told him, with a defeated sigh: "No, let's just do this in your office, sir."

After being on station for more than three years, beyond the time most Marine officers stay in operational assignments, I was offered some enticing posts for my next stop. I could train a reserve Force Recon platoon that mustered only one weekend a month on the windward side of Oahu in Hawaii. Also on the table was becoming the naval attaché in Hanoi, Vietnam, a job which largely consisted of entertaining dignitaries. Both would be vacations of a sort.

But how could I leave those men I had been with when they returned to combat?

There was one other option: I could remain with my platoon, but only serve in operations. In that role, I could hopefully help them succeed, and survive, for another deployment.

And that is what I chose.

When it came to combat, those days were over for me.

Or so I thought.

Targets on Our Backs

U pon its birth, MARSOC was an orphaned child. One that neither parent, Special Operations Command (SOCOM), or the
Marine Corps, wanted.

The Marines had always pushed back against the idea of an elite
within an elite, that any group within the Marines was somehow more special than the Corps as a whole.

After the 1941 attack on Pearl Harbor, when the name "Marine
Commandos" was suggested for an element envisioned as the American
equivalent of the British commandos, the Marine Commandant cracked:
"The term 'Marine' is sufficient to indicate a man ready for duty at any
time, and the injection of a special name, such as 'Commando,' would
be undesirable and superfluous." The unit was finally called the Marine
Raiders, but was disbanded only two years later, with commanders saying
that "handpicked outfits were detrimental to the morale of other troops."

Following the world-changing attacks of September 11, however,
Secretary of Defense Donald Rumsfeld saw the extraordinary effectiveness
of special operations forces—the Navy SEALs, the Army's Special Forces
and Green Berets, and the Air Force's Air Commandos—in the war on
terrorism and in Afghanistan and Iraq. He resolved to increase the number
of those forces under the umbrella of SOCOM, which had been formed
in 1987. Since the Marines did not have a special operations contingent,

no Marine command had ever been permanently committed to SOCOM. Now Rumsfeld wanted the Marines to pony up.

The Marine Corps was not happy. True, Force Recon was already elite, but at least we were under Marine control. Many within the Corps believed that Marines should support Marines, that a Marine special operations force such as Recon and Force Recon should work only as part of a Marine Expeditionary Unit. They felt that taking such an element away from a MEU and having it answer directly to SOCOM, would dilute not just the MEU but degrade the effectiveness of the entire Corps.

There was also the issue of power. Historically, Marines have been sensitive about being a branch of the armed forces within the Department of the Navy. Some believed that by ceding control over Marine personnel to yet another entity, SOCOM, the Marines would inevitably lose control over MARSOC—and that would insult the very core of the Corps.

So the Marines tried to stall.

Two years passed after 9/11 before the Corps reluctantly created a temporary unit, a platoon of eighty-six personnel known as Marine Corps Special Operations Command Detachment 1, based at Camp Pendleton, around a nucleus of Marines from the Force Recon community.

Det 1's deployment to Iraq in 2004 was considered a success. But a serious problem was exposed—Det 1 was seen as competition by those forces already in existence. As soon as Det 1 was placed under the command of the SEALs, its future was doomed.

Inter-service rivalry was not new. There is a famous photo of the Marine Brig. Gen. Lewis "Griff" Merritt in the jungles of the South Pacific during World War II sitting behind his desk, which had a sign on it that read: "We are fighting the Axis—not one another."

I understood. The SEALs and Green Berets had been doing special ops for decades and here the Marines, the new kids on the block, were competing with them for money and resources.

While the individuals in Det 1 did their jobs well, the unit did little to promote the idea of Marine special operations. The only purpose it ultimately served was to keep Rumsfeld at bay. But, eventually, tired of the unwillingness of the Marines to comply with his request, a vexed Rumsfeld kicked the Marine command in the jimmy. In late 2005, he ordered the defiant Corps to create a permanent unit under SOCOM. Thus the Marine Special Operations Company—MARSOC—was born.

MARSOC had a target on its back from the start. The Marines did not want MARSOC and SOCOM did not want to deal with the Marine holier-than-thou attitude. The SEALs and Green Berets wanted to keep the power and money afforded to special operations to themselves.

When the organizing body was labeled a Marine Special Operations Battalion (MSOB), it was widely scorned as the "Marine Sons of Bitches." Nevertheless, the first Marine Special Operations Command company was slated to deploy by early 2007.

As a young Marine major, I had no desire to be chopped up in the political and bureaucratic meat grinder that would be MARSOC. I was perfectly content in 1st Force Recon, where I had served since 2002, for my third, and probably final, deployment to Iraq. Though I would be at an operations center and not dug in with my platoon, I was very much looking forward to being around guys I respected and admired for one more go. We had stayed together not because of the financial bonuses other services offered but because we were completely committed to our comrades.

For my pre-deployment leave around Christmas 2005, a month before we were scheduled to go back to Iraq, I went to the Big Island of Hawaii, where my girlfriend Sugar Rae's family lived. Being Hawaiian, Sugar Rae exuded that "hang loose" vibe. She was laid back and happy. I loved that about her, maybe because she was so different from intensely serious Fred.

At her family's remote home, there was not a cell phone or internet connection to disturb the peace and quiet of country life. When we were dropped off at the Hilo airport to return to San Diego, I had wireless reception for the first time in a week. Sitting in the open-air waiting room, Sugar Rae laid her head on my chest as I caught up on my emails and phone messages.

"Congratulations, Fred," said a friend in a voice mail. "You are the first guy with orders to MARSOC."

I was blindsided. I was unaware that the leadership within the Corps had contacted Smith, my CO at 1st Force Recon, in its search for a Force

Recon major with significant combat experience. Though we butted heads during our deployment earlier in the year, he apparently had given me a glowing recommendation to Petronzio, MARSOC's freshly minted assistant chief of staff.

I understood what the orders meant—I would be wrenched away not only from my brothers in the 4th Platoon but from the family that was 1st Force Recon. To have spent such an intense part of my life with them and then be suddenly compelled to leave was horrible news.

"Who was that, Freddy?" Sugar Rae asked in her surfer girl accent.

I hesitated. Going to MARSOC also meant I would have to leave San Diego and move across the country to Camp Lejeune.

I didn't think our relationship could withstand my transfer to the east coast. No matter how much we wanted to be with each other, there was no ring on her finger, and having her come with me was a sacrifice I could not ask her to make.

After a few minutes of tortured contemplation, I told her about the assignment to take command of the first Marine Corps special operations unit.

"But the decision may not be final," I said, hopeful there was still a chance I could remain with 1st Force Recon and save what I had with Sugar Rae.

Upon returning to San Diego, I met with Smith.

"Sir, is there any way this can at least be delayed? I can deploy to Iraq and when we come back I can take over the second MARSOC company, the one that will be stood up here at Camp Pendleton."

"Fred, I wish I could," he said, clearly wanting to be helpful, "but I only rate two majors in the command. I have three and you've been here the longest. I'd love to take you to Iraq with us, but the needs of the Marine Corps come first."

Unsaid was that the other majors also did not want to move to Camp Lejeune, a place derisively referred to as "The Swamp." They were married, had children in school, and owned homes. I, on the other hand, was single and rented a small second-floor "Fonzie pad" (named for the attic space where Fonzie lived in the 1970s TV series *Happy Days*).

After I finished 1st Force Recon's pre-deployment workup, I would be given nine days to get to Camp Lejeune by early February. My platoon would go to Iraq without me while I created a new unit from scratch.

There was a lot of work ahead. Even if Sugar Rae joined me, she would surely find herself way down on my list of priorities. I knew it was unfair to string her along and pretend that we could stay together. When I kissed her in San Diego before heading out on my cross-country road trip, it was a goodbye kiss.

I had already thrown myself into the mission. My first call on behalf of Fox Company (Marine convention labeled companies alphabetically, so Alpha, Bravo, Charlie, Delta, Echo, Fox, etc.) was to Big Dave, who was now at 2nd Force Recon in Camp Lejeune.

"Are you interested?" I asked, offering him the post of senior enlisted advisor, the highest-ranking enlisted Marine, for Fox Company.

Young came from a Marine family. His father and his sister were both lieutenant colonels, and his two brothers were in Force Recon. To say that the Youngs believed in military service—and the Marines—was an understatement.

But Big Dave was wary of MARSOC too.

"Are you sure you're going to be the commanding officer?" he asked. "I'm about ready to drop my retirement papers. Call them and make sure. If you're going to be the CO, hell yeah, I'll go with you!"

I contacted MARSOC headquarters, and they confirmed that I was coming to command, not just to plan, train, and then hand off to someone else.

With Big Dave signed on, I asked him, "Who would you like to be our platoon sergeant?"

He said there was only one man for the job.

Gunnery Sgt. Mike Clarke was a gravelly-voiced hard-ass from Missouri with the nasty mug of a boxer who had been cut too often. He would look at you like he hated you because he did. But it was not personal. He hated everybody until you earned his respect. He had been in the Corps some twenty years, evidenced by his thinning black hair, and had ten overseas deployments under his belt, double what most of his peers could claim. He had fought everywhere from Somalia and Yemen to Iraq.

Gunny was not a big, muscular guy. He did not work out at the gym. But everything he did had a purpose for combat. He ran to develop stamina for long patrols. He did push-ups and sit-ups so he could carry heavy loads. He squeezed vise grips so his hands would be strong holding a weapon. He trained until he achieved mastery—and he trained the men he led to do the same. Clarke had won the award for Best Team Leader in 2nd Force Recon the previous year.

When I called him, he was training, as expected, taking a precision shooting course given by retired Army Special Forces guys in Arizona.

"Meet me at Camp Lejeune," I told him, adding, "Who's the captain you want to lead the assault platoon?"

He answered quickly: "Sid East."

East was cut from the same cloth as Clarke but looked as different as could be. East was as handsome as a movie star, one who always got the girl. But he never acted haughtily. He was always hat in hand humble. Raised by his mom in Philadelphia, he graduated from the Naval Academy. I gleaned from his combat record he was as courageous and gutsy as they come. I knew he would give everything he had to his men and the mission.

Clarke and Big Dave chose the remaining enlisted men from 2nd Force Recon to comprise East's 1st Platoon. These were not tender recruits; their average age was twenty-seven. They were experienced warriors, almost to a man combat veterans of Iraq. Each had enlisted as an infantry grunt but wanted to do more.

Each sought to serve in a unit where you could completely trust the man to your left and the man to your right. They wanted to serve alongside men who had joined the Marines for a compelling reason—to satisfy something missing in their lives.

The 2nd Platoon, our security element, would be made up of younger infantry Marines who had recently returned from a deployment in western Iraq. With the addition of a team of intelligence specialists and others, we would eventually be 115 strong.

I chose Devin Braden to be our air officer and forward air controller. He was one of the Marine F/A-18 Hornet pilots who provided air cover during my last Iraq deployment. I didn't want a transport pilot; I wanted someone who would call in an airstrike knowing what it was like to drop a bomb on the bad guys without injuring the good guys. I also wanted someone who could be available immediately and didn't need to deal with a wife and kids.

Making my way from Camp Pendleton, I stopped in Las Vegas, where he was at Nellis Air Force Base. I knew the bald-headed Braden was the man for the job—since he had no problem with my interviewing him at the Spearmint Rhino strip club. Why the heck not? We were Marines, we were in Vegas, and we were both single.

It was fortunate that, like me, he was not tied down with other responsibilities because he too was about to get very busy. I had him promptly check out of his squadron in South Carolina so he could attend a series of training courses around the country. He wasn't going to have time to visit another strip club anytime soon.

As I drove the length of the country, I visited special operations commands of the Air Force and the Army as well as the joint commands that included everyone. Consulting with them, I tried to corral the support of those who could help us with any potential mission.

Reporting to Camp Lejeune, I was informed that Fox Company would deploy with the 26th MEU in January 2007. I had eleven months to train up my men. Given the assistance everyone seemed willing to offer us, that seemed fair enough. I was also happy to learn that the 26th MEU's operations officer was Lt. Col. Don McQueen, my first company commander when I was a second lieutenant in 1st Light Armored Recon. He asked me to meet him at the Officers' Club at 5 p.m. to catch up.

What I saw driving there was an alien landscape to those of us from Camp Pendleton. Passing a river road base housing area on that unseasonably warm day, I noticed officers in uniform sitting leisurely at white-draped tables on a manicured lawn enjoying an afternoon picnic. Their tastefully dressed wives served them drinks and finger food on silver trays. For a hardworking middle-class kid from the Midwest, that Southern gentleman vibe spoke of a military upper crust I never knew existed. To me, it felt somehow inappropriate, even unpatriotic.

Besides myself, there was only one other man in uniform in the Officers' Club. Leaning his back against the bar, he had three stars on each collar. I knew that a three-star here had to be the II Marine Expeditionary Force commanding general. I had never met a general before.

I stopped sharply in front of him and greeted him in a robust voice: "Good evening, sir."

He glanced at me, read my name tape, and, strangely, said nothing.

I noted the name on his uniform, "AMOS," and excused myself to sit at a table to wait for McQueen to arrive. The lack of responsiveness from Lt. Gen. Jim Amos was curious, but I set it aside.

Talking with McQueen, I felt grateful to have such a strong relationship with the MEU's staff right off the bat. Maybe my trepidation about MARSOC was unwarranted.

But my first meeting five days later with Brig. Gen. Dennis Hejlik, MARSOC's commander, proved unsettling. Hejlik told me straight away that I was never to speak for him or use his name as my authority.

MARSOC was indeed an orphaned child, I said to myself.

When he asked if I had any questions, sitting kneecap to kneecap with him, I said I had three:

"First, what's our mission?" I wanted to know if we should focus on direct action raids, reconnaissance patrols, maritime boarding, or training indigenous forces.

"Second, who's the commander I'll work for while deployed?" Was the colonel in charge of the special operations forces overseeing the battlespace giving the orders, or the Marine colonel in charge of the MEU on the ships?

"Third, where are we going?" I didn't need a ten-digit grid coordinate showing the exact location, but I wanted to know the subregion. Knowing the threat environment was critical to tailoring our training and equipment for both the enemy and the terrain.

"Well," Hejlik said, "you're going to get on the ship and whatever comes will be like a regular deployment."

That was it? He had to realize there would be nothing regular about this deployment. I was dumbfounded.

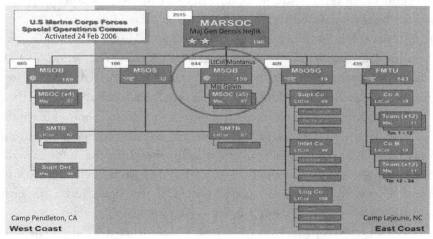

Marine Special Operations Command's Organizational Chart

Another meeting soon afterward brought together the MEU's leadership and Hejlik's staff to discuss how MARSOC was being rolled out. Many of the best men from Force Recon had been recruited to Fox Company, and some in the MEU were not happy. Usually dignified colonels and lieutenant colonels were shouting at each other.

I stood up and yelled over them.

"Gentlemen! Gentlemen!"

The room went quiet.

"I understand some of you think it's unfair for Force Recon to get ripped out of the MEU for the sake of MARSOC. But you have to understand one thing: MARSOC is happening. That is a fact and you'll have to deal with it."

"And you are who?" someone asked.

"I'm Maj. Galvin, commanding officer of Marine Special Operations Company Foxtrot."

No one cared. I was only a major. Ignoring me, they went back to arguing with each other.

That would never have happened at Camp Pendleton. On the west coast, if a young corporal had something to say, he would be brought in belt buckle close and listened to. At least that had been my experience. But on the east coast, it seemed to me rank was far more important.

I never felt I was better than the men I led. Most people think *gung ho*, the Chinese phrase the Marine Raiders picked up in World War II, describes someone who is motivated and enthusiastic. Actually, it translates as "work together." For MARSOC to succeed, we all had to work together.

Then McQueen broke some bad news as we left the room: He would not be deploying with us. He had been selected for command at our old unit, 1st Light Armored Recon. He was someone I trusted, but he would not be there to watch my back. The 26th MEU would be handed off to Col. Gregg Sturdevant, and until MARSOC was operational, my boss would be the CO of 2nd Force Recon—Lt. Col. Paul Montanus.

I had crossed paths with Montanus in Iraq when we did a right seat, left seat exchange—a couple of our 1st Force Recon leaders joining 2nd Force Recon for a mission and a couple of theirs joining us. I saw him utterly embarrass and humiliate his commissioned and non-commissioned officers (NCOs) in front of their men. They then had to try to lead their enlisted Marines into combat. It was a sorry sight.

Montanus loved the spit and polish, not the down and dirty. Marines beneath him privately derided him as a "perfumed parade princess," someone who looked and smelled good but had accomplished little.

Montanus had served a mere twelve months as a platoon commander at 3rd Recon before nabbing unprecedented back-to-back nonoperational assignments in Coronado, California, where he endeavored to perfect his performance as an athlete, running countless road races and triathlons. After Petronzio went from CO of 2nd Force Recon to assistant chief of staff of MARSOC, Montanus managed to slide into Petronzio's former post, despite his lack of credentials.

All decisions pertaining to MARSOC were in the hands of the leadership of MARSOC. Nevertheless, Montanus was peeved about what Petronzio was doing, particularly about choosing me as the company CO.

I suspect he had promised Ukeiley that he would be the first commander of MSOC-Fox.

After all, Montanus owed him.

Ukeiley had agreed to remain behind in the States as 2nd Force Recon's executive officer while Montanus deployed to Iraq. That was a sacrifice on his part. Having never deployed to a war zone, especially when there had been many years of combat operations, was crushing his chances for promotion to lieutenant colonel. An intelligence officer with a law degree, Ukeiley had never served as an infantry officer or a Recon or Force Recon platoon commander. He desperately needed to be deployed at the head of Fox Company.

But I was oblivious to any animosity from Montanus toward me. When he led 2nd Force Recon off the busses at Camp Lejeune after returning from Iraq, I was there, as a courtesy, to greet him and his men.

"Oh, Maj. Galvin," Montanus said in his nasally voice, "what are you doing here?"

"I'm here to welcome you and your Marines back home, sir."

"You're not here as part of MARSOC, are you?" he said, squinting.

I answered straightforwardly: "I'm the commander of Marine Special Operations Company Foxtrot."

It wasn't the answer he was looking for. Montanus had hoped to coerce and cajole Hejlik and Petronzio into changing their minds. It burned him to hear that the decision was final—and to hear it from me.

"Well then," he said, "remember you're working for me until MARSOC stands up. After this 96, come and see me."

After the four-day weekend, I respectfully waited at the door to his office the following morning. He did not show up. The next morning, as I walked into the headquarters building we shared, I intercepted him in the first-floor lobby.

"Oh, Maj. Galvin, what are you doing here?"

"Sir, I'm reporting as ordered. You asked to see me after the 96."

"Oh," he said and walked away without another word.

I followed him upstairs to his office and waited for him to get settled before doing what a Marine is supposed to do, bang on the hatch, the door, three times.

"Maj. Galvin, come in."

I sat down and began to detail my plans for the manning, equipping, and training of MSOC-Fox.

But Montanus was not interested.

"Maj. Galvin, you don't need to worry about a single thing when it comes to men and materiel because you will have the best. Let's face it," he continued with a cynical tone, "you have an easy job. All you have to do is train your Marines. That's it."

I sensed he was not paying me a compliment.

As soon as I exited, he immediately sent word to his staff to meet him in his conference room.

"Gentlemen, let me be very clear about two things," Montanus told them. "One, this is 2nd Force Recon and two, this is 2nd Force Recon. There will not be one person, there will not be one round of ammunition, there will not be one truck, there will not be one training request, there will not be any support, given to Marine special operations. I need to make sure you all understand that."

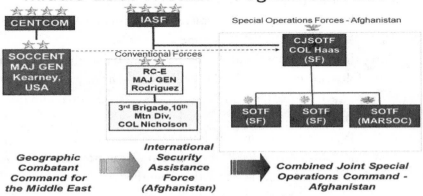

Central Command's Organizational Chart

I knew what he said because one of the men in the meeting was Big Dave! Montanus had not yet been told that I was poaching the only master sergeant on his staff. Big Dave walked directly from the conference room to our first-floor office and repeated to me every word Montanus said.

I picked up the phone and relayed to Petronzio the Montanus tirade. Petronzio exploded.

"That motherfucker! I thought he might act like that! Fred, I'm going to work this out. I'll get in touch with him and get back to you."

Montanus was summoned to Petronzio's office, where he was dressed down. But Montanus was given his pound of flesh. If Ukeiley could not be the CO of Fox Company, then Montanus insisted that he be our liaison officer. That way Ukeiley could notch his combat deployment—and Montanus could keep his hands in Fox Company.

I had won the first battle, but the turf war had just begun.

MARSOC was activated on February 24. Rumsfeld; Commandant of the Marine Corps Gen. Michael Hagee; Army Gen. Doug Brown, the commanding general of SOCOM; and Hejlik officiated at the ceremony. It reminded me of the wedding scene in *The Godfather*, with Rumsfeld as Don Corleone overseeing the forced marriage of the Marine Corps and SOCOM.

In Brown's speech that sunny morning, he said: "When the first Marine Special Operations Command company crosses the 30th parallel, you will be operationally tasked by the theater Special Operations Command." In other words, once we entered the Suez Canal in the Middle East, we would be controlled by SOCCENT, Special Operations Command - Central, headed by Army Maj. Gen. Francis "Frank" Kearney. That was the first time I knew for certain who was going to be our boss.

That also meant we were going into combat.

By giving us to SOCCENT, Rumsfeld made it clear that he was not going to allow the Marines to keep us stashed away, far from the action, on a ship with the MEU. So he had said, and so it shall be.

1st Platoon, Fox Company conducting sustainment training in Djibouti prior to deploying to Afghanistan

A reception followed at the Officers' Club. While the majority of the MARSOC headquarters staff congregated around Hejlik or the colonel in charge of their section, I gravitated to several Marine Raiders from World War Two who were in attendance.

The old Marines were glad to see the Corps truly become part of special operations. I was excited to hear their stories of the vicious hand-to-hand fighting with the Japanese in the South Pacific.

They were hunched over and hard of hearing now, but in their youth, they had experienced the dark heart of an enemy. They gathered around me to offer their advice.

"Major," said one of them, "make sure you kill them all."

The other Raiders echoed his words: "Make sure you kill them all."

1st Platoon, Fox Company conducting live fire training in Hawthorne, NV

100 Percent In

All eyes were on us—and I was going to make sure we didn't fail. Over the next eleven months, Fox Company trained from Fort Bragg, North Carolina; Fallon and Hawthorne, Nevada; Chesapeake Bay and Fort Pickett, Virginia; Avon Park and Hurlburt Field, Florida; and Fort Campbell, Kentucky, to Yuma, Camp Lejeune, ships at sea, and beyond. We did not know exactly where we would be going in the Middle East or what we would be doing. We had to be ready for anything.

We trained in the desert, the mountains, and even in civilian urban environments. In one exercise, the instructors wanted us to assault a very large complex rigged with IEDs, where "insurgents" had RPGs and machine guns. They presumed we would make a hard hit and run the ball straight up the middle. Instead, I had a foot patrol approach the compound with stealth through the nastiest possible terrain and use mechanical breaching tools to cut a passage through a fence.

We achieved complete surprise on the "enemy." When the instructors realized where we were, they had to shut down a civilian railroad line.

We trained with ships for search and seizure, and for amphibious operations; with vehicles to increase our off-road driving ability; and with aircraft, from fixed-wing attack jets and long-range bombers to rotary attack helicopters. We conducted live fire, close air support training with AC-130

Spectre gunships to ensure that every Marine, not just Braden, our air officer, was able to control that aircraft's fire support systems.

We employed so many resources of the Special Operations Aviation Regiment (SOAR) that senior Army Special Operations leaders whined that we were fighting above our weight class.

We planned, briefed, and executed full-mission profiles in every environment and with every service component of SOCOM. In those exercises, we often had to deal with sudden, unexpected events. The staff would also intentionally provide intelligence that was inaccurate, incomplete, or unreliable.

We practiced marksmanship too. The Corps took great pride in that skill. The sign over Stone Bay, the home of Camp Lejeune's rifle range, read: "You don't hurt 'em if you don't hit 'em," a quote from legendary Marine Gen. "Chesty" Puller.

We engaged man-sized targets with a service rifle at distances from 25 to 500 meters during day and night using both slow and rapid-fire. We were tested wearing full combat gear, stationary, walking, after sprinting, from behind, underneath and over barriers, with and without gas masks, and during live-fire obstacle courses, where Marines aggressively competed against each other to rapidly recognize and engage multiple targets in order to be named the platoon top gun. The turret gunners selected for each of our six convoy Humvees qualified with their machine guns during the workup and had to continue to meet the standard while in theater.

In decision making drills, we were required to immediately identify if any of multiple targets was a threat, then instantly address the most imminent threat before engaging each subsequent target within the kill zone—twice in the center of the chest (the organ cavity) and once between the eyes (the brain box) within 2.5 seconds. You never put your finger on the trigger unless you were up on the target and ready to fire. If someone "dropped a shot," he was taken out of the platoon until he succeeded in the drill.

Training also addressed the mental aspect of combat, "killology." The psychological, emotional, and physiological responses experienced during and after close-quarter combat were explored, including hormonal effects on the brain, vision, and manual dexterity.

Unambiguous personal and unit safety and accuracy were the goals, and each individual's mindset was closely scrutinized in the toughest conditions by instructors who watched from every angle. No quarter was given by the instructors. We wanted disciplined Marines, not lunatics with guns. If you couldn't hack the pressure, you were counseled. If you failed again, you were gone.

Typically during exercises and qualifications, a few Force Recon Marines in any platoon would wash out and be left behind. But, thanks to Clarke's tenacity, every one of our Marines graduated every course, which was unheard of given the high level of performance required. Our dedication paid off in spades—we did not have a single accuracy or speed issue and not one safety incident.

Some of the Marines thought Clarke was sadistic for pushing them so ferociously. Their wives or girlfriends were especially irritated at him because of the trips around the country and the otherwise long hours. They vented to Big Dave and to me about not having their men around to go to a movie or dinner or to watch a child's Little League game.

As far as I was concerned, my Marines were putting a down payment on their future survival. Sure, training robbed them of time they should have had with their families, but the return on that investment was a better chance of coming back from combat alive and well.

I never regretted training them too hard. I would forever regret it if they died because I didn't train them hard enough.

They all got along, which is not a given when you have a bunch of competitive alpha males trying to be the best they could be. Maybe because most of them were older, late twenties and early thirties, and many of them married, they were more low-key and laid back. Even the youngest, Walker, was married. There were not a lot of wild and crazy off-duty nights. I didn't have to babysit them to make sure they didn't get into trouble, which typically would have involved women and/or booze. We were usually too exhausted after a typical day to go out on the town.

Not that we were perfect. Klein, who was big and boisterous, seemed to invite trouble when he did drink. He kept an empty glass bottle in the back pocket of his baggy jeans just in case he needed to break it over someone's head in a bar fight. I was not surprised to hear he used it a time or two in watering holes around Camp Lejeune.

When an infantry Marine in our 2nd Platoon was charged with fighting a civilian—he was defending a woman the man had slapped—Montanus took the opportunity to ream me.

Exploding in rage in front of his staff, he railed that he ought to relieve me. Hearing about that, I went to his office and confronted him.

I requested that he relieve me immediately so that Fox Company would have the benefit of a new commander as early as possible before its deployment.

Put on the spot, Montanus lashed out.

"Never again ask me to relieve you of command," he said sternly. "I have the power to do it, you know, and the next time I just might take you up on that."

I would have been shocked if you had told me then that he would indeed have another chance to do exactly that.

For our final evaluation, we were tasked with an emergency assault of an objective-based upon time sensitive intelligence. Testing Fox Company's mission planning, command and control, and simultaneous mission execution capabilities, we were assigned one raid or recon mission every four hours for a grueling forty-eight straight hours. At any given time, we had three missions in the planning or execution stages. Passing with flying colors, Fox Company was certified as "special operations capable" to conduct direct action and special reconnaissance missions for deployments worldwide.

Senior leaders from Navy, Air Force, and Army special operations were astonished that the Marine Corps was able to successfully train a new special ops unit in less than one year. The message was heard throughout the special operations community—the Marines had landed.

Brimming with confidence, we were ready to rock 'n' roll.

The call sign I chose for Fox Company was appropriately in-your-face: Violent. Marine units with kinetic missions always had call signs with edgy names, such as Mortalis, Punisher, Vengeance, and Hitman. Call signs were not soft and cuddly, and ours didn't raise an eyebrow.

In retrospect, maybe I should have chosen a more politically correct call sign.

There were inklings that some at MARSOC headquarters would be obstacles to hurdle, rather than stepping stools to raise us up. Force Recon was lean and mean; MARSOC was fat and bloated. Led by a brigadier general (Hejlik) who had staff sections topped by seasoned full bird colonels, there were 197 Marines in the command unit. There was also a Marine Special Operations Support Group (MSOSG) to provide intelligence and logistics. Originally staffed with 315 Marines, the MSOSG quickly grew to 416, larger than that for all the Force Recon units combined.

Worse, our headquarters was littered with Marines who were unwilling, unable, or unwanted when others deployed to combat.

They were not at MARSOC to serve; they were at MARSOC to avoid serving. Not everyone has to be a fighter, but everyone should be willing to give everything they have to contribute to the success of the mission, to give themselves to something greater than themselves. These people were more interested in protocol than doing their utmost for men risking their lives on the front lines. They exhibited utter indifference to the seriousness of their jobs.

Not even the sight of flights regularly landing at nearby Cherry Point with caskets in the back of them, or a pair of Marines showing up at a widow's door in base housing with a folded flag, could change their selfish attitudes. They were attached to special operations only so they could look "special."

Petronzio was aware of the situation. Son of a Marine drill instructor who fought in Korea and Vietnam, the stocky officer grew up on Marine bases. The level of incompetence at MARSOC headquarters was such that he wrote in a letter to Smith: "You would not believe the stupidity I face here every day."

He could do little to help us. When I submitted a list of equipment I wanted, such as binocular night vision goggles for greater depth perception, upgraded weapon systems, vehicles able to withstand roadside bombs and mines, and advanced body armor, he barked at me: "Fred, the only equipment you need is already there in the 2nd Force Recon armory. That's what you will use."

We were also short on support personnel to accompany us on the deployment. Six was the minimum number required to sustain combat capability. We were assigned one—an inexperienced mechanic who had to keep forty-five vehicles, including sixteen Humvees, in working order.

I hoped Ukeiley might be of use, but he didn't spend a single day with Fox Company during our eleven months of prep. Instead, he wrote articles for the *Marine Corps Gazette*, obtained his private pilot's license, and delved into amateur mixed martial arts. His priorities began and ended with the man looking back at him in the mirror.

My protests only exasperated Montanus. Denying my requests, he pointedly suggested we spend less time training and more time "integrating" with his command.

He was also annoyed that Fox Company didn't celebrate the Marine Corps Birthday Ball, our high holy day, exclusively with his battalion. A couple of days after returning from training with SOAR in Fort Campbell, we did attend his affair, but we had our own celebration on the actual birthday of the Marine Corps (November 10) in Nashville.

The highlight of our event was the appearance of PFC. Chuck Meacham, a Marine Raider. We had spoken at the MARSOC activation ceremony, and I invited him to be our guest of honor. He genuinely inspired the Marines of Fox Company to prove ourselves worthy of carrying on the heroic tradition of the Marine Raiders from World War Two.

Montanus, however, felt I was trying to eclipse his own effort.

Maybe I should have stroked his enormous ego. Maybe I should have feigned interest in the design of his new battalion logo. Maybe I should have brought him flowers and chocolates.

In OCS, we learned about selfless service, not careerism, not about how to please our boss to get a promotion. Montanus had a rear echelon mentality. My men and I were going to the front lines.

Sure, I rubbed him and others the wrong way—I was persistent at best and overzealous at worst—but my sacred duty was to make sure we did our job for the people of America and my men came home to their families.

But where exactly were we going?

Most signs pointed to Iraq. By May 2006, the situation there was melting down, and every Marine in Afghanistan was being pulled out to reinforce our troops in Iraq. On the other hand, we could be sent to Yemen, or Djibouti in the Horn of Africa, or even to Afghanistan, where the Taliban were making a comeback, filling the vacuum we created by our withdrawal with brutal terror. When we were ordered to take two weeks of language training, we had to study three: Arabic (for Iraq and the others), French (for Djibouti), and Dari (for Afghanistan).

As far as I was concerned, two weeks of a foreign language was just enough to get us into trouble. You could learn some useful commands, such as "stop" or "put down your weapons," but you couldn't hold a conversation. Being misunderstood when you had to make split-second decisions was a recipe for disaster. I would rather rely on an interpreter. But we took the courses and waited to be told our destination.

Wherever that was, I was going to be gone a long time, probably seven months. Whenever I went on a deployment, I would give my girlfriend at the time the option to gracefully and amicably back out of our relationship. That only seemed right, for both of us.

I did not want to give Holly that option.

I had met Holly Rochester four years earlier in Yuma. She was an intelligence officer, a first lieutenant, at a time when there were few female Marine officers. Originally from upstate New York, she had been in the Reserve Officer Training Corps (ROTC) in college and then graduated from Officer Candidates School in Quantico. She was smart and hardworking, qualities I really admired. That woman could brief a room of Marines like few male officers.

Confident and clear, she truly was impressive. You did not find women like her trolling bars in San Diego.

You rarely found women at all at the Yuma Air Station, such a desolate base in a desert town that it was called a "man ranch." More than a hundred of the Marines' best pilots, all of them men, would train there. They were jet jocks, and they were fueled by testosterone.

Some sported the "Maverick" or "Goose" cool guy look from the movie *Top Gun*—the Hollywood leather jacket and embarrassingly tacky aviator glasses. Some even carried business cards displaying their aviator wings to hand out to women. Those gold-colored wings earned the name "golden leg spreaders" for a reason.

One of only three females on the base, Holly was the best looking by far. In her mid-twenties, like most of the pilots, she was a Katie Holmes type, not a blonde bombshell but a cute girl next door, tall with black hair. A female unicorn in a world of men, she was the belle of the ball.

But I was at Yuma to work. It was 2002; I was a captain, in my early thirties, and completely professional. During the six-week course she took, we never spoke to each other except as teacher to student. I was aloof and didn't make a move on her. Because of that, she thought I was a jerk.

A few months later, when I was a 1st Force Recon platoon commander at sea around the Persian Gulf, she was on the intelligence team that deployed with our task force. Working together on the same ship every day for several weeks, we came to admire each other's capacity for focusing on the mission—and also grew increasingly attracted to each other.

But we kept our feelings to ourselves. We never talked on a personal level, never had a date. Though we were subsequently stationed at the same base in Al-Anbar Province at the height of Iraq's insurgency, we were separated by our undivided devotion to our jobs, not to mention a great deal of concertina wire.

Then, six months after being assigned to stand up MARSOC, Holly emailed from Virginia. She was taking an intelligence officer's course and wanted to visit me over a weekend. She came down to Camp Lejeune with a male officer friend of mine, who was in the course with her, and they stayed at my rented townhouse. My friend and I racked out on a couch and an air mattress downstairs; I gave Holly my bed upstairs.

By the time we took a four-day trip to Washington, DC, over the 4th of July, we were officially dating. When we were both given another 96 for the Marine Corps Birthday, I flew to Yuma, where she was now an instructor and a captain, and we attended the Marine Corps Ball together.

We were falling in love.

With Fox Company's overseas deployment looming, I did not want to let her go.

"I'm one hundred percent in," I told her. "If you want, we can pick up where we left off when I get back."

"I'd like that too," she said with a big smile.

We spent a joyous Christmas holiday together before Holly left on her own much shorter forty-five-day deployment, a once-in-a-lifetime opportunity to support Special Forces missions in Iraq.

She was not at Camp Lejeune the morning of Wednesday, January 3, when Fox Company gathered together with our loved ones—wives and children, moms and dads, brothers and sisters—for Hejlik's stirring send-off speech before we were bussed to Norfolk, Virginia to board the *USS Bataan*.

"We still don't know where you'll be going," he said to the assembled crowd. "Well, we may know, but there's no certainty. What I do know is that some of you, many of you, won't be coming back."

I shook my head in disbelief. Did our general, our leader, just say what I think he said? My Marines looked at each other and wondered if that was the most asinine thing we had ever heard. What kind of pep rally was this? Why would anyone say that? You *never* say that in front of families!

With Hejlik's words ringing in our ears, Fox Company set sail for war.

Level Zero

After a few days crossing the Atlantic, we finally learned our destination: Afghanistan.

Nearly all of us had been to Iraq; only a few had been to Afghanistan. Our advance echelon and intelligence element, which had hung back at Camp Lejeune, quickly flew into Jalalabad to set up our base, which we named Camp Raider.

Meanwhile, the Navy let us know quickly that we were just passengers on this ship. To allow the *Bataan*'s sailors to do their work without interference during the day, we set up a vampire schedule.

At sunset, with nearly all the sailors in their bunks, we began eight hours of training and instruction, including required classes on the law of war and the ROE. Each night, we also conducted tactical clearing drills across the decks of the ship before transitioning to the flight deck for live-fire training until sunrise. We would then collect all the brass—the rifle and pistol casings—and complete a rigorous physical fitness regimen.

Hanging up our sweat-soaked clothes, including our black silky gym shorts known as "Ranger panties," we hoped they would dry out during the day while we grabbed a little shuteye. They never did, and the odor that followed us became an unavoidable curse of cramped ship life. Combined with suffering the rolls and yaws of being at sea, even Filthy Fred was looking forward to reaching the Mediterranean, where we could have our first port call, at Palermo, Italy.

Until then, we trained and enjoyed mealtimes on board with an unexpected shipmate—Dr. Thomas H. Johnson, a white-haired, spectacled professor from the Naval Postgraduate School who was an expert on Central Asia and was on his way to Afghanistan. As soon as we were told Fox Company would end up there too, I asked him to share his knowledge of the country's history and culture.

Johnson loved the Afghan people and would occasionally dress in their traditional garb for our dinners together. He emphasized that Afghanistan was different from the Iraq we knew. Thanks to oil, Iraqis had some wealth and education; Afghans were agricultural, poor, and illiterate. While most Iraqis were moderate in their religion, most Afghans leaned toward the radical. Both were tribal, he said, but Afghans were even more fiercely and pridefully family-oriented. He found Afghans to be noble people.

While I was dubious of the hospitality Johnson said the Afghans would show us, the daily reports sent by our advance team said there was also little hospitality awaiting us from Haas, the Special Forces commander, and his staff in Bagram. Apparently, Haas and his Green Berets were expressing a decidedly disturbing hostility towards Fox Company.

But we were at war with an enemy intent on destroying us. To me, there was no place for an Army-Navy football game in a combat zone. I hoped they would be more welcoming once the rest of us arrived.

After three days of liberty in Palermo and Marmaris, Turkey, we transited the Suez Canal and finally disembarked from the *Bataan* in Djibouti. In early February, we flew into Bagram, where we discovered that we were *Task Force* Violent.

Haas had directed his staff to designate us a task force—a not so subtle sign that we were on our own. He also ordered, despite being known as Fox Company during our entire workup, that we use our call sign for our unit name.

Haas took me into his office and showed me a map on a table indicating where we were to operate within AO Bulldog—a hastily scribbled circle around the infamous Tora Bora cave complex in the White Mountains.

I assumed that Area of Operations "Bulldog" was named by Ukeiley. The Army would certainly never have used that name since the bulldog was the mascot of the Marines, and Ukeiley was the only Marine who interacted with the Army staff. Besides, he'd shaved his head and thought he looked like a bulldog.

Haas was very familiar with eastern Afghanistan. As an Army special forces lieutenant colonel, he was prominently featured in Sean Naylor's 2005 book *Not a Good Day to Die*, which chronicled Operation Anaconda in the Shahikot Valley in 2002.

Haas knew that Tora Bora was where bin Laden was last seen—and that five years later, he was no longer there. If he were, Haas would have sent his own Green Berets to ferret him out. He also knew Al-Qaeda and the Taliban were no longer using ratlines to summit the White Mountains near Tora Bora as part of their infiltration routes to and from Pakistan. Why would they? They had Highway 1, Hell's Highway.

Haas was limiting us to the Tora Bora area to distract us and occupy our time. It was a red herring. He was keen enough about military politics to understand that success and promotion did not depend on what you did right but on not doing anything wrong. Haas was due to retrograde back to the States in late March, and he hoped to safely run out the clock. He would be rewarded for not taking risks, for not breaking anything. He did not want Fox Company to screw it up by, well, actually doing something.

What occurred later that day underlined his intention.

After reuniting with our advance team in Jalalabad, we learned that Marines training Afghan forces had been hit by an IED at an isolated desert outpost to the south. I notified CJSOTF-A that Fox Company, with our technologically advanced gear, was able to identify the bomber—and that he was one of the Afghan troops! Not only that, but he was still on the base! If we moved quickly, Fox Company could prevent his escape.

The CJSOTF-A staff responded with a firm "no."

Under no condition were we to intervene, they said. They wanted the perpetrator to establish a pattern before apprehending him. That was like hearing a police chief say he knew who the serial murderer was but wanted to wait until he killed again to be sure. It was outrageous and a huge disappointment.

In the military, you kill a plan by taking away its logistics.

All you had to do was look at Camp Raider.

What had not been stripped clean by the French troops who preceded us had been trashed. We had 115 men but no place to sleep, forcing us to hire local carpenters to build bunks. We had a well for drinking water but, finding it contaminated with fecal matter, had to scavenge bottled water. We had two generators for electricity but were not allotted fuel to run them. We had our mechanic but no equipment to service our vehicles. We did not even have guards. We hired presumably friendly Afghan civilians who, of course, stood around the camp looking like Taliban because they had no uniforms.

Instead of lending us the support personnel we needed, Haas sent, of all people, an Army chaplain!

I am a man of God, and I welcomed having services and the availability of religious counsel. Every day, I told my Marines that Chaps was there if anyone wanted to meet with him.

But the guy was goofy, ten-thumbed, corny, and sappy.

That did not go over well with my brutally earthy Force Recon barbarians. They made so much fun of him that an unhappy Chaps bolted in a huff and complained to Haas, who was offended we didn't appreciate his gesture.

Army Maj. Sebastian Johansson, an experienced logistics officer, showed up out of the blue one day and offered to help. I welcomed him with a grateful handshake and a hopeful smile.

But despite his nonstop energy and nose-to-the-grindstone approach, he too ran into a stone wall.

"Something as simple as the cereal," he later told the COI. "(The Marines would) try to get (boxes) from across the street. Couldn't get them. (They were told) 'we have a box here, but we're going to use it for our guys. You don't get any.'"

When he pleaded directly to MARSOC at Camp Lejeune, he earned scornful phone calls from Haas' staff about bypassing protocol.

"We're going to do it all from this end," Johansson was told by CJSOTF-A.

"Okay, fine," he said. "Who's gonna do it?"

"Well, we don't have anybody to do it right now."

Air Force Col. Patrick Pihana, Kearney's chief of staff, would later testify that Marine special operations was greeted with open arms! CJSOTF-A "did a great job of bringing the Marines on board, getting them received, staged and moved further on to their mission...once they came into theater. So it was a big challenge but everybody jumped right on it and treated it like another special operations mission... (This was) a service that we were welcoming into the fold, so to speak."

Not exactly.

The reality was that "MSOC-Fox was, in essence, pushed on (CJSOTF-A), which created a lot of friction and enhanced animosity," explained Johansson at the COI. "(Fox Company) was set up for failure as the CJSOTF, SOCOM and MARSOC knew what they needed to do and didn't do it... They put Fox Company into an AO with no support, which truly made it challenging to be successful."

Big Dave was more direct: "My personal gut feeling is that they really didn't want us to do well."

During the COI, Petronzio recalled a meeting years earlier when Det 1 was being formed. He said he was "sitting in an office of special forces colonels who had no idea who I was. I was not in uniform, I did not look like a Marine... It was a huge, snickering joke about how they were going to kill this process... That culture is out there...and we're going to have to fight through it just like we're going to have to fight through it in our own culture. We still have a bunch of Marines who don't think MARSOC is a good idea."

Even for those in our corner, it was apparent that our mere arrival was the only definition of success, our "mission accomplished." Ukeiley said as much. All they wanted was a trouble-free, uneventful deployment that would encourage SOCOM to bring in another company and maybe, eventually, the Marines would be accepted into the special ops community.

In other words, avoid making waves and maybe they will ask us to the next dance.

Col. Sturdevant was asked by one of my attorneys at the COI if it was his decision to starve MARSOC of men and materiel.

"No, it was not my decision," he answered nervously.

"Then if it was not your decision, it must have come from above you, is it safe to say?"

"Yes," Sturdevant said without elaboration.

"And if it came from above you," the attorney probed, "then it's safe to say that the order to not support them came from a general, correct?"

Sturdevant was again brief: "Yes."

He was circumspect because no one wanted to name names; no one wanted to piss off a general. But I suspect the general in question was Amos, commanding general of the II Marine Expeditionary Force, whom I'd met, however briefly and coldly, at the Camp Lejeune Officers' Club.

I would discover why Amos might have made that decision to leave us hanging out to dry only much later.

What I knew, at the moment, was that Fox Company was all teeth and no tail, shooters without enablers. We desperately needed an advocate at CJSOTF-A, someone who would fight for us so we could fight for everyone.

Ukeiley, stationed at CJSOTF-A headquarters in Bagram, was supposed to be that person. But he never ventured out to see Camp Raider in person and instead seemed intent on undermining us from a distance.

Inadvertently copied on an email sent by Ukeiley, Johansson was surprised at "the negative light that (Ukeiley) was shedding on MSOC-F.... He was not representing MSOC-Fox's best interests."

After much prodding, Ukeiley delivered, sort of.

"I get a semi (trailer) full of dry goods," remembered Johansson with a smirk. "The dry goods were five, ten pound bags of flour, five gallon cans of cooking oil, stuff we couldn't use. We had no cooks, we had no kitchen." Much like sending Chaps, the Army provided support that was not supportive.

Johansson did scrounge up uniforms for our Afghan guards, but he had a tough time getting a replacement for the torn, bloody camo jacket Klein was wearing when he was hit by shrapnel from the IED. The jacket had been taken from Klein for evidence, and Johansson contacted the CJSOTF-A supply staff to requisition a new one.

"Sorry," they said. "Talk to MARSOC."

He phoned Camp Lejeune.

"Sorry," MARSOC said. "Talk to CJSOTF-A."

Finally, an exasperated Johansson phoned a sympathetic Camp Lejeune gunnery sergeant who agreed to drive to the base exchange store, purchase a replacement jacket using Johansson's credit card number, and ship it to Jalalabad.

Though we were dealt a difficult hand, Johansson believed Fox Company dealt with the situation "as best they could." He was impressed with how we went about our business. We were confident, he said, but did not show "bravado," adding that I ran a "very tight ship. There wasn't any screwing around. They were focused on their mission."

We remained highly motivated. My Marines worked each day planning and rehearsing possible missions, conducting live fire training, and updating our intelligence.

"Why aren't you getting up into Tora Bora?" a dissatisfied Ukeiley asked. "You're not doing what the colonel wants."

If only we had helicopters, we could. Eggbeaters were key to inserting small recon teams into the mountains. We were excited when a helicopter visual reconnaissance mission was finally granted and was told that subsequent insertions had been preapproved. The men were charged up.

After that preliminary flight, I requested helicopters to take us into the mountains. We were denied. Day after day, I requested them and, night after night, CJSOTF-A canceled them at the last minute.

After three weeks of game playing, I met with Haas and dropped a dime on his staff.

"Sir, I have been asking and asking and asking, and your staff is not playing fair," I said in frustration. "They are not providing anything we need."

He said he would look into the issue, but sounded less than eager. He could have told me he was going to order them to fulfill my requests. He did not.

Not surprisingly, his staff was angry that I had gone around them, and they made sure I felt their wrath.

"How dare you go to the colonel!"

"Well, this is how it works," I shot back. "I'll try to work with you, but if you're an obstacle, I have the right as a commander to go to my commander and let him know."

That didn't help my cause. I wasn't trying to make enemies, but I guess I did.

To facilitate accomplishing anything, anything at all, I was more than willing to ignore Haas and special operations and prostitute ourselves out to the regular Army. I wanted to be relevant while we were there. By the middle of March, we would need to start packing up our gear to fly out of Afghanistan.

When John Nicholson, a very politically well-connected Army colonel, arrived with his brigade in late February to take over the battlespace that included AO Bulldog from a Marine infantry battalion, I thought we might be set free once and for all.

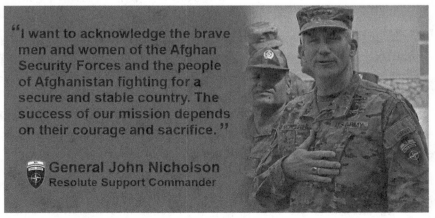

"I want to acknowledge the brave men and women of the Afghan Security Forces and the people of Afghanistan fighting for a secure and stable country. The success of our mission depends on their courage and sacrifice."

General John Nicholson
Resolute Support Commander

Gen. John Nicholson, U.S. Army, ISAF Commander (Courtesy of International Security Assistance Force (ISAF) Public Affairs Officer)

The bony, thin-lipped Nicholson seemed amenable to Fox Company working with his units, acknowledging that we were "bringing very unique capabilities that no one else had on the battlefield."

But the Army wanted to go easy. Nicholson, like Haas, did not want us to conduct raids, patrol through villages or perform any offensive operations. He did not want us to even look like we could have an offensive mission.

"We are totally different," he said. "We befriend the population. When we go into a village, our men are not even allowed to have a machine gun on top of the turret. We replace them with a spare tire."

Nicholson was punch drunk on the counterinsurgency (COIN) strategy advocated by the newly minted four-star general who had recently been put in charge of all coalition forces in Iraq, Army Gen. David Petraeus. That same strategy was also being applied to Afghanistan—and Nicholson was fully on board with its "killing with kindness" doctrine. The mindset was to "first do no harm" and then win over the hearts and minds of the civilian population. The latter, Nicholson said, was "the center of gravity" for winning the war in Afghanistan.

Petraeus had laid out his beliefs in *Counterinsurgency*, the joint field manual written under his direction and published under his name and that of Mattis, representing the Marines, in late 2006.

In one chapter, titled "The More Force Used, the Less Effective It Is," they wrote: "Any use of force produces many effects, not all of which can be foreseen. The more force applied, the greater the chance of collateral damage and mistakes. It also increases the opportunity for insurgent propaganda to portray lethal military activities as brutal."

Another section read: "Not only is there a moral basis for the use of restraint or measured force; there are practical reasons as well. The COIN force does not want to turn the will of the people against the COIN effort by harming innocents.

"Discriminating use of fires and calculated, disciplined response should characterize performance in COIN, where kindness and compassion can be as important as killing and capturing."

Public opinion was in favor of almost anything that might wind up the wars in the region, particularly during a contentious presidential campaign year pitting John McCain and Barack Obama. COIN was offered as the magic potion that would achieve that goal. If COIN's "soft" approach ended the intractable conflicts in Iraq and Afghanistan, Petraeus and Nicholson would-be heroes.

A political animal rather than a warrior, Nicholson was the quintessential "red carpet Ranger." He had served only a fourteen-month tour as a rifle platoon leader but soon boasted a far more politically powerful post in the 82nd Airborne Division as the commanding general's aide-de-camp, a role he would later fill for the Secretary of the Army. He then served as a special assistant to the Commander in Chief, U.S. Army Europe, and the Seventh Army, Germany. Among his primary duties was to be the commander's speechwriter.

It was no surprise that he was given such cushy assignments. His father was Army Brig. Gen. John W. Nicholson and his uncle, Jim Nicholson, was an Army colonel and decorated Vietnam veteran who was chairman of the Republican National Committee before serving as ambassador to the Vatican. While Fox Company was in Afghanistan, Uncle Jim was Secretary of Veterans Affairs in the cabinet of President George W. Bush.

Maybe if my eyes had been opened earlier to the politics of the military, I would have tried to ingratiate myself with Nicholson. But I guess I am just not the sort of guy who kisses rings.

With Nicholson hitching his wagon to COIN, what Fox Company had trained for nearly a year to do—direct action—was off the table.

The U.S. taxpayer had paid to send a company of special ops Marines into a war zone halfway around the world, racking up a bill of more than $15 million on training and equipment, just so we could stay inside the wire. When we did leave the wire, we were to be relegated to Level Zero missions, missions that posed so little threat of upsetting the apple cart that they did not even require coordination with Nicholson's Task Force Spartan.

Everyone in Fox Company was disheartened, but there was nothing we could do.

Then I heard that someone else might want our services. With the scuttlebutt circulating that Fox Company was looking for more substantial missions, another government organization (which I cannot name here) reached out to us. Needing an assault element to conduct a raid in Nuristan to the north, where insurgents were about to encircle one of its outposts, that other government organization came to us only because it had nowhere else to turn—the Army battalion commander in that area had denied its request for an infantry unit to ward off the attackers.

It wasn't the first time he'd balked at taking action.

He had previously refused to deploy his troops to defend a resupply convoy headed to his base despite desperate pleas from the besieged Afghan drivers. When the commander finally did send soldiers their way, they were from the Afghan National Army. As a consequence, the supplies were captured. So were the drivers. When the Taliban discovered they had contacted the American base for help, they cut out their tongues.

I briefed Ukeiley and the CJSOTF-A operations staff and received permission to conduct a coordination meeting with the other organization at a camp in Nuristan. News of my arrival there sent the Army commander into a panic, and he reported to Nicholson that I was conducting an unauthorized recon on his turf. When I heard that, I knew I had to scramble to quell the alarm.

I called Haas, who was my boss, and told him I was only having an initial meeting to see if the operation was feasible and that no plans had been developed or submitted. I made it clear that the Army commander's accusation that Fox Company was conducting a clandestine mission was completely false.

Haas accepted my explanation, but when I requested his permission to continue cooperating with the other organization, he shut me down with a "No." He said he'd recently been burned collaborating with them. After a mission failed because of what he said was their screwup, they had blamed his Green Berets, and he was not happy about that. He ordered me to return to Jalalabad that night, which I did.

The next day, his Green Berets assaulted the enemy around the other organization's besieged camp and the outpost was secured. It seemed Haas didn't have a problem working with them after all. And he had *no* problem telling me one thing and doing the opposite. Obviously, the only "problem" he had was with Marines in special ops.

The next morning, Montanus called me at 3 a.m. from Camp Lejeune, as he did routinely. During those calls, he would analyze and criticize everything going on with Fox Company, wanting me to do this or that. This time, he complained about our call sign, Violent. He was concerned about the optics—"violent" was too, well, aggressive.

"I don't like that word," he said. "Change it."

But while in Afghanistan, I was not working for Montanus.

He was now the CO of the 2nd Marine Special Operations Battalion, which had been activated when 2nd Force Recon was deactivated, but he had no authority over our unit while we were deployed. He could not legally order me or even influence me to do anything.

Nevertheless, I tried to get along. Maybe Filthy Fred and Fightin' Fred could be Friendly Fred.

"What would you suggest?" I asked.

"Personally, I like 'Dagger,'" he said.

Of course, he did. His 2nd Force Recon had been Task Force Dagger when in Iraq (there had also been a Task Force Dagger with Haas in Operation Anaconda).

The following day, we went on another Level Zero mission and, because Ukeiley was copying and forwarding all of my emails to him, Montanus saw that we were still Task Force Violent. He phoned me again at 3 a.m.

"Don't forget where you came from," he snapped, "and where you're going back to!"

He was unaware that a unit commander could not arbitrarily change a call sign. The previous night, I had indeed dutifully requested a new moniker—Raider—from the theater four-star general's communications staff. But the process was lengthy and would not be completed before we left Afghanistan.

I was proud to try to resurrect that name. After the incident on March 4, among the first emails I sent were to a couple of those World War Two

Marine Raiders I had met at the activation ceremony for Fox Company. I wanted to let them know that, despite what they might see in the press, we had flown their flag and been true to their name.

From February 10, when we touched down in Afghanistan, through March 3, we conducted twenty-nine missions, all Level Zero—local patrols, recons, meet and greets with tribal elders, and intelligence gathering.

On our thirtieth mission, on the morning of March 4, we were ambushed.

Under Pressure

4 March 2007
Jalalabad, Afghanistan

Little did I know that even before Fox Company made it back to base that day, local tribal elders had contacted Afghan "stringers" who sent news of the incident to international journalists based in the country. Within half an hour, freelancers working for AP, a photographer, and a television cameraman, arrived on the scene. The reports were incendiary, lighting a fire under the populace and Afghan politicians.

The news stories, coupled with rapidly spreading rumors, fueled a tirade launched by the elders at the Provincial Governor of Nangarhar, Gul Agha Sherzai. On March 5, about fifty elders met with Sherzai and told him about the horde of drunk Marines who threw a grenade to make it seem like a bomb went off and then went door-to-door wildly firing at civilians.

A former *mujahideen* and warlord who helped American forces capture the city of Kandahar from Taliban forces in 2001, Sherzai was a political ally of President Karzai and had officiated over the opening of Highway 1 in 2006 with Karzai in attendance. But Afghans were increasingly displeased with Karzai's corrupt administration. That May, anti-American and anti-Karzai rioting in Kabul left at least seven people dead and dozens injured. Both Karzai and Sherzai were facing enormous political pressure. When the elders presented Sherzai with a handy escape valve for their pent-up anger—blame the Americans—he gladly passed on their account of the incident to Karzai. Recognizing possible political advantage when he saw it, the cunning Karzai immediately called the U.S. ambassador, Ronald Neumann, and demanded a halt to all U.S. military actions.

"We will not accept civilian casualties on our soil during the fight against terrorism and we cannot tolerate it," Karzai told his parliament, condemning our response to being ambushed and offering his condolences to the victims' families.

Though what happened behind the scenes was out of my view and above my pay grade, I can only imagine senior U.S. military, Department of State, and Department of Defense officials scurrying to contain the damage to their policy of winning the hearts and minds of the populace. Faced with a head of state fuming about a violation of human rights by American troops, they instantly began smoothing ruffled feathers. In an attempt to appease Karzai, they promptly gave him what he wanted by agreeing to pull back on military activities, at least temporarily.

But, I wondered, would our leaders ultimately stand strong and support Fox Company, or would they cave and sacrifice us to the withering criticism of world opinion? Would they consider the men of Fox Company disposable, acceptable collateral damage in a war of words?

As far as I was concerned, my Marines had performed precisely as we had rehearsed during the workup. We had successfully reacted to a complex ambush (one involving explosives, gunfire, and tactical maneuver, and sniper fire), overcome degraded communications due to the blast, and replaced a wounded Marine during the mission. Despite being bombed, shot at from multiple positions, blocked from exiting, and swarmed by a mob of men, we had suffered only one minor casualty.

Addressing the platoon to kick off our debrief, I said, "This was our first contact with the enemy. You did a phenomenal job today. But let's not be overconfident. Spring is almost here, and that's the fighting season. This will not be the last time we confront the enemy."

East then described what he had seen and done during the mission. He was followed by each team leader, in order from Vehicle One to Six. The debrief covered everything before, during, and after the ambush—planning, rehearsals, inspections, staging, movement and action, contact and response to the enemy, and retrograde.

I didn't hear most of it though. Not long into the reporting, my watch chief pulled me out of the debrief and handed me a phone. On the other end was a major in Nicholson's office, and he was livid. Nicholson, unaware that we had a patrol in Bati Kot, had lit him up, asking, "Why are they up there? We don't need help in that area!"

The major, in turn, screamed at me: "The colonel wants to know what's going on, right now! You are to report to him immediately!"

Nicholson was irked that he didn't know Fox Company was on a mission until twenty to forty minutes after we had been attacked. He was especially disturbed that we hadn't informed him of "troops in contact" in an expeditious manner, that I hadn't made him aware of the situation without delay. Nicholson was convinced that Fox Company had purposely kept him in the dark.

When he then learned we had previously conducted twenty-nine missions but he had been informed about only five, he was furious. Being the mindless, aggro Marines that we were, he feared we had gone completely rogue, doing whatever we damn well pleased.

But Haas was my commander, not Nicholson. Nicholson acknowledged at the COI that he "did not have command authority over those units... Even mission approval was not my purview.

"But the intent...(was to) develop a cooperative working arrangement between all CJSOTF forces and my force." He felt he had been left out of the loop.

I told Nicholson's major that we had just returned to base and started our debrief. When I had complete, accurate information, I would let him know.

As soon as that call ended, the CJSOTF-A watch officer was on the line. He was in a panic too, demanding that Haas be informed of exactly what had happened. I told him the same thing—we were working on it, putting together slides and a storyboard in PowerPoint, and I would pass on the information as soon as possible.

But now, I was sensing that these fires needed to be doused right away before they spiraled out of control. I instructed East to draft an updated situation report and send it to Haas in short order, and I left the ongoing debrief and drove across the airfield to Nicholson's office to personally relate to him what I knew at the time.

He appeared to have calmed down. Though he had issues with what he felt was our lack of communication with him, he was supportive of our actions during and after the ambush.

"Hey Fred, whatever you need to do to get out of a gunfight," Nicholson said, "I'm not going to question you. I got it. You're on the ground. You're in the fight. You're in an ambush. You've got to get out of there."

I sighed with relief. I took Nicholson at his word that he would give the benefit of the doubt to anyone caught in a VUCA environment— Volatile, Uncertain, Complex, and Ambiguous.

"And what about the accident when you returned?" he asked.

"Sir?"

To get to the fuel farm across the airfield, you had to drive past a little bazaar that had been set up by locals selling trinkets. A female Army soldier on a Gator, a utility all-terrain vehicle, was zipping around the bazaar on a shopping trip and ran into Vehicle Two, which Ortega was taking to be refueled. I didn't know anything about the collision, including that she had injured an arm until Nicholson brought it up.

After having withstood a bomb blast and a gun battle, the accident seemed rather minor. When I saw Ortega a few minutes later, I told him to check on the injured soldier and apologize, regardless of who might have been at fault. I figured that issue was taken care of.

It was not. Nicholson would use the incident against us at the COI, claiming I told him Ortega should be forgiven for the accident because he was "juiced up" after the ambush, like we all were. None of that was true. On the night of March 4, however, I took comfort in the belief he would stand behind us.

I drove back to our side of the airfield and called Bagram, giving Haas and Ukeiley a verbal account of the ambush.

Haas said he too understood the situation but added that Kearney, the commander of SOCCENT, would likely want to investigate the incident. Fair enough. Investigations were not uncommon and their number was increasing thanks to recent battlefield episodes.

No event upset the public more than that of Pat Tillman. A famed professional football player, Tillman had patriotically joined the Army Rangers after September 11. His shooting death in Afghanistan in 2004 was first blamed on the Taliban. But, in fact, he was killed by friendly fire, information that was covered up by senior Army general officers for weeks after his widely broadcast memorial service. The Tillman affair was a public relations nightmare for the Army. It also proved a personal disaster for several high-ranking officers, including four generals, who received career-stunting reprimands for their errors.

The message to all commanders was clear—the only way they could never be wrong was to aggressively investigate anything with the slightest whiff of wrongdoing and immediately let the public know the results. And that is what Kearney would do with Task Force Violent.

The March 4 ambush couldn't have come at a worse time for the Corps, which was reeling from three sensational high-profile civilian killings in Iraq—in Fallujah in April 2004, in Haditha in November 2005, and in Hamandiya in April 2006.

Lt. Ilario Pantano was leading a platoon from 2nd Battalion, 2nd Marine Regiment, against a suspected enemy compound near Fallujah when a vehicle emerged containing two Iraqi men. His troops stopped the vehicle and handcuffed the occupants. Pantano stayed behind while the rest of his platoon searched the compound, where they discovered a cache of arms.

When his men returned, the Iraqis had been shot to death.

According to Pantano, he had unbound the Iraqis, and they began talking to each other. When they moved towards him, he felt threatened and ordered them to "Stop!" in both Arabic and English. When they did not, he shot them.

He later stated: "I then changed magazines and continued to fire until the second magazine was empty... I had made a decision that when I was firing I was going to send a message to these Iraqis and others that when we say, 'No better friend, no worse enemy,' we mean it." "No better friend, no worse enemy" was a slogan popularized by Mattis, then commanding general of the 1st Marine Division. Pantano was putting his words into action.

An NCIS probe led in early 2005 to two charges of premeditated murder. Pantano was ordered to an Article 32 hearing, effectively a preliminary hearing under the Uniform Code of Military Justice. He could have faced the death penalty if later convicted at a court-martial. But when an autopsy confirmed Pantano's account—that the Iraqis were shot while moving toward him—all charges were dropped.

Two years after, several Marines grabbed an Iraqi man from his home in Hamandiya while searching for an insurgent and dragged him away. They threw him into a hole created by a previous IED blast and shot him multiple times in the head and body. The troops then attempted to cover up the incident by placing an AK-47 and a shovel next to his body to suggest he was shot while digging the hole for another roadside bomb. Several Marines were subsequently court-martialed.

Meanwhile, the Haditha mass killing was still on the front pages. In December 2006, four of those Marines were formally charged with murder, and the battalion commander and three other officers with dereliction of duty.

Just three months after those charges were filed, a suicide bomber attacked my Fox Company convoy driving down Hell's Highway and we were accused in the press of killing and wounding innocent men, women, and children. Already in the crosshairs of the media, Congress ,and the public, the Corps was being denounced once again.

Even so, I felt satisfied we would get a fair shake, particularly after Haas assured me that he would push hard for a senior Marine infantry officer with combat experience, someone who had been at the nasty end of an explosion or gunfire, to conduct the Article 15-6 investigation. But, he said, Kearney would have the last word on who that would be.

I instructed my men to not talk about March 4 with anyone, including each other, and definitely not with me. I did not want to be seen as influencing them on what to say or not say. We all knew what happened on the patrol. All we had to do was be honest with the investigator.

Perhaps Haas did not push hard enough. That afternoon I was informed by Ukeiley that the officer chosen was Pihana, Kearney's chief of staff and that he would fly from their headquarters in Qatar and arrive in Jalalabad on March 8.

Col. Patrick Pihana comments during his change of command at 18th ASOG, Pope Air Force Base, NC (Courtesy of 18th Air Support Operations Group Public Affairs Officer)

I was suspicious. Not only was the appointment quick, but it was extremely unusual that someone with Pihana's level of responsibility—fifteen thousand special ops forces spread from the western border of China to the Horn of Africa—would be rushed in from out of the country for such an investigation.

You don't need a sledgehammer to pound a tack. Besides, he wasn't a Marine and had no infantry combat experience. What would an officer in the Air Force know about how Marines fight on the ground?

Pihana's appointment was my first clue that Kearney's investigation might be neither fair nor impartial. But Kearney's was just one of many agendas working against Fox Company.

On the night of March 4, I emailed three Marines I considered mentors and told them about the ambush and how we responded in very loose detail. I also wrote: "The media is probably mentioning several versions of the story. We have one version and it's the truth from our men and myself who were there... Our men did an amazing job, none sustained more than a scratch and we killed several people who were trying to kill us. The investigation will prove exactly that.... Let the Raiders and Force Reconnaissance Marines and Corpsmen know that we will never let them down."

The email somehow found its way to more than a dozen other people, including Hejlik, MARSOC's commander. He was seething, believing that I had revealed tactics and procedures. He fired off an email to his assistant: "We are providing information to the enemy on how successful his TPs were... I NEVER want to see this kind of bullshit again - ever!... Get ahold of Maj. Galvin and I want his email recalled—now!... IF any of you have any doubts on how pissed off I am about this then you need to come and see me."

In truth, my email was harmless. What riled Hejlik was that I had sent an email outside my chain of command. He was determined to teach me a lesson about who was in charge.

I also sent an email via the classified internet to Holly. Using a classified computer might be unusual, inappropriate, or even illegal, except for the fact that we both held Top Secret security clearances. After I took Fox Company to Afghanistan, we would often communicate by classified email. On March 4, I simply told her we had been in a firefight, and we had done everything correctly. There was nothing to worry about.

Wrong. I had a lot to worry about.

That afternoon, I was visited by an operative from another government organization. He had met with a Bati Kot tribal elder and wanted to know if what the Afghan said was true—that my Marines were drunk, had slammed into a car on the road, and then tried to cover up the accident by faking a car bombing by throwing hand grenades! There was more:

The elder also said that not only did my Marines shoot at everyone on the street, but we also went into homes, stores, and other buildings and shot people there too.

I was shocked and also distressed. I was shocked at what the elder said but also distressed that someone from another U.S. government organization thought there was the slightest chance that what he said was true. The tale was ridiculous from the start. Drunk? Where would we get the alcohol? Not that we would ever drink while on duty anyway, but it was nine o'clock in the morning! I told him that nothing remotely like what the elder said had actually happened.

But now I knew that the events of March 4 were not just being falsely recounted by the Afghans and the media, but we were in the crosshairs of our military too.

Did they truly believe that our Marines would shoot and kill Afghan children including an infant, as well as women and elderly men, during an ambush in broad daylight? Or were they taking advantage of an opportunity to sensationalize a juicy story by sacrificing truth for sales?

Or was doubting our account simply in their best interest, the interest of their careers—truth be damned?

I hoped the truth would win out, but I also knew that it didn't always.

In the Penalty Box

Soon after the explosion, a man identifying himself as Qari Sajjad telephoned the AP and claimed to speak for Hezb-e-Islami Gulbuddin (HIG). He said the breakaway faction of the Taliban-linked group once led by Younis Khalis, a former *mujahideen* commander, was responsible for the blast that "destroyed two vehicles, killing or injuring American soldiers." Sajjad said the attack was revenge for "cruel acts" done to Afghans by U.S. forces. He identified the suicide bomber as an Afghan named Haji Ihsanullah, a forty-five-year-old with a white beard.

A few members of the Afghan National Police (ANP) and the squad of Gabel's MP patrol we had seen rehearsing and which followed us out of the Torkham Gate base, arrived within fifteen minutes after Fox Company departed the area. A second MP squad was on site within thirty minutes. Gabel herself, who had been on another mission, arrived about an hour after that.

Concerned that the crowd which had gathered was growing hostile, and not wanting to aggravate the situation further, her soldiers secured the site but took a backseat to the ANP and Afghan Border Patrol, who soon had one hundred members cordon off the area and begin an investigation.

One of her squad leaders attempted to treat the location as a crime scene, which they were trained to do in the military police, but it was difficult.

"I tried to keep all of the local national forces busy since usually they would get on the scene and try to pick up evidence from the site," said the staff sergeant. "I did see local national police picking stuff up and kicking things around on scene, at which time I instructed them to stop." Other than a torso, without head or limbs, found on the south side of the road some fifty-feet from the site, he did not see anyone dead or injured, neither did any of the other MPs.

Gabel asked the ANP to search the hill area for shell casings, but they returned without any. One of her sergeants, however, did find casings on the far end of the bridge; among the trees along the road, north and south; on the north shoulder of the road; and on the south, on or near the centerline of the road. Due to security concerns with the increasingly agitated villagers, none of the MPs ventured past the bridge.

"We collected all the brass that we could find," Gabel testified, "both 7.62 and .50 cal." The expended casings, about 75 of the 7.62mm and about 50 of the .50 caliber, were placed in plastic evidence bags.

The MPs did not recover any brass from within the Prado but they were able to examine the vehicle.

"It was heavily shot," Gabel said. "I would say in the range of probably 200 bullet holes within that Prado. There were bloodstains inside the vehicle, but neither I, nor my soldiers saw any bodies or any unusual items inside the Prado to include weapons or cash or anything that would be viewed as unusual, except for the fact that it was so heavily shot."

Gone were the bodies of the three men who were presumably killed.

As two MPs took photos to document the state of the SUV, a freelancer, Rahmat Gul, also began snapping photos.

"Two soldiers with a translator came and said, 'Why are you taking pictures? You don't have permission,'" Gul recounted to the AP.

One of the MPs grabbed the camera from Gul, deleted the photos, and returned it to him. When another soldier later told him that it was okay to take photos, Gul began again. But the first MP returned and angrily demanded he delete those photos too. Gul hesitated and, he claimed, the soldier raised his fist as if he was going to strike him.

A freelancer shooting video for the AP and a reporter for the Afghan channel Ariana Television alleged they had similar encounters with the MPs. The television journalist said, "They warned me that if it (the footage) is aired...then, 'you will face problems.'"

Both the AP and the United Nations Assistance Mission in Afghanistan (UNAMA) protested the intimidation to the coalition military as the stench of a cover-up of yet another atrocity by the American military filled the air from tiny villages in Afghanistan to powerful newsrooms in world capitals. One story that spread like fire on social media charged that the Marines in the ambush had returned to the "scene of the crime" to clean up incriminating evidence and that it was Marines who confiscated cameras from journalists!

Nicholson did not ride to our rescue by responding with the facts. Letting the Marines take the brunt of those inflammatory accusations was convenient since those interfering with the media were Army MPs, and they were his responsibility.

By the time he authorized an investigation—which determined, of course, that my Marines were nowhere near the site when the press arrived—the controversy had subsided. Nicholson had deftly deflected any criticism, and I began to wonder how supportive he truly was of Fox Company.

Two days after the ambush, East and I were in our unit's Jalalabad operations center briefing Nicholson, Haas, and Brig. Gen. Joseph Votel, the deputy commanding general overseeing the U.S. military in eastern Afghanistan. Hoping to persuade Votel to let Fox Company integrate more fully with Nicholson's brigade for future operations, I presented a comprehensive summary of our training and capabilities and a short account of what occurred on March 4.

Strangely, none of them asked any questions.

I found out why when Haas took East and me outside and told us that he was putting Fox Company in the penalty box. While Pihana was conducting his investigation, no one involved in the March 4 incident would be allowed to leave the base without his permission and, even then, he would restrict Fox Company to missions between Jalalabad and our forward base at Khogyani, about fifty miles of dusty nothingness to the southwest. Haas said we could draw up and submit CONOPs only for missions in that corridor.

We were not the only ones sent to the penalty box—so was everyone else. Until the anger in the streets of Jalalabad and other Afghan cities subsided, all American and coalition troops were confined to their bases.

That was exactly what the Taliban wanted.

Though they lost in the field, the Taliban still achieved their goal— they were free to do as they wished, without interference—by winning the battle of public opinion. That was possible thanks to a surprisingly savvy information operation.

The objective of an information operation, quoting from our own doctrinal publication, was "to influence, disrupt, corrupt, or usurp the decision making of adversaries and potential adversaries while protecting our own." Among the typical tactics were "fake news" or "spin."

The Taliban understood they could not defeat us militarily, not with their weapons of choice, IEDs and RPGs. But another weapon cost them little and produced a far greater yield—the media.

Our Afghan-born interpreter, Adnan Ali, who was sitting in Vehicle Three next to Milton, told us that by the time we arrived back at the base following the ambush, the Afghan guards at the gate had already heard damning news reports about Fox Company. I didn't realize the enemy was sophisticated enough to be able to manipulate the media that quickly against us. That had never happened in Iraq. But in Afghanistan, the media had been weaponized.

Milton, who was on the Fox Company intelligence team, said at the COI that the Taliban "know how to use the media, manipulate the media. In my opinion, way better than we do…. If there's a big attack and a big incident that occurs, you can pretty well bet that a reporter with at least some inclinations toward insurgency is going to be there relatively quickly to get their side of the incident."

The Taliban had AP and Reuters on speed dial. Calling international reporters directly, their story was instantly relayed via the proverbial "anonymous spokesman" to the public via the internet, radio, television, and newspapers.

International reporters also used "stringers," locals they paid to be journalists on the scene. The Taliban, in turn, would pay those same stringers to pass believable but biased information on to the reporters.

The Taliban could make charges without having to prove them. The international media would often broadcast that information despite little or no corroboration from more reliable sources.

Retired Army Lt. Col. Ralph Peters wrote in the *New York Post* in September 2008 that "over and over again, terrorists and their sympathizers claim that every successful American air strike or raid massacred a wedding party or a family gathering.... The global media treat the terrorists' or local thugocracy's claims of American barbarism as incontestable facts. They dismiss our military's statements to the contrary as 'obvious' propaganda. The terrorists know what they're doing."

The coalition, on the other hand, usually didn't fully respond to the media to counter accusations before completing an investigation. The Taliban realized it would take the coalition weeks, and sometimes months, to do that. As Winston Churchill once said, "A lie gets halfway around the world before the truth has a chance to get its pants on."

"The insurgents know that all they have to do is get it out there and the international press will do the rest," said Army Gen. Dan McNeill, then the commander of the coalition, NATO's International Security Assistance Force. "Some of it has been misinformation, some of it disinformation, and some of it just not accurate. The difficulty for me is that once those get out there, nobody wants to refute it. The insurgent is skilled at information operations, there is no question about that."

Sometimes, the Taliban's purpose was to neutralize an uncooperative warlord by revealing information. Whether false or true, that would prompt U.S. forces to arrest him. Sometimes the Taliban planted misinformation about their own activities or future plans to lure coalition forces into deadly ambushes.

Sometimes, the information provided to international reporters was meant for the Afghan audience, such as to convince them that an attack was a coalition attack when it was actually the Taliban fighting a rival.

Sometimes, as in our case, the objective of the information operation was to capture the attention of the world, stoke controversy, and incite such hatred towards us that we were thrown into the penalty box.

Islamists were eager to get the story out that our troops were wantonly killing civilians—and others were eager to believe them. Mass protests would follow, leading to propaganda victories. By the time an authoritative report was finally released, the vast majority of the Afghan population would never see it. If they did, they would discredit the findings, having by that time been saturated by the Taliban's misinformation.

Such tactics gained them a significant advantage not just in public opinion but on the ground. For fear of being on the front pages, which might lead to being investigated and prosecuted, our leadership hesitated to go on the offensive.

Battalion commanders reduced aggressive actions, particularly in major population centers, where the demonstrations would be the largest and the voices the loudest. By refusing to do much more than create daily storyboards to talk about what they intended to do, and rarely did, some commanders successfully avoided controversies that might damage their careers and reputations.

They avoided defeat, but also victory.

I was chomping at the bit to get the Fox Company investigation over and done with as soon as possible so all of us could get back onto the ice. We were particularly antsy to get back in the saddle because my executive officer and company intelligence officer, Capt. Jerry Goldman had received information that the Taliban were readying a coordinated attack against our base in Jalalabad. They planned to ram the front gate with two suicide vehicle bombers in succession, followed by rockets and mortars and a surge of jihadists. They wanted to retaliate for the March 4 incident.

That's what we picked up the Taliban saying. I thought they might be trash talking, trying to scare us or wear us down by applying constant pressure. Whatever the case, I wanted to put them to the test and take the battle to them anyway. We knew the identity of the Taliban leader boasting about the coming attack and even the building where he lived.

But until we were let out of the penalty box, we couldn't head back to the Bati Kot area. We had to sit tight. Hopefully, the Taliban were blowing smoke and we wouldn't be attacked before we could eliminate that terror cell.

I emailed East that it was "criminal that we know where these guys are and they (our commanders) want to wait for them to blow us up before they get the point."

He shot back with grim humor: "Maybe we should get drunk and go on patrol... At least if we get blown up again, that's one less suicide bomber for Nangarhar."

But time was running out. We had only a few weeks left in Afghanistan before we would retrograde out of the theater.

Pihana arrived in Afghanistan on March 6 and flew to our location in Jalalabad to begin his investigation on March 8. I was happy to hear him say he wanted to meet right away with the thirty men on the March 4 patrol, and I assembled them in the chapel that night.

He introduced himself as Col. Patrick Pihana but added that we should call him "Pat."

We were absolutely floored. He acted like a substitute teacher in high school trying to buddy up to his students. A squirrelly looking, prematurely gray, desk jockey, his credibility did not improve when he noted that he was an Air Force officer—and we noted that he was wearing the new camo uniform for the Army!

"I do not know what it's like to experience what you Marines did," he continued, trying to be sympathetic. But admitting that he'd never been in combat didn't help his standing in our eyes.

He told us he would interview each Marine and each would then write a sworn statement. If a Marine didn't want to be interviewed, he said he would order him to at least write a statement.

The Marines in the room looked questioningly at each other.

Was that not compulsory self-incrimination? Since our arrival at boot camp, we were taught that was illegal.

But we were anxious to give Pihana the true story of what happened and get back to work, and whatever could make that happen was fine with us. We wanted an end to the stories about cowboy Americans ruthlessly shooting innocent civilians and threatening to delete photographers who didn't delete their photographs. I figured the investigation wouldn't take long, maybe wrapped up in forty-eight to seventy-two hours, given what our Marines had said in the debrief—bomb, ambush, fire back, exit. Simple enough.

All thirty Marines, including me, trooped one by one into a small, sparse room with a desk and two chairs. Pihana asked questions, and we answered them. Many of the interviews were annoyingly interrupted when Pihana had to leave the room to answer calls from Kearney, who evidently was keeping a close watch on the investigation. Returning, Pihana would light-heartedly joke about "pesky generals."

Pihana acted very chummily toward me, but I felt he was all too obviously playing both Good Cop and Bad Cop. He never advised any of us of our legal rights, which is what an investigating officer must do if he believes a criminal act may have been committed, and yet his threat that he would compel a statement was a red flag. But we willingly made and signed statements anyway.

Frustrated by sitting on our packs, I tried to get CONOPs approved to get us back in the game. But if there was any reason to turn us down, no matter how insignificant, from a misspelled word to incorrect font size on a PowerPoint slide, that is what CJSOTF-A did. Undeterred, East and I, along with Clarke and Big Dave, worked around the clock until we eventually had three CONOPs that were impeccable.

The missions were decidedly risk-averse, conducted under the cover of darkness during a single night and not unlike what we had accomplished in training. One squad would dismantle a weapons cache recently discovered at a remote desert location, weapons that might be used in an attack on our base. A second squad would drive to Khogyani to tow a disabled five-ton truck back to Jalalabad. The third squad would travel between Jalalabad and Khogyani to covertly collect intelligence.

On March 9, the day after our interviews with Pihana, we received the go-ahead from CJSOTF-A to conduct the operations. The street protests had stopped; we would be the first off base missions in the province. But the Marines from the March 4 patrol were to remain behind the wire, in the penalty box, except for personnel approved by Haas for Explosive Ordnance Disposal (EOD) and a Quick Reaction Force (QRF).

East was in charge of the intelligence mission to Khogyani, but he could not accompany that squad.

"Sir," he asked me, "can they do anything else when they're out there?"

"No, Capt. East," I answered sternly. "It's not that I don't want to do something more too, but that's it, Jalalabad to Khogyani and back."

Prodded by Goldman, who had always impressed me as being overly ambitious, East asked me twice more about the parameters of that mission. Twice more, I told him what we were allowed to do and that I could not, and would not, cross the line in the sand drawn by Haas.

That night would turn into a tragicomedy of errors.

The squad sent from Jalalabad to recover the weapons cache was the first to leave the wire.

Only a few minutes later, an Army battalion commander, Lt. Col. Christopher Cavoli, one of Nicholson's subordinates, called me in the operations center.

"Fred, it's nine o'clock. I'm tired but I'm woken up now and I'm unhappy," he said, fuming. "Tell me why we're getting word from the locals that you've shot some guy in the face with a shotgun!"

"Sir, what? A shotgun?"

I had heard nothing from the squad about gunfire. But without any further discussion, I ordered the mission aborted.

"What the hell happened?" I asked the squad's lieutenant upon his return.

He explained that while traveling down Hell's Highway, and despite wearing night-vision goggles, the lead Humvee had to swerve to avoid a fifty-five-gallon drum filled with rocks sitting in the center of the road. During the day, the drum had served as a blockade for a Taliban checkpoint. With American troops behind the wire and nowhere in sight, the

Taliban could demand payment for safe passage. Our patrol was the first to head down that section of Hell's Highway since March 4.

The second Humvee in the convoy was forced to suddenly swerve as well—and rolled over onto its side. The squad cordoned off the area before hooking up a winch to turn the chariot back onto its wheels.

And in the darkness, a vehicle approached at high speed.

Following the EOF procedures, a Marine fired a pen flare.

But the vehicle did not stop.

Another Marine fired a round from a sniper rifle into the pavement in front of the vehicle and when it still didn't slow down, a second-round into the windshield.

The vehicle came to a sharp stop.

"Hey, man, after you fire a weapon, you need to let me know," I told the lieutenant.

"But in Iraq we'd get in firefights all the time. We didn't report every..."

"This is not like your last deployment," I said. "We trained differently. When you have contact, it's 'observe, engage and report'—observe what's going on, engage if you need to, and report *immediately*. That's how it goes."

I got on him but didn't want to kick him in the junk too hard. He had a lot to learn, but he was teachable.

"And someone got shot in the face?" I asked.

"The driver took some glass shards from the windshield," the lieutenant said. "That's all."

I did not have to ask about a shotgun. I knew nobody in that squad fired a shotgun because no one in that squad had a shotgun. Another squad did, but sharing weapons was not something you did in the military.

I phoned Ukeiley with the information I received and then turned my attention to East's patrol, which had left on the intelligence mission.

Within seconds, Ukeiley was back on the phone and I was thrust into an administrative version of hell, a barrage of calls and emails demanding the intelligence patrol also return to base.

Ukeiley said that CJSOTF-A had received not one but two CONOPs for East's mission! The brief I had submitted had six slides, but a second one had thirty-three slides, including a route I did not authorize that led the squad into an area near the Jalalabad airfield. As soon as I saw the second CONOP, I realized East's objective—the house of the high-value terrorist who may have been organizing an attack on us. Buoyed by all the equipment available for the approved mission, East had taken on an unapproved mission—getting close to that Taliban and putting ears on what he was up to.

When your troops are operating deep in a battlespace and are unable to communicate with you, a commander has to trust them to do the right thing on their own. I could supervise East all I wanted but, if he meant to keep his plan a secret from me, there was no way I could know about it once his patrol was out there. East slipped up, though, when CJSOTF-A was erroneously sent the actual route as well as the one I had approved.

With the best of intentions, East was being mission-aggressive. I thought Goldman was more selfish than anything else. Angling to be the next MSOC platoon commander, he wanted to make a name for himself by landing a big fish. Whatever their different motives, each felt it would be better to ask for forgiveness later than ask for permission beforehand.

I ordered the patrol back to the base, short of its intended destination.

What more could go wrong? Well, how about Ukeiley telling me there was now going to be a second investigation, this one solely about March 9!

"Yes," I said, resigned, and, after taking a breath, added that our towing convoy had departed from Khogyani.

I should have remembered that bad things happen in threes.

As the convoy left Khogyani, the brakes on the vehicle being towed seized up, causing it to slide in the thick muddy terrain and tip over onto its side, which caused the tow truck to roll over too. Realizing that every subsequent movement of my men would be examined under a microscope, I contacted Ukeiley to request that the staff in Bagram approve one of our elements from Jalalabad to assist and reinforce the squad. Ukeiley told me we were good to go.

Fortunately, no one was seriously hurt, and by the early morning hours of the next day, the vehicles were back on their tires to continue their journey to Jalalabad. But the incident contributed to the undeserved innuendo spread by Ukeiley that Fox Company could do nothing right and that I'd lost control of my men.

As quick as he could, Ukeiley made sure Haas knew that he was blameless regarding the unapproved intelligence mission.

"Sir," he said, "I have no fucking clue what this is about. I did not have anything to do with this."

When Ukeiley recounted his statement at the COI, Lecce interrupted.

"Hold on, I know this is getting you emotional, but try to watch the expletives here."

"Yes, sir."

Lecce offered Ukeiley a graceful way of excusing his profanity in court.

Giving a wink and a nod, he asked, "I take it you were quoting verbatim at that moment?"

A chastened Ukeiley looked at him for a second before replying.

"Yes, sir," he said with embarrassment.

East met with his Marines who conducted the reconnaissance patrol and told them that Haas and Nicholson were asking about the two briefs with different routes and that if any of them asked to tell them their route was from the airfield to Khogyani, not in and around Jalalabad.

Gunnery Sgt. Caden Gardner, who had served that night as my senior watch officer, immediately took East aside.

"I told Capt. East that I think he made a mistake," he said at the COI, "and that I was going to instruct my Marines to tell the truth."

East returned to his squad and told them to tell the truth.

I chewed his ass up one side and down the other. He had disobeyed my direct order. I had trusted him and he had deceived me. On a personal level, he had let me down, and that hurt.

I rarely used foul language in front of my Marines, but I dropped the f-bomb on him.

"How fuckin' stupid can you be!"

I could have relieved him of his command on the spot. But I did not.

This was a Marine who did three combat tours as an infantry officer in six years and had nearly died after being shot in the right thigh with an Iraqi 12.7mm heavy machine gun round that nearly blew off his leg during

Operation Phantom Fury in Fallujah in 2004. After almost bleeding to death on the spot, he was transported to a medical facility where surgeons recommended amputating his leg. East somehow convinced them to insert a titanium rod and save his leg instead. But he was assured that he would never walk properly again. They suggested he apply for a medical discharge and leave the Marines.

East rejected their opinion and, defying their prognosis, completed a grueling rehabilitation, which ended with him being able to walk normally. He not only remained in the Marines, but he trained for and passed the punishing Force Recon indoc and was selected to be a platoon commander at 2nd Force Recon. He then went on to graduate from the Corps' most challenging gut check, Amphibious Reconnaissance School, before I chose him as the first platoon commander at MARSOC.

East was a hero, a stud, and a true patriot. If someone else wanted to punish him, that would be their decision. I would not.

Then the hammer came down on Fox Company.

Kicked Out

That night Nicholson fired off emails to his bosses—Votel and Maj. Gen. David Rodriguez, who led the Regional Command- East— requesting that they order Task Force Violent to cease all operations in his AO Bulldog. We were not to leave the wire for any reason until further notice.

The next morning, March 10, after spending all night reporting on the events to Haas' staff, Ukeiley, Nicholson's staff, and even Montanus, I trudged to Nicholson's quarters just after 8 a.m. and banged three times on his hatch, hoping to speak with him.

There was no answer. No one seemed to know where he was, or at least didn't want to tell me. When I finally tracked him down by phone later that day, he said little and, without explanation, refused to meet with me.

I also attempted to speak with Hejlik in Camp Lejeune, but his executive assistant was not able to or didn't want to, bring us together on the phone. I sent him a detailed email regarding the difficulties we had faced in Afghanistan and requested a conversation with him. He never responded.

Someone else had already been in their ears—Ukeiley.

The previous night, after cleaning up the mess of three missions gone haywire, I opened a damning email from Ukeiley listing the failures of Fox Company, and especially mine as a leader, from the minute we landed in Afghanistan. He ripped me a new one, blaming me for not supporting

Haas when the CJSOTF-A staff was doing everything they could to help Fox Company. A livid Ukeiley said I was slapping Haas and CJSOTF-A in the face with my bad attitude.

I expected as much from Ukeiley—he was injected into the special operations hierarchy dominated by the Army and he "Army'd up," as Marines will say. His sabotage included blind-copying the scathing email to Hejlik and Nicholson, as well as Haas and every member of the CJSOTF-A operations staff. Of course, he also sent it to Montanus. The email eventually even made its way to Brown, the SOCOM commanding general.

"Did you mean to embarrass Maj. Galvin with that email?" Lecce asked Ukeiley at the COI.

"No," he answered shamelessly.

"What was your intent with that email?"

"I was frustrated. We were failing, and that means 'we' collectively... MSOC-F was built to do direct action. That's what they spent ten months doing, I mean, prepping to go into places in Baghdad, fight their way to a target, prosecute the target, fight their way back. And they were put into a situation that was probably as far removed from what they had anticipated as, I think, possible....

"(CJSOTF-A) were very set in what they were going to do," he continued, "and the MSOC was trying to push to do something else. And it was as if everybody was talking and nobody was listening.... Every time it was 'get back in your box.'"

Ukeiley charged ahead.

"Point blank he (Galvin) said, 'Hey, I want to conduct raids every night, every other night... I want to do what this thing was built to do.'"

"What was CJSOTF's response?" Lecce asked.

"They didn't want to hear that... Maj. Galvin wanted to do a raid... and I went into the J-3's office and he (the operations officer) said, 'Get the fuck out of my office.' And then on the other side, I couldn't get Maj. Galvin to see that even though he had the best of intentions as far as what he wanted to do, he was losing the most important thing, which was the trust and confidence (of his commander)... It spiraled down so quickly that you're at the point on March 9, how the fuck—excuse me—how did we get here?"

Haas sent Kearney a summary of the Ukeiley email. That was the last straw for the SOCCENT commander and Kearney promptly issued an order for our redeployment.

Panel member Daniels asked Ukeiley: "Did it ever cross your mind that you are writing Galvin's relief (removal) with this email?"

"No, sir. I did not think that because I wouldn't have written it if that was the case."

Porter was incredulous. He looked directly at Ukeiley and jumped in:

"If you had questions about stuff like that, you get your butt on a helicopter and fly out to Jalalabad and speak face to face with that officer.... You are aware that these emails you sent are what got Fox Company kicked out of Afghanistan!"

"Yes," Ukeiley meekly confessed.

On March 11, Haas sent his deputy commander, Army Lt. Col. Richard Wendell, to deliver the bad news.

Wendell was a butterball, the most obese military officer any of my Marines had ever seen in uniform, one he could barely fit into. Only seven days after the ambush, only two days after Pihana had begun his interviews, Wendell stood in front of Fox Company and crudely announced in his Southern drawl:

"Y'all fucked up, and we're kickin' y'all out!"

He seemed peculiarly upbeat. Wendell saw us as blunt instruments who could not comprehend the finesse of special operations. He was pleased to get rid of this company of Marines.

"Y'all been redeployed out of Afghanistan!"

At the COI, Col. Hill, who guided our training, said, "There's a lot within the special operations community that say 'Marines should never be a part of that organization and look what happens. First time we sent a Marine unit out, this happens right here, and I told you we should never have invited those guys into the club.' So you always had the Marine haters, and they would spin this to their story."

It seemed terribly unfair. During the same period, CJSOTF A under the leadership of Haas was investigating several of its Green Berets for illicit drug use and sales, prostitution, the cutting off of the ears of Afghan civilians, and other egregious and intentional high crimes. Yet, there was no talk of tossing their entire units.

Here we thought we were doing something great and important for our country, serving as the tip of the spear in a very dangerous part of the world, and now, we were being ridiculed and booted out.

Following Wendell's visit, we withdrew our men from Khogyani, sullenly gathered all our equipment, and waited for planes to fly us to Bagram. I was on the last flight, accompanied by Big Dave.

When we landed, Ukeiley boarded the aircraft. He had a grin on his face.

"Hey, how's it going?" he said, putting out his hand to shake as if we were buddies.

"Do you really think I lost control of my unit?" I asked, refusing his hand.

He stammered.

"I can't believe you did what you did," I said. "You're disgusting."

"What do you mean?"

"You know what you did," I said, revolted by the betrayal of his email.

As I pushed past him, I asked, "Does Haas want to see me?"

"No," he answered sheepishly.

"Then I don't ever want to see you again," I said, and walked off the plane.

Big Dave and I spotted Pihana standing behind a chain-link fence. We yelled at him to get his attention, but he acted as though he did not hear us. We shouted louder and louder until he could no longer avoid acknowledging us.

There were no pleasantries when he walked to us. I simply asked him about the status of his report.

"I handed it over to Col. Haas," he said. Why he first reported to Haas instead of Kearney, who appointed him, was curious and has never been explained. But Kearney received it soon enough. In any case, if there was a bowl of water for Pihana to physically wash his hands of us right then and there, he would have done so.

Meanwhile, Kearney was trying to make it appear in the media that he was allowing due process to take place. In reality, he was doing nothing of the sort.

His spokesman told *The New York Times* on March 23 that Kearney "opened the investigation and ordered the Marines involved to remain in Afghanistan until it is complete." The next day, *The Washington Post* reported that all of Fox Company was indeed being ousted.

Marine Unit Is Told To Leave Afghanistan

By Ann Scott Tyson
The Washington Post
Saturday, March 24, 2007

In an unusual move, Maj. Gen. Francis H. Kearney III, who commands U.S. Special Operations forces in the Middle East and Central Asia, ordered the 120-strong Marine Corps Special Operations Company to leave Afghanistan because the incident so damaged the unit's relations with the local Afghan population that it could not carry out its mission, the officials said.

"General Kearney decided they could no longer effectively conduct counterin-surgency operations, and so that's why he decided to move them out of there," said Lt. Col. Lou Leto, a spokesman at Kearney's command headquarters in Tampa.

Afghan President Hamid Karzai criticized the U.S. military reaction, and the incident sparked large anti-American protests.

> Kearney ordered an Article 15-6 inves-
> tigation, in which an investigating officer
> conducts an inquiry and reports back to the
> commander, to begin soon afterward, Leto
> said.
>
> The investigation and abrupt removal of
> the unit, known as MSOC- F, is doubly sig-
> nificant because the company was composed
> of some of the most experienced, highly
> trained Marines.

Yet Kearney had already ordered all of Fox Company out of Afghanistan on March 10, an order conveyed by Wendell the next day.

The first large group of my Marines flew out of Bagram and landed in Kuwait on March 23. Kearney ensured that everyone in Fox Company was out of Afghanistan by March 31.

Ironically, the day the last member of Fox Company left Afghanistan, our personnel support of five men, from the minimum support package of six that we had requested for months, finally arrived—just in time to create a total of 120 members of Fox Company dismissed from the country.

Soon after we were gone, Klein's new jacket arrived too.

Flying into Kuwait, Fox Company was billeted at the Udari Range, a staging post in the country's northwest. As we waited for our next assignment, we learned that Montanus and Hejlik would also be arriving and would pay us a visit. I thought they might be coming to hear our side of the story of March 4 in person. But I received a heads-up call from a friend at MARSOC headquarters tipping me off that they had another mission.

"You could feel the headman's axe hanging," said Big Dave at the COI.

Montanus took East and me aside outside the barracks. "Nobody will ever say that you did anything wrong tactically, Fred," he said to me, "but you are a field grade officer and as a field grade officer you have to be political and that is where you have failed."

He turned to East and asked, "Is it true? Is it true your Marines were drunk and throwing grenades?"

We protested our innocence but knew that whatever we said would hold little weight with Montanus.

On Tuesday, April 3, he ordered me to bring Fox Company together in formation. Montanus stood off to the side of my Marines and, lacking the guts to do what a superior officer ought to do in such a case, he instead ordered me to announce that I was being relieved of command.

I had never seen or heard of a commander being relieved in public quite like that. It was the most demeaning thing I have ever done.

"I am honored to have served as the Fox Company commander," I told my Marines, trying to hide my anguish and remain stoic. "I am honored to have had the privilege and responsibility to lead men of your caliber and commitment."

They stared at me and I could see their jaws clench. They were angry and confused.

"But I have lost the trust and confidence of our leaders," I continued, "and have been relieved of command."

In the awkward silence that followed, I turned sharply and marched away with Big Dave at my side to a waiting car that hastily drove us to Kuwait International Airport, from where we would fly to North Carolina.

I was devastated. After twenty years in the Marines, I had no idea what the future held in store for me. Court-martial? Prison? Would I lose my family of blood brothers? What then? I had no answers, only questions.

I heard that Hejlik arrived later and addressed my men, saying that Fox Company had worked very hard but "the situation doesn't look good."

Concern crossed the face of every Marine gathered before them, especially those who had fired their weapons on March 4.

"If we find anything wrong," Hejlik added, "those responsible will be going to prison for a very long time."

Afterward, the somber company filed into the chow hall, sitting at tables alongside other Marines, including Hejlik.

Gen. James F. Amos, commandant of the Marine Corps, awards the Distinguished Service Medal to Lt. Gen. Dennis Hejlik, commanding general of Marine Forces Europe and Marine Corps Forces Command, for forty-four years of service to Corps and country during Hejlik's retirement ceremony at Marine Barracks Washington July 23, 2012 (Photo By: Sgt. Austin Hazard)

"Where's Sgt. Klein?" the command sergeant major asked the Fox Company Marine next to him.

Klein, who was two tables in front, recalled that "my buddy pointed directly to me and he (the sergeant major) looked directly at me, smiled and just shook his head up and down and then instantly looked down and returned to eating his food with a haughty smile. At this point, I made up my mind that I was going to directly ask Hejlik about what was happening."

Klein and Lester approached the general outside the chow hall. They came to attention, saluted, and requested permission to speak. Hejlik told them, "At ease," and they stood at parade rest.

"Sir, if you wouldn't mind," Klein said, "could you explain what you meant when you said the situation didn't look good."

Hejlik glanced at the names on their uniforms.

"Yes, Sergeant, it doesn't look good for either of you two. There are inconsistencies with the statements in the investigation, things that don't add up. If we find that you failed to tell us something about any civilian who was killed, then you're going to Leavenworth."

They could hardly believe their ears. No one, certainly no general, throws the word "Leavenworth" around lightly. Leavenworth, Kansas, has the military's only maximum-security prison, the only one for those convicted in a court-martial for violations of the Uniform Code of Military Justice, the only one for enlisted men serving sentences of more than ten years, the only one for commissioned officers, and the only one for anyone convicted of offenses related to national security.

"Well, sir," asked an uneasy Klein, "what do you recommend we do?"

"You're being sent back to Camp Lejeune," he said perfunctorily. "That's all I can say right now."

Klein was sure that was a signal that he was going to be court-martialed and end up in prison.

He shuddered when he later was told that Hejlik had put on hold his expected Purple Heart.

"Receipt of a Purple Heart award requires that a service member's actions following a distinguishing act are honorable," said Maj. Cliff Gilmore, the MARSOC spokesman, in the *Marine Corps Times*. "Maj. Gen. Hejlik will not make a final decision regarding possible presentation of personal awards in this situation until the investigation is complete."

A campaign to slander Fox Company was also underway, fueled by anonymous sources with axes to grind. Some had their chance to pile on in a March 30th article in the *Marine Corps Times*:

Readiness of ousted spec ops unit questioned

The recent expulsion from Afghanistan of the Marine Corps' first special operations company did more than just put the relatively new leatherneck command in the spotlight. It has made many question whether the company was up to the task in the first place…

Some Marine combat veterans say the recall of the 120-man company is a "black

eye," an "embarrassment" and a public humiliation that could do irreparable damage to
MarSOC…

    Some worry that the incident smears the
good name and service of others serving in
MarSOC…

The article quoted a couple of unnamed commentators on the internet: "If the original report is true," wrote one, "then the MarSOC Marines effed up very, very badly and honestly looked like a bunch of college guys, not highly trained professionals." Another said that a "field grade officer who worked in MarSOC last year referred to the company as 'a bunch of Keystone cops.'"

The article's contention was absurd—our training had been stellar—but the mere fact of its publication indicated just how rancorous the subject of Marine special ops had become, and how malicious the haters were towards Fox Company.

Another sign of trouble to come arrived on April 11 when Kearney's SOCCENT command issued a press release repeating allegations that on March 4 at least ten civilians were killed, including "several women and children," and thirty-three wounded. In speaking with the media, Kearney labeled the incident as "catastrophic…from a perceptions point of view."

The Army general also noted that "seven journalists, representing eight different media outlets, complained that U.S. Marines and Afghan forces confiscated their equipment to delete any images."

If he didn't know, he should have that Army MPs dealt with the media at the site, not my Marines. Yet he laid the blame squarely at the feet of Fox Company.

What was in Pihana's report that made the general so confident that he could publicly tar and feather us before the COI even began?

Not being privy to a copy, I did not know. But clearly Hejlik and Kearney, among others in power, were not only disowning us, but they were also throwing us to the wolves.

A Rush to Judgment

Kearney gave *The Washington Post* a glimpse of what was in Pihana's report, telling the newspaper: "We found...no brass that we can confirm that small arms fire came at them. We have testimony from Marines that is in conflict with unanimous testimony from civilians at the sites... (The investigating officer) believes those folks (the Afghans) were innocent.... We were unable to find evidence that those were fighters."

The consequences of such a conclusion, that we were murderers, were very serious for us and the Corps. Kearney had effectively tossed "innocent until proven guilty" in the gutter.

No one in the military chain of command was willing to stand up and defend us, including the Marine leadership—not Pace, not Conway, not Hejlik. Any of them could have said there would be no comment until the investigation was complete, but they chose not to. They were covering their butts, trying to get ahead of bad news.

For the first time in my career, the Marine values of honor, courage, and commitment rang hollow.

Only one man of prominence had our back and objected in public—Walter Jones, a Republican member of the House Armed Services Committee whose district in eastern North Carolina included Camp Lejeune. I had never met him and neither had any of my Marines, but he spoke up for us loud and clear.

"I was shocked because of my great respect for the Marine Corps and special ops," Jones told the *Military Times*. "My disbelief was such that I just had to give the benefit of the doubt to these Marines. And then when the Army came out with their press release...almost like they weren't upset that they had to ask the Marine Corps to leave (Afghanistan), I was very incensed."

Jones didn't know if we were innocent or not. But he knew people were jumping to conclusions and that was not right. He wrote to Secretary of Defense Robert Gates and Army Secretary Pete Geren, furious that "not only has the presumption of innocence been discarded, but the reputation of these Marines may be maligned."

Nicholson's apology to the Afghans, he added, amounted to a public execution.

"This statement, among others, is contemptuous. To convict these Marines in the press before the investigation has even been completed is irresponsible. Our military service members, and certainly these Marines, deserve far better.... You must restrain your officers and enlisted personnel from commenting to the press on this incident until the investigation has finished and all the facts are available and verified. Due process has been disregarded!"

Jones, like all true leaders, led from the front, as did another Congressman, Rep. Dana Rohrabacher (R-California).

"No one should ever ignore when our people are acting in an illegal or immoral way," Rohrabacher said, "but neither should commanding officers try to demoralize them by exaggerating any fault they find and giving the benefit of the doubt to the enemy, rather than to our own people."

Suddenly, the Marine leadership could not backtrack fast enough. One day after Jones' remarks, Hejlik posted on the official MARSOC website the following question and answer:

Q. "Does MARSOC have a response to allegations of the MSOC Fox ambush?"

A. "We do not discuss the details of ongoing investigations because of due process. We are absolutely committed to ensuring our Marines are treated with the presumption of innocence."

One more day and Conway retreated too, telling reporters that Nicholson's statement that the March 4 incident was a "stain on our honor" was not appropriate.

"I would just as soon that no one—in any chain of command—apologize or talk about 'terrible, terrible mistakes' or those types of wrongdoings," Conway said. "I think he (Nicholson) was premature to apologize." He told the *Marine Corps Times*: "As has historically been the case, a service member under investigation or undergoing trial is innocent until proven guilty. And too much in terms of declaration of guilt and apologies has already been said."

I'm convinced they retreated because they realized they were in grave danger of committing the crime of undue command influence.

As Abraham Lincoln said, "Nearly all men can stand adversity, but if you want to test a man's character, give him power." Given the complete obedience of subordinates to superior officers, and the power superiors hold over assignments, promotions, and separations, what a superior says might greatly influence the actions or decisions of the military justice system. To discourage undue or unlawful command influence, there are rules against it and penalties if proven. A verdict can even be vacated or a case dismissed.

But neither Kearney nor Nicholson stepped back from their statements. So Mark Waple, my civilian counsel, working alongside Jack, my military attorney, wrote a letter to Maj. Gen. Scott Black, the judge advocate general of the Army, asking him to muzzle them, citing Article 37 of the Uniform Code of Military Justice regarding command influence. We assumed Black conveyed the message because Kearney and Nicholson stopped commenting on the case in public.

We needed experienced hands, and Waple and Jack certainly fit the bill. Waple, in his early sixties, gaunt, with thinning gray hair and glasses, looked like a college professor. In fact, he was a West Point graduate and a former Army infantry officer and judge advocate before he resigned and went into private practice. Jack was his mirror image—stout and bald, a fierce pitbull of a Marine—but equally experienced.

East's military defense counsel was Maj. Scott Woodard; Knox Nunnally was his civilian counsel. A prominent Houston attorney, Nunnally was the father of one of East's Naval Academy roommates who had not only served with East as an infantry officer and platoon commander but was wounded by an Iraqi IED the same day East was grievously shot in Fallujah.

Before I lawyered up, I found civilian attorneys for all five of the enlisted Marines. This was not about jaywalking; all of us could be facing capital offenses. After East phoned me in Kuwait and relayed that Hejlik had announced that "if we find anything wrong, those responsible will be going to prison for a very long time," I said to East, "You tell those Marines to not worry about a single thing. I'll take care of them."

I arranged to have their legal fees paid thanks to someone else recently labeled a war criminal—Ilario Pantano.

After hearing about the MARSOC 7, he called me and we met at a Starbucks in Wilmington. I knew that consulting him would be seen as controversial. After all, he shot those two Iraqis forty-five times. But I needed to help my guys, and I accepted his advice as well as his offer to assist us with funds from his Defend the Defenders foundation.

"Take care of my men," I told Pantano, refusing any money for myself. "We'll get through this together."

A few days later, when East, Lester, Klein, Walker, Clarke, and Pratt walked out of the terminal at the Raleigh airport, I was the only Marine standing there to greet them. No one from MARSOC headquarters welcomed them home after an overseas combat deployment. The Corps' cultural philosophy of "never leave a Marine behind on the battlefield or at home," a philosophy I adhered to, had been replaced by the slogan on a Home Depot bumper sticker—"Do It Yourself."

I picked them up in a motor pool van and drove them to the base. Along the way, I tried to buoy their spirits by telling them about the lawyers I had hired. But the specter of going to prison darkened their faces and their mood. Even the usually carefree, no worries Pratt was noticeably unnerved.

After I brought them to our compound at Camp Lejeune, a Marine chaplain arrived to counsel us about our return to the States. He preached to the seven of us about what a wonderful and joyous time this was as we reunited with our loved ones.

He must have been the only person in the Marines unaware that we had been thrown out of Afghanistan and were back in the States because we were being investigated for murdering innocent men, women, and children.

The men sneered, and the meeting was quickly over.

The rest of Fox Company would return from Afghanistan like Marines should, making an amphibious landing from the *Bataan* onto the beach at Camp Lejeune. But even this arrival was a bit unconventional—NCIS was waiting. They commandeered Vehicle Two and removed its turret panel and the driver-side ballistic windshield, sending them to the U.S. Army Criminal Investigation Laboratory in Forest Park, Georgia for further examination.

As Fox Company walked around the base, I noticed that Marines would recognize us and awkwardly turn to head the other way to avoid interacting with us. If we neared them, they would immediately stop any conversation they were having and shoot us sideways glances after we passed. When we entered an office, everyone would suddenly fall silent. We had become radioactive—do not touch for fear of contamination.

Occasionally, we overheard what they were saying about us, about the disgrace we'd brought on the Marine Corps' proud history, on the Marines that I loved. The humiliation ripped me up inside. But rather than discouraging me, their accusations, spoken and unspoken, only made me want to fight back harder. I embraced the PMS, the Pain, Misery, and Suffering like I had when I was a roper.

A couple of days after we returned, I was looking out an upstairs window of the 2nd Marine Special Operations Battalion's operations center when I saw an unusual sight—a Marine MP patrol car sitting at the entrance to our parking lot. A minute later, another MP car drove up behind the first, and together they sped toward our building. As they reached the front door, they slammed on their brakes and two MPs rushed in like a SWAT team dodging bullets.

They hustled up the stairs to see Montanus, but he was out of his office. So they gave his executive officer (XO) the long-awaited copy of Pihana's investigation and the accompanying report.

They also announced that a criminal investigation had been authorized by Mattis.

Apparently, armed MPs were the delivery messengers because of worry about the reaction to the news from the murderous, half-crazed Marines of Fox Company.

After the MPs hastily retreated from the building, the XO called me in and informed me of the investigation, adding that I was supposed to promptly contact NCIS to provide them with a statement about March 4 to complement the one I had given Pihana. But he could not let me see the report, much less give me a copy.

As I stood there, disappointed that so many forces were lining up to steamroll us, Montanus returned to his office and was told what had transpired. Unlike me, he didn't seem particularly concerned. He assured me that Fox Company had a tremendous support network at MARSOC and offered our Marines the opportunity to enjoy some time off by using post-deployment leave. When the investigation was over and we were cleared, he vowed that he would assign my Marines to Hotel Company, which would deploy to Afghanistan later that year.

"I'll look after you like you're my own sons," he said.

Given my experience with Montanus to date, I had no reason to believe anything he said. And Montanus didn't have any sons.

I proceeded to the NCIS office as instructed and banged on the hatch three times. I told the agents that I had been directed to make a statement to them but, since I had yet to read a copy of Pihana's report, I was refusing to do so.

The next day, Petronzio asked me to meet him, along with East and Clarke, not in his office but behind the base movie theater. We skulked around as if we were in a spy film—except we were all Marines at Camp Lejeune!

"You didn't get this from me," he said in a whisper and surreptitiously handed us a copy of the report.

What I read made my heart sink. Pihana recommended not only that Mattis launch a criminal investigation by NCIS but that the MARSOC 7 be charged with negligent homicide and dereliction of duty.

Trying to head off a trial, Waple suggested I take a polygraph test right away. He said he believed everything I told him, "but it's a different story if you have to go to court and convince a jury. There is no guarantee that the truth wins." If I could unequivocally demonstrate through a lie detector test that the MARSOC 7 were innocent, the military hierarchy might relent and shove the entire incident into the thankfully forgotten past.

The test was administered by Terrence Vincent O'Malley, a recent president of the American Polygraph Association and the gold standard of polygraphy.

Meeting in his Fayetteville office, I noticed the autographed photo on his wall of actors Robert DeNiro and Ben Stiller, who sought his input for the lie detector scene in the movie *Meet the Parents*.

When "(Galvin said he) did not observe any civilians killed during the 4 March 2007 ambush," O'Malley's conclusion was "no deception indicated."

When "(Galvin said) Marines under his command did not fire on civilians during the ambush on 4 March 2007," his conclusion again was "no deception indicated."

We had the results reviewed and validated by both the assistant commander of the Criminal Intelligence Service of the Texas Department of Public Safety (who was a past president of the Texas Association of Law Enforcement Polygraph Investigators) and an investigator with the Georgia Department of Public Safety (who was a past president of the Georgia Polygraph Association).

They all agreed: I told the truth. The report was sent to Hejlik and Mattis.

But a general, like the Pope, never admits to a mistake.

In fact, taking the polygraph, and passing it, probably ticked them off. Having kicked us out of Afghanistan, it would be scandalous if it was discovered that we didn't deserve to be given the boot. Sweeping the results under the rug, the rush to judgment continued.

Gathering the MARSOC 7 at my apartment off base, one of our civilian attorneys clued us into the harsh reality of the investigation and possible court case to follow.

"Who's the youngest?" asked Phil Stackhouse. Walker raised his hand. "Who has kids?"

The grizzled Clarke raised his hand, as did Walker, who had a son, just one-year-old.

Stackhouse pointed to Walker.

"They will come after the weakest link," he warned. "They will dogpile you."

Stackhouse knew that being a parent in the military, especially a relatively new one, made you vulnerable. With your rank and pay at risk and the possibility of going to jail, you had a strong incentive to do or say whatever an investigator or prosecutor might "suggest" in order to save not only your future but that of your family.

Walker was the sort of guy who always wanted to do the right thing. Distressed about any effect on his wife and child, feeling responsible for them, he hoped he wouldn't have to choose, as Ortega had, between his family and his fellow Marines.

So we teamed Walker with Stackhouse, who'd just retired from active duty in 2006 after twenty-two years as a Marine lawyer and had recently been honored with the Outstanding Career Armed Services Attorney Award from the Judge Advocates Association. He had also been Pantano's lawyer. I was confident he'd be able to fend off the attack dogs they would set on Walker.

Not being married, and not having children, I was in a different boat. All I had to think about was myself—and my men.

I felt certain Holly could deal with whatever came her way.

I didn't think she would be painted with the same MARSOC 7 brush simply because we were together. I wondered though if she too saw those sideways glances and heard what was being said behind her back about her boyfriend.

If she did, she never told me. When I spoke with her each night on the phone while she was in Yuma, we didn't talk shop. I didn't ask for her help as an intelligence officer either, despite our Top Secret security clearances. I didn't want to do anything that might jeopardize her career. Without my saying a word, she understood what I had to do to protect her.

Soon we connected in North Carolina and drove to upstate New York so I could meet her parents. She was very close to them and gaining their approval was essential to cement our relationship.

That wasn't a problem. Her dad had been an officer in the Navy and we got along straight off. Her family was military through and through.

He told me that when Holly was only a little girl, she said to them, "Mom, dad, I know what I want to do."

"You know what you want to be when you grow up?" they asked anxiously.

Holly looked up at them with her big brown eyes and said with single-minded conviction, "I want to join the Marines."

How many ten-year-old girls say that? Taken aback, they asked her, "Why?"

"Because," she answered, "if I can make it in the Marines, I can do anything."

She was one determined little girl, and she grew up to be a very determined Marine.

Filthy Fred and Fightin' Fred aside, I'm actually kind of a romantic guy. I took Holly and her parents to Niagara Falls to stay at a hotel overlooking picturesque Horseshoe Falls and at a restaurant that night, in front of her parents, asked her to marry me.

When she said, "Yes," I thought marrying her was the best thing that could ever happen to me.

We scheduled the wedding for the following spring.

Presumably, by then, we would know any ramifications from the ambush.

We put our faith in an organization that was almost sacred to us. Though I had been anxious about what might happen, I hadn't truly believed our country's military leaders, our Marine leaders, would turn their legal guns on us.

Pantano predicted otherwise.

"They will sic the dogs on you," he told me, adding ominously, "and when the machine comes after you, they can make you look pretty bad."

After getting my hands on Pihana's report, I spent the night poring over it. Alternately angry and frustrated, I furiously scribbled notes about lies and misstatements. At 3 a.m., I finished reading the last page, and the message was clear: East and I had fought our country's enemies both on and behind the front lines for years, and now our country was sending in the Marines to take us down.

We had been betrayed.

The fight was on, and I remembered the words of my Infantry Officer Course instructor:

"If you get into a knife fight, you are going to bleed."

A Lot of People That Died That Day

7 January 2008
Camp Lejeune, North Carolina

We won one small battle in the beginning. Our civilian attorneys needed security clearances to defend us. Without them, they would not be able to review certain documents, interview certain witnesses, or even be present in the courtroom if upcoming testimony was labeled "classified." Clearance would take four to six weeks. That blew up the prosecution's tactic of drowning us with a flood of documents. A November 1st start date was no longer on the table.

But East and I did have Top Secret clearance, so we could at least read the documents—though we couldn't tell our civilian attorneys what was in them in detail.

Wading through the material was daunting. After twelve-hour workdays—we were still Marines with jobs to do—East and I would spend each night digesting hundreds of pages in an attempt to summarize the classified portions for Waple and Nunnally. We burned the candle at both ends trying to counter the sheer size of the prosecution's manpower and resources.

Finally, more than ten months after the ambush and half a world away, East and I had our first day in court.

We would be in the same courtroom, at the same time, side by side, and prosecuted by the same legal team for the United States government. We were always called "defendants" and our lawyers "defense counsels"— curious titles for a "fair, impartial and unbiased fact-finding panel," per the COI's instructions.

Maj. Philip Sanchez and Maj. Kurt Sanger, the Marine lawyers assigned to the case, were not officially called "prosecutors" but rather "counsels to the court." Yet, their witnesses were called "prosecution witnesses" in the court transcripts. I will call Sanchez and Sanger "prosecutors" throughout this book because that is what they were. If it looks like a duck, walks like a duck, and talks like a duck, it's a duck.

Walking to the base's court building that Monday morning, breathing the brisk winter air, I crossed paths with Montanus.

He shook his head with disapproval, with a disgusted look on his face. I saluted and he did the same, but he seemed ashamed we were wearing the same uniform.

"Sometimes the enemy does not play fair." I'd learned that too in my Infantry Officer Course, and I was reminded of it when the media photographer snapped my photograph before I entered the building. Two officers on trial, accused of being responsible for killing nineteen Afghan civilians and wounding another fifty, was front-page news. But allowing the media access to photograph both me and East was extraordinary.

It was also disconcerting. It was damaging enough to be identified in print; now, our faces were everywhere.

I'd never had my photo published in a newspaper before. This was not how I imagined the circumstances for my first time.

After entering the building and peeking into the room on the left, where investigators had set up their command post, I walked into the courtroom on the right and sat at the defense table with East and our lawyers. In front of us was the three-member panel that would determine our fate.

Questionnaires had been sent out across the east coast Corps to select the panel members. They had to be lieutenant colonels or colonels from the combat arms profession (infantry, artillery, or armor) and with combat experience.

Col. Mark Porter looked more like a civilian CEO than an infantry officer with twenty-two years of service. His expertise was in organization, mainly on the east coast, but he had served in combat twice in Iraq, where he was also an operations officer. Since he was the senior colonel, he was selected as the COI's president.

Col. Eric Daniels was also from the infantry. Before becoming an officer, he started his career as an enlisted Marine, working as a court reporter. With twenty-seven years of service assigned to bases on both the east and west coasts, he had served in combat three times, including twice in Iraq, once as a battalion CO, and had been deployed to Afghanistan as an executive officer. He knew about sacrifice: His older brother had been a twenty-one-year-old Marine who died in a helicopter crash in Vietnam.

Lt. Col. Steve Morgan was in the artillery before becoming an intelligence officer. He had thirty years of assignments under his belt at bases across the U.S. and overseas. Each time he was in combat, he was awarded the Bronze Star with valor, once in Afghanistan and once in Saudi Arabia/Kuwait.

Lt. Colonel Steve Morgan, USMC (Ret.) comments supporting Fox Company's exoneration at a U.S. Congressional press conference (Courtesy of *Stars and Stripes*)

Morgan wore a constantly sour look to match a cranky attitude. He had good reason. He was the only panel member with up close and personal combat experience in Afghanistan. During a 2004 deployment to Paktika, as the CO of a Provincial Reconstruction Team, his convoy was ambushed by a numerically superior enemy force firing from concealed positions as close as ten meters away. Half his unit was killed or wounded. Morgan fought back heroically while at the same time treating his casualties and reorganizing his men to return to their base. I hoped that at least he would understand what had happened on March 4.

What I didn't know was that, as the COI began, Morgan thought we were guilty.

"When I walked in there," he later told the *Military Times*, "I was ready to send these guys to the brig (given) everything I had known and some of the read-aheads that I had received to prepare myself.... I had this notion in my head: Maybe these guys did what it had been said they'd done."

Major Fred Galvin, USMC entering courtroom with his military and civilian defense counselors (Courtesy of the *Jacksonville Daily News*)

Besides, Nicholson had already said we were guilty.

"Why would the commander make such a strong statement," Morgan asked himself, "if he didn't have substantive facts to back it up?"

The prosecution was confident too, enough so that a few of their attorneys celebrated their role in one of the most notorious war crimes trials in memory by bringing their wives or girlfriends as spectators that first day. The well-dressed women gaily chatting before the court was called to order reminded me of the elegant southern belles I'd read about who picnicked on a hill as they watched the savage Battle of Manassas play out below them during the Civil War.

East and I said little to each other beyond the greeting we would give every day: "Shields up!"

In the recently released movie *300*, the Spartan warriors thrust their shields over their heads to protect themselves as they faced the onslaught of the massive Persian army at the Battle of Thermopylae in 480 BC. We felt as overwhelmed as they did. I prayed every day that we would not suffer the same fate, being slaughtered to the last man.

East and I wore our camouflage utility uniforms to court. That was not a choice; our commanders told us to wear them, it was an order. At the time, we didn't think anything of it and we complied, but it was significant.

In most Marine Corps trials, including the Haditha and Hamandiyah cases, the accused wore their service uniforms. East and I were decorated combat veterans who proudly wore our awards for valor and service on those uniforms. But Marines didn't pin them to utility uniforms, except during an awarding ceremony. As a consequence, we walked into court past the mass of assembled photographers and journalists, without those medals and ribbons.

The Marine command didn't want to look like they were putting war heroes on trial.

They intended to control the optics, control the narrative. They were waging an information operation not unlike what they would employ against an enemy—or like what the Taliban were doing to our troops.

Clarke wanted to influence the optics in our favor by encouraging other Marines to stand in front of the court building in a show of support. But I was adamant there be no such demonstration, no such fanfare. I told him we were not going to play those games for the media. East and I would take the high ground.

The Court of Inquiry was ordered into session, and the raspy-voiced Lecce, the legal court's advisor, rattled off the ground rules. Prosecutor Sanchez followed with a few brief comments in a calm, soft-spoken tone matched by gentle flourishes with his hands.

Our defense's opening statement was anything but gentle.

Jack politely greeted the panel—and attacked. Before he was a Marine, he had been a college football linebacker, and even in this courtroom, he was trying to sack the quarterback.

"Witnesses that will take the stand will tell you that the two majors sitting here beside me, have knowingly made false statements to third parties."

Nodding towards Sanchez and Sanger, his impassioned voice rose with indignation: "They've specifically attempted to deceive MARSOC enlisted Marines and officers by participating in and actively interrogating Marines with NCIS agents while wearing civilian attire, failing to inform them of their officer status!"

We had discovered that prosecutors Sanger and Sanchez were the unidentified men who sat in on many NCIS interrogations, notably at those of Ortega and Ruiz. Lecce was occasionally included as well. Neither Ortega nor Ruiz had their lawyers present.

Jack roared as he vigorously shook the wooden courtroom podium like a Southern Baptist preacher saving souls.

"They LIED and attempted to deceive those witnesses using statements or evidence THEY created!"

To punctuate his point, he lifted the podium a few inches off the ground and slammed it down.

"The general principle is SUPPOSED to be 'fair and unbiased,'" he raged, unintentionally spewing spit in the direction of the prosecutors, who slinked down in their wooden chairs. "And it's SUPPOSED to be presenting the government's evidence, not creating it!"

To prove the point to the panel, we had repeatedly requested the audio and/or video of the interrogations, particularly of Ortega and Ruiz. But we were denied each time. Nevertheless, Jack demanded that the panel sanction the prosecution and ban Lecce from the courtroom.

He also asked that the panel dismiss the case that night.

"The bottom line is that 4 March 2007 was a valid shoot," he said firmly. "No ifs, ands, and buts about it. And if you conclude after reading all the evidence, after listening to all the testimony of those Marines on that patrol, and you conclude that it's a valid, lawful, professional shoot and it was justified under the Rules of Engagement, then I believe that this Court of Inquiry is closed."

Jack was an unstoppable force of nature. After the session was recessed, I figured we would hear within hours that the case was dismissed.

But the cards had already been dealt.

The following day, the prosecution called its first witness: Milton, our Fox Company human intelligence specialist. After the deployment, the tall, solidly built Alabaman had left the Marines and joined the Army Corps of Engineers. He testified in a suit and tie.

"I really felt," he said with a wistful sadness in his voice, "that there was a lot of people that died that day that, you know, probably didn't need to."

I stiffened. One of my own Marines was testifying under oath that we had killed innocent Afghans.

The Crime Scene

I gripped tight the arms of my chair. How could Milton possibly say what he said? Knowing what actually happened, how could he possibly believe what he said?

Milton went on to paint us as bad guys from the start of our deployment. He told the COI that during operations before March 4, the platoon threw rocks at vehicles that did not obey hand and arm signals to move off the road. The same thing happened on March 4 as he sat directly behind East in the rear passenger seat of Vehicle Three.

Milton told the panel he had asked East: "Hey, sir, did you see that?"

"What are you talking about?"

"It looks like the gunner in Vehicle Two just put a huge hole through that guy's windshield," Milton said he answered. "That is the kind of stuff that is going to get us blown up out here."

According to Milton, a Green Beret team at Jalalabad had told members of Fox Company that throwing rocks was what they had done in Iraq to keep civilian vehicles from harassing a convoy. Rock throwing became an unauthorized step in the laundry list of EOF responses that ratcheted up in violence from non-lethal to deadly. In Iraq, drivers typically responded by moving to the side and stopping.

Not so, as we learned, in Afghanistan. The drivers there had more, well, attitude. It was part of their national character to be rugged and fearless. They felt we were on *their* road in *their* country and they had as much right as anyone to drive on it any way they wanted. Drivers would refuse to pull over, stop or even slow down. The more adventurous would not only keep coming closer but go faster and weave between our vehicles. They were fools, but most of them were harmless fools.

"Maybe honestly he (the driver) doesn't know what he's doing and he's just acting like a jackass," Ruiz explained at the COI. "Should I shoot him just for that? I'll pay for somebody's windshield in place of somebody's life."

Milton and the prosecution made it appear we were being mean and petty, somehow disrespectful of Afghan culture, if not committing a human rights violation, when we threw a rock—and we deserved to get blown up if we did.

I suppose it's all a matter of perspective. If you are David slinging a stone at Goliath, you're an underdog hero; if you're a uniformed American behind a machine gun, you're a bully.

Following his warning about retribution, Milton recalled that the Marines in our turrets went back to hand motions. But soon after, there was the explosion, "a pretty big fireball," he said. Once the smoke began to clear, he heard gunfire but could not tell who was firing at whom. East then gave the order to "move out," and the convoy continued forward.

After Milton heard over the radio that Fox Company was taking fire from a hilltop, he recalled East saying to Ruiz, his gunner, "Let it ride."

Milton assumed that order meant to fire away. But "let it ride" could have meant "forget about it," because Ruiz did not shoot.

Regardless, Milton was certain others in the patrol did fire, including two he personally saw discharge their weapons at vehicles on the road—Walker in the back of Vehicle Two and the recovered Klein.

"It seemed like after the attack a lot of those hand and arm signals had been replaced with gunfire," he testified. "Sometimes the pattern of gunfire would be like a warning shot and impact the road right in front of the vehicle, trying to get them to move to the side of the road. Sometimes the pattern of gunfire would impact directly across the hood of a vehicle that was oncoming. And then in some instances it looked like the pattern of impact went directly across the windshield, the hood, or the cab of the vehicle."

He added that he was "pretty upset" about that.

"At the time, I knew there was an inherent danger, but I thought it was a little bit excessive."

He said the shooting stopped only after East gave an order to "cease fire."

Then Milton dropped his own bomb: "There was a lot of people that died that day that, you know, probably didn't need to."

Milton's account perfectly fit the prosecution's scenario: We were struck by an IED and we freaked out, recklessly firing on anyone and everyone over the next several miles as we hustled out of the area.

The damning Afghanistan Independent Human Rights Commission's report agreed, quoting one Afghan eyewitness saying that "a coalition forces vehicle arrived at my fuel station and opened fire on me and on laborers working beneath the bridge." Another said he was traveling in a car some ten miles from the bomb site: "There is no reason why they should have fired on the car, we were quite a long distance away."

The report went on to say that "no evidence was found that any of the vehicles or persons fired on away from the main VBIED site posed a threat to the American convoy or were anything other than civilians... (and) no kind of provocative or threatening behavior on their part preceded the attacks."

According to the commission, whose conclusions were parroted in *The Washington Post* and *The New York Times*, we spun out of control.

I thought having an Afghan testify might help us, and Ali, our interpreter, would fit the bill. He might give an eyewitness view different from that of Milton. At least I hoped he would.

But despite numerous requests that Ali be called as a witness, the government said that was not possible—because they were unable to find him.

We were also stonewalled when we asked for Kearney and Hejlik to be called into court. Neither appeared, though Hejlik agreed to answer a few innocuous questions submitted to him in writing (see Appendix II), rather than being asked tougher questions under oath by our lawyers.

Pihana too refused to appear in court despite the proximity of his Tampa office to Camp Lejeune, but he did testify via a live video teleconference.

He said that, at first, he believed my Marines; that after inspecting Vehicle Two, he'd concluded that we had indeed been subjected to small arms fire and a complex ambush, prompting our deadly response.

"I was pretty convinced...(especially) when I looked at the (vehicles)... Here was damage to the windshield, here was, you know, impacts here and there... I thought, oh great, you know, it looks like it's going that way."

He also had in hand the report of a specialized post-blast analysis team that inspected and took photos of Vehicle Two within the first hour of the patrol returning to Jalalabad.

Navy Petty Officer 1st Class Brett Childs, an EOD technician, noted the impact areas on Vehicle Two, including the presence of the tip of an AK-47 round.

Pihana then brought in Sgt. 1st Class Andy Moon, an Army EOD specialist, to be his subject expert. Onsite within forty-eight hours, Moon inspected Vehicle Two both the night he arrived and the following morning. He found impacts on the turret shield and the left and right front windshields. He had no doubt that the impacts were from small arms fire and not from the blast.

Not only did the windows have divots on the outside and halo effects on the inside but, Moon testified, "the grouping is too tight (to be caused by a bomb explosion)... It wouldn't be all together. You might have two or three really close together. It wouldn't be all the same size (either)."

The AK-47 fragment, however, was gone. By the time of Moon's initial inspection, all the vehicles had been pressure washed and cleaned in anticipation of our next mission. Perhaps the fragment had washed away.

To help determine the direction of fire, Moon put a pen into the bullet hole in the turret shield. He also recreated the turret's position at the time of the attack.

"We had the gunner (Klein) line up exactly where the turret was," Moon explained, "and from that and the direction of fire, we derived that the bullet impacted most likely from the northern direction of the road... The gunner happened to get lucky and didn't get struck by the bullet." He estimated that the bullet was 5.56mm or 7.62mm fired from a distance of between 350 and 450 meters.

"And you told them (the Fox Company Marines) what you thought were impact rounds from small arms; right?" asked Woodard, East's military attorney.

"No."

"You did not?" Woodard pretended to be surprised.

"No," answered the by-the-book Moon. "I did not inform the Marines at that point in time what I thought was what on the vehicle. That would actually try to sway their opinion on what actually happened. What I do is when I'm actually interviewing people, I get their statements, I take what I have, and when I get back to the office I will sit down with my team and we'll try to figure everything out from the evidence that we received."

In the meantime, something happened to change Pihana's mind.

He said that visiting the scene and interviewing Afghan witnesses prompted doubts that we had taken small arms fire. He then re-examined Vehicle Two.

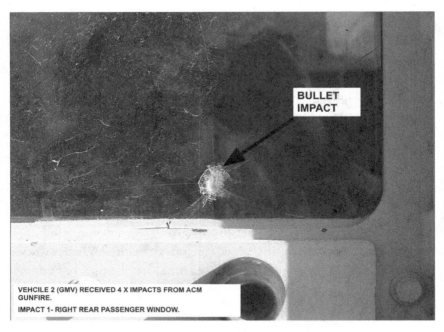

VEHCILE 2 (GMV) RECEIVED 4 X IMPACTS FROM ACM GUNFIRE.

IMPACT 1- RIGHT REAR PASSENGER WINDOW.

VEHCILE 2 (GMV) RECEIVED 4 X IMPACTS FROM ACM GUNFIRE.

IMPACT 2- RIGHT EDGE OF GUNNERS TURRET GLACIS. PASSED THROUGH EDGE OF GLACIS.

Images of bullet impacts on multiple sides of Vehicle Two

"I stood around to the side of that glacis (the sloped plate of armor at the front of the vehicle) and looked at it and went, 'Wait a minute. That (bullet) didn't come from the front (the north).'"

He put his pen in the hole and came up with a different result than Moon.

"The evidence," Pihana crowed proudly, "does not support his theory."

Instead, Pihana said, the bullet impact was from friendly fire.

Taking his cue from an Afghan witness, he reckoned that Walker, the rear compartment gunner in Vehicle Two, turned toward the front and accidentally shot his own turret, which was directly in front of him at point-blank distance.

"I thought these are experienced operators who know what incoming rounds sound like, who have been in this before," said a disparaging Pihana. "And when I first took on the investigation, I was sure, based on just the initial reports I was hearing, that I would find evidence (of enemy fire)... That was kind of eroded by the fact I thought people further back in the convoy may have heard, when they heard weapons fire, outgoing weapons fire instead of incoming weapons fire."

He also took the word of Milton that the impacts on the passenger side window of Vehicle Two existed prior to departing on the patrol. Pihana surmised that all the other impacts were from the blast, not from incoming shots, no matter what Moon thought.

"They look just more like a hot material of some kind ejected possibly from the blast, impacting the...front windshield," he said with an air of authority, "and then splattering on impact and solidifying."

"It is true, is it not," Waple asked Pihana pointedly, "that this is your first attempt ever in any kind of investigation to make that kind of expert analysis?"

"Yes," he conceded. "All I had to go on was the information from the experts I talked to, from photographs that I obtained and just my own judgment."

He declared, "If they sat on that spot for one to eight minutes, and were taking fire from all the directions that they described, especially from the Prado, it was inconceivable to me how I could not find more physical evidence of the convoy being struck by multiple fires."

Waple proffered an alternative explanation, one Pihana himself suggested in his report.

"Even you in your conclusions said they (the Afghans) might have been bad shots," Waple said. Being under fire and running around while taking cover does not help accuracy.

"That is possible," countered Pihana. "(But there was) a large volume of fire being reported. If there is no impact, then a logical conclusion is they weren't fired upon."

He said he climbed trees alongside Hell's Highway with a hand-held metal detector searching for small arms bullet fragments but came up empty. He was, however, given a .50 caliber SLAP round, which an Afghan dug out of a wall. SLAP was the acronym for Saboted Light Armor Penetrator, armor-piercing ammunition used by NATO troops. The source of that round, he said, had to have been our convoy.

"We found no physical evidence to support such an (incoming) attack occurred," he said with assurance. "Nobody ever saw anybody fire on the MARSOC convoy, to include...contractors affiliated with USAID working in a riverbed. They were right there where there were reports of enemy combatants.... Nobody saw shots (from Afghans)."

One of the NCIS agents who testified, Marine Chief Warrant Officer Vic DiVicenzo, was of the same mind—there was no forensic evidence to support the idea that a complex ambush occurred. Even the Afghan commission had left some wiggle room, writing in its report that "there was some limited physical evidence available suggesting that a complex ambush really took place at the site of the incident."

When he and other NCIS investigators arrived in May, they went to the blast site for about an hour. They examined a small portion of the highway but did not go to the hillside, the riverbed, or the gas station. None of that mattered much anyway. It was two months after the ambush. By then, the "crime scene" had been contaminated, with evidence undoubtedly taken, moved, or destroyed.

But, DiVicenzo emphasized, they did interview reported eyewitnesses and victims of the attack and "most of the people," he said, "regardless of whether they were at the VBIED site or whether they were down the road in Bati Kot or traveling in a taxi cab, most said the same thing in terms of the use of force that was done by the coalition forces...all the firing came from the gun trucks. Nobody—of all the people that we interviewed, we never identified a single Afghan person not affiliated with the convoy, whoever said that they saw enemy fire."

DiVicenzo noted there were inconsistencies in the statements given by my Marines to Pihana and NCIS about being fired upon. One saw one thing, while another did not.

Pihana agreed: "There were impressions or perceptions that the convoy was taking fire from multiple locations that did not exist or at least were not supported by the evidence I found or didn't find."

Neither he nor DiVicenzo accepted what my Marines told them.

"We're trying to fit the pieces together," DiVicenzo said, "and many of them just don't fit." He then presented to the panel a list the prosecution had instructed him to compile of those inconsistencies.

Pihana insisted that though we were in a heightened state of alert, worried about a follow-on IED, the vehicles that continued to come our way, including the Prado, did not pose a danger and should not have been fired on.

"The Marines told you that the drivers of these vehicles to the front of them were driving wildly and pretty erratically after the blast went off, did they not?" asked Waple.

"Yes...that is the Marines' perceptions."

"And your perception, not being there," Waple said sarcastically, "is that is not true; correct?"

"Correct," Pihana answered, gritting his teeth. "Death and bombing and destruction is an everyday occurrence in Afghanistan... When something like this happens, if it didn't happen to you, best to get out of the way and head on home about your business.... They would continue to go on with their normal driving, which in Afghanistan, if you've never been there..."

He paused a moment to glare at Waple.

"(It) can look pretty bizarre to us... It would almost appear that every vehicle that came toward the (Humvee) vehicle...was a threat, which I don't believe was supported by the evidence at all."

"Were they just shooting at everything they saw?" Waple asked, dripping with doubt.

Pihana knew he could not go that far.

"It just didn't look like there was enough discrimination," he said, "if you will, to, you know, to stop the firing. It got out of control."

Milton said he heard East admonish the Marines to stop firing unless they were being engaged, which the prosecution interpreted to mean they *had* been firing without being engaged. Sgt. Jose Obregon, the driver of Vehicle Four, said he heard East say over the radio, far down the road, to "cease firing warning shots," which the prosecution interpreted to mean we *had* been firing warning shots and were now moving on to lethal shots.

DiVicenzo said he came to conclude that, without provocation, we had killed and injured innocent civilians.

He claimed he was uncomfortable coming to that conclusion.

"Being put in the position of finding, potentially finding fault with your comrades in arms, if you will, no, that did not excite me."

But, he added, he could not excuse firing at civilians.

"I mean you get hit, you're not sure what happened, here's a vehicle moving, you just got hit, you suppress. Right, wrong, or indifferent, it happened. It's part of combat. People make mistakes on the battlefield. I completely understand that…(the officers) wouldn't have a whole lot of visibility on what gun trucks One and Two were doing from their perspective…

"My concern is as they traveled down the road—and this is where I have a hard time grasping the escalation of force…whether they were warning shots or purposely in the vehicles. That, to me, is where I have issues, personally, as a Marine with what occurred."

DiVicenzo seemed uneasy about his withering testimony.

"My father is a Marine, I come from a Marine Corps family," he said. "Quite honestly, when I got this case, my intention was to go over there and attempt to exonerate the Marines. I wanted to do that."

Hoping for the tearjerker clincher, the prosecution hooked up a live video feed from Jalalabad Airfield and brought in a handful of the Afghan witnesses NCIS had interviewed, assisted by an interpreter.

The first three were Lt. Col. Ziudin, an officer with the ANP who was not at the ambush site that morning, his brother Nangyli, and the brother's son, Nasurtullah. It took a short while to bring in Nasurtullah because he was paralyzed and had to be wheeled into the room on a hospital gurney.

Nangyli recounted that he was driving a red van he was using as a taxi. Inside were six passengers besides his nephew. After he stopped the van, the Americans fired at "all those vehicles that were parked along the road. This convoy they were shooting almost to everyone along the road, everyone."

Among those fired at was a small bus next to Nangyli's van, and he and Nasurtullah were hit by one of the 7.62mm rounds from our medium machine gun. He said he was wounded in the leg and his son in the neck, causing his devastating paralysis.

"How many U.S. vehicles did you see that day?" asked panel president Porter.

"Three."

"Did you see any Marines out of vehicles?"

"At the beginning when they were asking us—by their hands to don't come," Nangyli said confidently, "that I saw them. Yes."

As Porter continued his questioning, Sanger grunted. He did not look pleased with the direction the testimony was taking. He knew we had not exited our vehicles.

Trying to gain clarity, Porter asked, "On top of the vehicles, or outside the vehicles on foot?"

"They were out at the front of the vehicles on the road," Nangyli remembered.

"Walking?" said a bewildered Porter.

Nangyli attempted to elaborate: "I saw them standing, not walking."

He said the convoy then drove past his van.

"What happened to the three Marines that were on the street walking?" Porter asked.

Nangyli looked puzzled.

"Maybe those guys jump into the vehicle (Humvee)."

Sanchez shook his head, wondering why they had invited Nangyli to be a witness.

Porter continued: "Where were the holes in the vehicle (the red van)? The bullet holes?"

"The front window of the vehicle has one hole that's where the one bullet get into the vehicle, hit me, and after went to the back seat and hit (Nasurtullah)," he said mournfully. "The same—we think is the same bullet."

The other men in his van were uninjured. One, an older man sitting in the front seat, drove them to the closest hospital.

Lecce tried to get the testimony back on track for the prosecution.

"Did you—on the trip to the Ghani Khail Hospital, did you see any other wounded Afghans or damaged vehicles?"

"Yes, sir," Nangyli said with certainty. "I saw maybe more than fifty people that they were wounded and there were two vehicles before me, two or three vehicles after me, you know. I saw a lot of injured people there."

Lecce probed further.

"Did you also see injured people at the Ghani Khail Hospital?"

"A lot. Yes."

"Did you see any other wounded Afghans?" Lecce asked.

"I had five other Afghans, they were wounded with me in the same room."

"Did you know if there were any other, any wounded, in other rooms?"

"I think, yeah," he offered. "There were about thirty-seven wounded, and I was told twenty deaths."

Lecce asked Nangyli if he was aware of any injuries that occurred farther down Hell's Highway towards Jalalabad.

"Yes, I was aware of some injuries and deaths maybe fifteen kilometers away."

With a satisfied Lecce starting to thank him for his testimony, Nangyli jumped in:

"From my side, I forgive them with my heart. I hope that somehow it gets to help me out to take my son all down to the U.S. for the further treatment. Because you are the prosecutor, then I have no other way to raise my voice. And now we're thinking that the crime took place, and now it is going to be proved too. I want help for my son to become better and become healthier. And I think I deserve it, and you guys are the only ones I can raise my voice to."

With that plea ringing in the ears of the panel members, Nangyli left with his paralyzed son Nasurtullah. It was a sad sight, one that made Fox Company look irredeemably heartless.

We were being hit from every direction, in court and the press.

Even the front page of the *Marine Corps Times* proclaimed "Meltdown at 'Task Force Violence': Uncovered – the hidden story of the MarSOC Marines who shamed the Corps."

Marine Corps Times **front cover, three months prior to the Court's verdict**

The article began: "They were supposed to be the fewest of the Few and Proud, quiet professionals trained for sticky covert missions. So when Marine Special Operations Company-Fox—the first of the Corps' new spec ops units to deploy for combat operations—left for Afghanistan in early 2007, the Corps expected nothing less than total success.

Then the unit bent every rule that wouldn't break, ticked off every commander in the theater, alienated the local population, violated direct orders, caused an international incident, and allegedly killed as many as nineteen Afghan civilians and wounded dozens more."

We were being bloodied.

Apologies and Cash

At sunrise each day, I found myself beside my bed on my knees, praying that God might protect me.

It was all I could do to fight the sense of being vulnerable, of being powerless. It's a feeling you never want to have in combat, a feeling I last had as a thirteen-year-old with my father.

I had thought I was tough. I had survived being bombed and shot at. But now I felt a dread I couldn't shake.

It was brutal to watch a team of Marine prosecutors portray my Fox Company Marines as killers of innocent civilians, and East and me as the officers who made that happen. And there seemed to be little I could do about it.

One thing prevented me from falling into a depression during the darkest days of the trial—my concern for the well-being of my Marines. I had more to think about than just myself.

The public didn't know their names, but their families, friends, and acquaintances knew they had been in Fox Company, knew there had been a supposed massacre in Afghanistan, knew they had been kicked out, knew that if East and I were convicted at a court-martial that they would be next. I worried about how they were dealing with that uncertainty about the future. East and I were taking the heat in the COI, but they too were squarely in the crosshairs of the legal system.

Beyond their careers, livelihoods, and freedom, their sense of self-worth was at stake. All of us had experienced a breach of faith, not unlike the victims of sexual abuse in the Catholic Church. We had put our trust in something greater than ourselves and that trust had been violated.

I wanted to check in with them, keep track of how they were doing, so every week I threw some steaks on a grill and invited them to my place for a barbecue.

As if leading men into combat, I put on a brave face, trying to show confidence myself and give them confidence in turn. If Fightin' Fred looked afraid, they would be afraid too.

During officer training, we were taught to look your men in the eye when you spoke to them. So I smiled, looked each of them in the eye, and assured Lester, Klein, Walker, Clarke, and Pratt that everything was going to be okay.

Truth is, I was just as scared as they were that our lives could very well be ruined forever.

East was not at the barbecues. He did not want to see the other Marines at less than his best. Barely thirty years old, he had been diagnosed with cancer. His doctors were convinced that the trauma of the COI had triggered the appearance of that disease. East was not the only one suddenly suffering physically. After noticing that Clarke seemed more distant, more detached, than usual at one barbecue, I discovered that he had been diagnosed with diabetes, which doctors said was brought on by stress.

Lester was peculiarly quiet too. He had left the Marines after the deployment, as he'd always intended. But rather than his exit lifting the cloud that followed him, his gloominess grew darker and turned to paranoia. Because of the notoriety of the trial, he feared being identified and violently attacked by a religious fanatic. Lester worried that a homegrown jihadist would hunt him down in retaliation, sneaking up behind him and blowing his head off in a misguided attempt at payback.

Some were better at hiding the stress than others. Pratt didn't seem to have a care in the world and Walker, while concerned about his wife and child, was taking everything in stride.

Klein, however, was not very good at burying his emotions.

He was angry about what was happening. I did what I could to calm him, including keeping him away from chugging too many beers. I was worried about him.

Privately, I was mentally, physically, and emotionally exhausted. I wore the same unperturbed façade I had learned to put on for so many combat missions. But beneath the surface, I struggled.

I had loved and respected the Marines since I went off to boot camp. But when I looked around the courtroom, I was disappointed that no Marines came by to silently offer encouragement. I had told Fox Company to stay away, but other Marines, particularly from the MARSOC headquarters building only a mile and a half away, could have shown their faces.

No one did.

The family I so much wanted, and had been part of for more than twenty years, was determined to leave me behind. The lack of brotherhood was devastating. I never thought so few would care.

Perhaps they were afraid of showing us support. After all, the command hierarchy, including the Army's Kearney and Nicholson, said they believed Fox Company had killed innocent people. And Nicholson not only had offered his widely broadcast apology but he'd put American money where his mouth was.

On behalf of the U.S. government, Nicholson paid *solatia*, an Afghan custom considered an expression of condolence for deaths, injuries, and damages. He authorized disbursements of up to $2,300, the equivalent of four and a half years income for the average Afghan, for each of nineteen "dead" (given to the next of kin) and the fifty "wounded": $466 to anyone who suffered a serious injury and $233 to anyone claiming a minor one. Payments were also made for property damage, such as to vehicles.

Nicholson, via a live video feed from the Pentagon, explained at the COI that for Afghans "death is a part of their everyday existence. I mean, one out of every five of their children die before the age of five. So they are pretty accepting of death. What they are not accepting of is when someone is killed, their honor has been stripped of them and then their honor must be restored... There is a couple ways that honor can be restored. One way is through the apology and *solatia*."

173

The *solatia* list was created by the province's governor and included anyone he said was a victim. Every civilian on every casualty list was named solely on the word of the victim, witnesses, or family members. Though he had the power to remove names, Nicholson committed to the governor's list as submitted.

But the civilian casualty count, which did not include the suicide bomber, an enemy combatant, was a moving target. No two reports had the same numbers. The initial report from the ANP said sixteen were killed, including a woman, a three-year-old child, and the three men in the Prado, and at least twenty-eight injured. The United Nations Assistance Mission in Afghanistan tallied seven dead and twenty-four wounded.

Haji Liwani Qomandan's Blue Prado which was the only vehicle displayed in the press after the 4 March 2007 ambush (Courtesy of *Associated Press*)

Pihana testified that, "Gut feeling, I can look you in the eye and say that I'm comfortable, at this point in time right now, six to seven deceased. In terms of wounded, fifteen to twenty."

The Afghan commission said there were twelve dead and thirty-five injured. According to the commission, the deceased were:

Name	Father's Name	Age
Abdullah	Mira Jan	60
Fazil Rahim	Abdullah	35
Atequllah	Gholam Hazrat	40
Zarmina	Taher Khan	35
Entezaruding	Jamaludin	1
Robina	Unknown	4
Khanul Tera Gul	Unknown	19
Shin Makhe	Unknown	65
Zarpadshah	Unknown	70
Farid Gul	Kateb	18
Farid	Gul Zada	25
Nasrat	Ziaudin	25

No one knew the exact numbers—because neither the dead nor wounded were verified with physical evidence.

Incredibly, Nicholson blamed Fox Company for not confirming the number of dead and injured on March 4.

He said it was difficult to determine how many people were injured or killed because the Marines left the area after the incident. Unlike what the Army would have done, he expressed with pride, the Marines did not stay to count the dead, help the wounded, and secure the area.

"We would stay and remain on the battlefield," Nicholson said, puffing out his chest. Leaving the scene of a gunfight is "something we never do," he went on, stressing that his Army brigade was trained to "remain in possession of the battlefield."

I was flabbergasted by Nicholson's arrogance, not to mention his ignorance of the tactics recommended following an ambush.

The 2006 *SOCOM Combat Convoy Handbook* said that the proper reaction to an ambush was to "identify the source by calling out left/right/front/rear; return fire on the move, drive through the kill zone, establish fire superiority, assault through, withdraw as applicable." The 2005 *USMC Convoy Operations Battle Book* advised that "a convoy commander that is ambushed along an intended route may have guidance to push through the kill zone or stop and assault the enemy."

Neither manual said one word about stopping and treating the kill zone as a crime scene. That was the job of the MPs—and the Army MPs at the scene were under Nicholson's command.

In fact, not a single death or injury caused by a Marine bullet was confirmed by physical evidence to any investigator—not even those of the three men in the Prado. There was no corpse with a bullet hole, no photograph of a corpse with a bullet hole, no autopsy indicating a bullet hole, no body exhumed to reveal a bullet hole. Nor was there any documentation of a bullet wound on any survivor.

One MP who arrived within thirty minutes of the blast said, "Besides the dead guy on the south side of the road I didn't notice any additional Afghanis who were injured or dead." Another stated that he too saw only the one headless corpse.

Local doctors could not say with any confidence if they treated anyone for wounds caused by gunshots and, specifically, Marine gunshots.

Dr. Amangul Amani testified via video teleconference that on the morning of March 4, three bodies were brought into his Ghani Khail Hospital between Bati Kot and Jalalabad but he was unsure if they were victims of shootings. The Nangahar Public Health Division told NCIS that they were taken away without permission before being identified and examined.

The translator jotted down on his transcript of the Public Health Division interview: "The answer above sounds fishy. They are hiding something. Those bodies. Could have been Taliban, or the attackers who fired at our forces after the explosion."

Amani said that he normally saw ten to twenty injuries a day from accidents, bombings, and gunshots. On March 4, he saw twenty-three patients, of which eleven were sent on to Jalalabad Hospital. Of the remaining twelve, most had glass cuts. Whether they were due to a bomb or a gunshot or another cause was unknown.

One patient suffered what appeared to be bullet entry and exit wounds, and one woman lost fingers from a gunshot, but who was responsible was unknown. A ten-year-old boy suffered head trauma when he hit his head on the back of a car seat as the vehicle abruptly stopped. He remained in the hospital three days, the longest of any patient treated after the ambush.

The hospital's emergency room physician, Dr. Fazel Rahim Shagwali, testified that he operated on two patients that day but did not recover anything from them that could be identified as bullet fragments.

The translator was highly skeptical of the numbers of casualties provided by the Afghan National Police too.

"If the hospitals did not have the total number of dead and wounded, how did the police get them?" he wrote in his notes. "If the police saw the bodies and injured why didn't they secure the area and not let anybody touch or take the bodies away? The hospital authorities must know something they are hesitant to express.... There are a lot of discrepancies in answers to the interrogator's questions.... The numbers given by each police section are not corresponding with each other."

Waple challenged Pihana.

"And yet all of that testimony (of the Marines) you chose to not believe and to believe the testimony of Afghan witnesses." He shook his head. "How many Afghan witnesses did you talk to?"

"There were probably eight to ten."

Waple was confounded by the low number.

"Did you, in any way, attempt to verify any of the stories related to you by the Afghan witnesses?"

Pihana looked surprised.

"No, there wasn't time to do that."

The attorney continued as if he did not hear him.

"For example, the witness that related to you that a woman was killed in one of the cars, did you ever go and verify that a woman was actually killed?"

"No," an irritated Pihana answered. "The day I got there, one of the reports (was) that a female had been killed northwest of the site out in the field, (and) was being buried that day.

So not a good time to go to a funeral and interview someone."

Waple handed Pihana off to Jack, who asked about the minibus that, according to the Afghan commission, was shot up, killing four people, including a one-year-old child.

"Is it true that when you finally found the driver of that bus that he testified to your agents that the bus was not shot, that there was no damage to the bus, and that he drove it off the road and ran it into a tree? And as far as he knew, all his passengers left and ran off and took taxis back to where they were coming from?"

"I believe that's true," said Pihana meekly.

What about the ANP officer's brother and nephew who were supposedly shot, paralyzing Nasurtullah?

As soon as Nangyli had said there were only three U.S. vehicles, instead of six, there were doubts about his truthfulness. When he then said that some Marines stood on the road in front of their vehicles to wave off approaching traffic, a ridiculously dangerous tactic we would never do, his testimony was easily dismissed.

There was the same lack of solid evidence for vehicle damage.

Despite NCIS asserting that we shot up every vehicle over six miles (twenty-four vehicles according to one report and eleven according to the ANP and the *solatia* list), the MPs reported no more than three such vehicles—the taxi and white Toyota, both next to the blast site, and the Prado. One MP did not recall seeing any damaged vehicle other than Qomandan's Prado. Another said he only observed a white and yellow taxi with a shattered windshield but "the taxi was too far away for me to tell what caused the damage." A third MP told NCIS that the only damaged vehicle he saw besides the Prado was a white van that the ANP released to the owner, who drove it away before the MPs could examine it.

Media reports claimed shot up cars were strewn all along Hell's Highway, but the photograph of only one was seen over and over again in newspapers and on television—that of the Prado.

Using Pihana's "logic," there should have been "evidence" of far more damaged vehicles if my Marines had been firing like madmen.

Nevertheless, Nicholson said accepting the governor's list of victims was meant to "rebuild the relationships (with the area Afghans) as quickly as possible… I'm much more interested in making payment(s) so I can resolve the situation here and calm (it) down so that my unit could continue to operate."

Despite his belief that we were guilty, he acknowledged that he never read any part of the investigation, including the preliminary investigation.

"I talked to Col. Pihana a little bit about it," he said rather offhandedly, "but at that point, as you can imagine, this thing was starting to assume a pretty high level (of) visibility, I think that you are all aware. So at that point—and frankly, you know, I'm still fighting the campaign. My world did not revolve around this incident and its aftermath."

Greasing Afghan palms with *solatia* soothed the angry locals. *Solatia*, Nicholson seemed to say, was like paying protection money to organized crime: If you pay the mob, they will allow you to continue to operate your business.

"(We) were working directly with that tribe to convince them not to plant poppy, and not to harvest it," Nicholson said. "When this incident occurred, it stopped that effort dead in its tracks… When you stop operations during the harvest, you essentially give the enemy a free ride… because of the restriction on our freedom of action that resulted from this incident."

Rather than blame the knee-jerk reaction by American officials to criticism from Karzai, the politically savvy colonel was blaming Fox Company for causing the halt in military operations!

At the first, largest and most elaborate of two *solatia* ceremonies, Nicholson made his public apology. Some 250 people, including victims and tribal leaders, were in attendance on May 8 at the Nangahar governor's palace grounds, where a meal was served and turbans and prayer rugs were presented by the Americans as gifts.

"Everybody who's anybody attends these events," said Air Force Lt. Col. Gordon Phillips, who took over as the Provincial Reconstruction Team commander in Nangarhar one week after the ambush. "This thing is huge."

Testifying at the COI by video from Afghanistan, Phillips added that when he arrived at his post, he ran into "a great deal of hostility" and concern about March 4 from villagers: "It was the hot topic."

He said they would continually berate him with: "Who is accountable?" The Afghans were "looking for justice to be served," he said, and he promised them that "an investigation would be forthcoming."

Solatia, our swift removal and the prospect of a trial threw Karzai and the Afghans a few bones, proof that the U.S. was sensitive to the feelings of the Afghan people and was taking serious action regarding their concerns.

Jack asked Nicholson: "There was great political pressure from the (Afghan) government, from the president's palace on down for something to be done about this. Would you agree with that?"

A prickly Nicholson shot back.

"It wasn't 'something needed to be done,'" he said, "it was that we needed to address this with the people.... That's why this process we are going through today is so important, because this is part of the justice that is expected by the Pashtun people...in terms of understanding what happened, and that those who caused this are held accountable for it, and then that restores the honor of that particular tribe so that they can resume cooperating with the government.... If their honor is not made whole, then they are obligated to fight you and exact a similar toll as what you took from them."

Jack, offended by that answer, bristled.

"My question to you," he asked Nicholson, "(is) what about our honor as Americans? I mean, did anybody apologize for an IED attack on our convoy?"

Nicholson looked annoyed.

"Well, the enemy did that, not the civilians," he replied. "The enemy, the vehicle-borne IED, the guy who drives into the area from outside the area and detonates himself. So the population is not responsible for that, the enemy is." He stiffened. "We don't apologize for killing this enemy. We just kill them."

Nicholson added that, unequivocally, the U.S. does not pay *solatia* to the enemy. Capt. Dana Ross, an Army intelligence officer on Nicholson's staff, testified that the names on the *solatia* list had been vetted to sift out possible terrorists.

After all, it wouldn't look good if it were discovered that money from American taxpayers ended up in the pockets of the bad guys.

Ross detailed that he ran the *solatia* names "through multiple query search engines for which intelligence information is stored, intelligence information that's collected from agencies from both on the strategic level down to the patrol leader level…. We entered the names, variations of the names with wild cards, searching for any of these individuals to pop up with reporting throughout the Nangarhar region and the surrounding area of interest. And none of the names popped up as being in any of the reporting data."

We needed to show, Nicholson reiterated, that America cared about innocent Muslim lives, about innocent Afghan lives—for their sake as well as ours.

"We were deeply ashamed," Nicholson said, "because Americans don't kill innocent civilians. Period. And when they do, if we expect to win this ideological struggle that this war is being waged over between the extremist elements who are trying to convert the modern Muslims of the world into extremists, we have got to stay on the moral high ground. And you do that by when you make a mistake, you own it, you fix accountability for it, you fix the problem, and then you move on. And if we fail to do that, we're going to start down a slippery slope and we're going to lose this war."

Holly was my only sanctuary, though she was thousands of miles away at her duty station in Yuma. Coming home after a long day, I would call her and we would talk about our wedding plans. I wouldn't rehash what had happened in court. I didn't want to talk about things that would bring me down, and I didn't want to bring her down either.

Holly reacted less like a fiancé and more like an indomitable Marine. That was okay. All I needed to continue to trudge uphill was her saying, "I believe in you, Fred."

Rules of Engagement

"We're surrounded. That simplifies the problem."
—Attributed to "Chesty" Puller

T he mild-mannered Waple didn't look like a boxer, but he approached our case like a fighter preparing for a championship bout.

Getting up before sunrise to take long jogs and eating just one
meal a day, he stayed physically fit to help him mentally focus on our case.
When he counter-punched, he was rugged and relentless, firing back with
everything we had.

Waple charged that Pihana's investigation was "one-sided, hurried,
inaccurate..." and his report's conclusions "very much flawed and incorrect."

He noted that the most significant and credible ordnance expert,
Moon, vehemently disagreed with Pihana.

"He wanted me to back up his opinion," Moon said at the COI of
Pihana. "He tried saying what he had thought actually happened on the
site. He didn't think that there was any gunfire at the vehicles due to the
interviews that he had performed on site with the local nationals. Basically,
he just tried persuading me. He kept saying the same thing over and
over again, 'Well, this is what I think happened because this is indented
this way.'"

"He made you feel uncomfortable?" asked Waple, aware of the awkwardness of an NCO butting heads with a full bird colonel, even if one was Army and the other Air Force.

"Yes," Moon admitted.

Regardless, Moon was so convinced of his findings and objected so strongly to Pihana's that he wrote a statement detailing them and submitted it to the colonel.

"I write it exactly the way I see it," he said. "I did not adjust my memorandum for him."

Did Pihana take into consideration Moon's findings?

"I did consider them," Pihana said, "but based on the evidence, at least the evidence I developed later, the evidence I found appeared to rule their conclusions out." He dismissed Moon's analysis of the bullet impacts as a "theory" and did not include Moon's account in his final report.

He also ignored, or did not pursue, other evidence that conflicted with his own "theory" about what happened on March 4.

He never asked any other Marine in Fox Company, including our mechanic or our logistics liaison Johansson, whether there were bullet impacts on Vehicle Two before departing on the patrol, as Milton said there were.

If he had, he would have heard what the mechanic and Johansson each told NCIS—they saw bullet impacts on Vehicle Two only *after* Fox Company returned.

Neither did Pihana include in his report the result of his inquiry into the SLAP round he uncovered.

I was more than a little surprised when I first heard about the SLAP round after returning to Camp Lejeune. I didn't think we had that ammunition with us. When Petronzio was told of the possibility, he asked Clarke to immediately contact the Fox Company ammunition NCO, who was still in Kuwait, to check his records. He confirmed that no SLAP rounds were ever broken out for our use. The reason was simple: We didn't expect to face an armored vehicle threat.

Petronzio relayed the information to Pihana. But only the accusation that Fox Company had fired the round appeared in his report.

Weeks later, Waple asked Pihana at the COI: "Didn't you learn from Col. Petronzio…that the patrol did not have any SLAP rounds issued to it on 4 March 2007? Do you remember that discussion with Col. Petronzio?"

Backed into a corner, Pihana pled ignorance. "Actually no, I don't."

His competence took another direct hit when Jack asked why Pihana did not trek up the hill, where my Marines said they saw muzzle flashes, to search for evidence of fire.

Pihana replied that he accepted what the ANP told him—there was no brass there.

Jack followed up: "That particular evidence you took it at face value with no verification?"

Pihana had no choice but to answer, "Without verification, yes."

Gabel reiterated that her MPs gathered up brass, both 7.62mm and .50 caliber, up to 350 meters from the blast site. NCIS files confirmed that the MPs also notified NCIS that they had recovered brass in the dry river-bed forty-five meters due north of the western edge of the bridge.

That was vital information. When firing a weapon, the expended shell casings remain around the weapon, the point of fire, not at the target, the point of contact. Since we never got out of our vehicles, our brass would have been found around the blast site and on the road. If there was brass in the riverbed, there must have been someone firing *from* the river bed—and that would be the enemy.

If those casings were from 7.62x39mm ammunition, that too would prove that the enemy had fired at us, since they used Soviet-made ammunition of that caliber while the U.S. used 7.62x51mm.

But there was a problem. The casings were gone.

The MPs had stored them in evidence bags at Camp Torkham. Gabel testified that when Pihana finally contacted her eight days after the ambush, she told him about the evidence. His inexplicable response was that he "didn't want the brass."

About nine weeks later, a day or so before NCIS was scheduled to show up at her post for interviews, Gabel said she was searching the camp's burn pit, where they incinerated their garbage, for items unrelated to our case—and stumbled upon thirty-four .50 caliber casings and thirty-two metallic connector clips used to hold .50 caliber ammunition together. Spent casings were not supposed to be disposed of in a burn pit, and certainly not casings that were potential evidence.

But an MP working the night shift during a camp clean-up had emptied the trash into the burn pit. "Purely by accident," Gabel said, the evidence bags were in that trash. While the .50 caliber pieces, which were likely from our machine guns, were retrieved, placed in two plastic evidence bags, and handed over to NCIS, none of the 7.62mm brass was salvaged. It was never determined if those casings had burned up or were otherwise lost—and Pihana never mentioned in his report that evidence which might have supported our innocence had mysteriously disappeared.

"Our guys would not shoot for the hell of it," asserted Ruiz at the COI. "Vehicle One and Vehicle Two had our most seasoned team leaders. I know if we fired back, we took bullets first. I didn't see nobody shooting at me (or) I would have returned fire (too). It was controlled fire... I firmly believe those team leaders would not let those guns engage if they did not see a threat."

Pihana didn't explicitly call the Marines of Fox Company liars, but he rejected what my Marines repeatedly had said—seventeen reported hearing small arms fire, ten reported seeing small arms fire, and eight saw enemy shooters.

"I don't believe the Marines were intentionally lying to me," Pihana told the court. "I believe that what they gave me was their best account of what happened that day... But how do you account for whether they believed, or they did not believe, they were being fired at? That I cannot explain."

"Their understanding of the Rules of Engagement was what?" asked Nunnally.

"Basically, self-defense Rules of Engagement is what I got from all the Marines," Pihana replied. "Some people were almost able to quote it verbatim what the ROE was."

There was no question in my mind we knew the EOF and ROE virtually by heart. We had taken numerous classes about them on board the *Bataan* and several times more while in country. They were addressed in our briefings before nearly every mission. We were even given a card, the size of a business card, with the ROE printed on it, which we were supposed to keep with us and consult as needed.

I cannot reveal our ROE, not even today. That might tell our enemies exactly how far they could go before we would respond with lethal force. That would encourage them to approach that line in the sand with full confidence we would not retaliate. What I can say is that if we felt threatened, whether by a hostile act or hostile intent as judged by a reasonable person, and taking into account all the circumstances, we could fight back. The ROE has always assumed an inherent right to self-defense, though the nature, scope, and duration of that response must be appropriate.

"Appropriate," however, was a gray area. There was no hard and fast definition that applied to every real-world situation. A gunner forced to respond seconds after a bomb explosion, for example, could very well find himself in a courtroom trying to justify his actions.

Spotlighting the Prado, Nunnally suggested to Pihana that "if the Marines are telling the truth—they say the Prado was moving towards them after an IED that presents a threat, they see people firing from that Prado, they see people in that Prado that have weapons in their hands— then that is a threat that they are entitled to fire at to defend themselves under the Rules of Engagement; that is correct, is it not?"

"Your key word in that statement was 'the truth,'" replied Pihana. "Whether or not the Marines believed or saw anything, that I could not determine.... But, again, there was no evidence to support that."

"Col. Pihana, assuming that they *are* correct," Nunnally asked with steel in his voice, "they have every right to fire on that vehicle, do they not?"

Pihana bobbed and weaved.

"The Rules of Engagement state that in self-defense, if you are fired upon, then you can return fire, yes, to protect yourself."

Nunnally would not accept his generality.

"Please, sir," he insisted, "is the answer to my question, 'Yes, they do have the right to fire on that vehicle if their statements are true?'"

Pihana refused to give in.

"*If* their statements are true," he said, enjoying the sparring. "The statements the Marines told me, I believe, they think is the truth in their minds, but not mine."

Pihana appeared pleased that he had dodged Nunnally's right uppercut.

The slick Texas lawyer turned away, as if defeated.

Then, as if another question had just occurred to him, he slowly swung back to face Pihana.

"You believe that the Marines *perceived* they were taking fire or *perceived* they heard fire?"

"I believe that the Marines perceived they were taking fire," he said matter-of-factly. According to Pihana, the gunners shot because they *thought* they were being fired on when, in actuality, there was no threat—including from the men in the Prado.

Nunnally feinted with his left.

"Based on the *perception* that a Marine believes he's being fired at, in your understanding, can he return fire?"

"Yes," Pihana casually answered.

And Nunnally hit him square on the jaw.

"And if it was only a perception," he asked, "then there wouldn't be any physical evidence?"

The courtroom fell silent. Not a paper rustled. The prosecutors froze in place. The panel—Porter, Daniels and Morgan—turned toward Pihana.

After contemplating the pivotal question for an eight count, he curtly responded, "That's correct."

Pihana's entire argument suddenly went up in smoke.

Whether we took fire and there were bullet impacts to prove it, or the gunners thought we took fire but the lack of bullet impacts proved that we had not, my Marines had every right to shoot back.

But there was no knockout.

Regardless of the ROE, and the lack of a definitive casualty count, Pihana said, the end result still stood: We had fired indiscriminately at civilians, and killed and injured unarmed men, women and children. As the Afghan commission put it, we had committed "a serious violation of international humanitarian law standards."

That was the bottom line.

The Ones Who Were
Shooting at Us

N CIS relied heavily on Pihana's report because its own on-scene
investigation in Afghanistan was severely limited.

They arrived on May 2, two months after the incident, by
which time memories of witnesses were no longer fresh and there had been
plenty of time for them to be influenced by the media, tribal elders, the
Karzai government, the Taliban, you name it. And the NCIS team was
allowed only one hour at the site of the ambush. One agent, Chief Warrant
Officer Darryl Jackson, called the situation "kind of ludicrous."

He saw no evidence of small arms fire on the road or on trees by
the side of the road. He did not examine the nearby riverbed or hillside.
Jackson said he was told by the Army, upon whom NCIS relied for support, that "there wasn't security to allow us to look at other alleged attack
sites. We asked for three days; we asked for three separate trips. We were
told we had sixty minutes."

But Phillips, who provided the ground security team, told a different story. He testified that the NCIS investigators *asked* to remain in Bati
Kot for only sixty minutes and that he would have provided security for
as long and wherever NCIS required. He maintained that there were no

Taliban-controlled villages in Nangarhar Province and, following the *solatia* payments, his soldiers were "able to pretty much operate freely."

Somebody was not telling the truth.

Only Phillips had a motive to be dishonest: Like Nicholson, he needed to paint a peaceful picture of the area, no matter how far that was divorced from reality, because that justified the COIN strategy.

Phillips was a true believer, claiming with unshakable confidence that the prospect of Afghans receiving money did not expand the *solatia* list or color the testimony of witnesses.

The fact is most people in the world will say what you want to hear when offered money to do so. I can only guess how many people in New York or Los Angeles would line up at a government agency and swear that there was death or injury to a relative or damage to a car if they didn't need any proof and the reward was four times their average annual salary. A whole lot, I bet.

For anyone not beholden to COIN, there was no question that the *solatia* system incentivized claims of death, injury and property damage. One NCIS agent testified that "anyone that you interviewed would almost always ask for money or you know, 'How do I get reimbursed for my damages or my injury?'"

The translator for the hospital staff interviews concluded in his notes that, "It sounds like there is some kind of conspiracy going on… They are trying to rob us here. I think they have all ganged up in conspiracy in anticipation of receiving money from the Americans."

Remember Rahmat Gul, the freelance photographer who arrived on the scene within an hour of the ambush and charged that the MPs took his camera, deleted the photos and threatened him?

Initially, he said he didn't witness the explosion and shootings. He later said he saw both—and that he was injured too! Three times he asked coalition authorities by phone to be compensated for his injury. Finally, when he was connected to an NCIS agent to investigate his claim, Gul hung up. Nonetheless, his name was included on the *solatia* list.

Our lawyers noticed something else suspicious about that list, something none of those who vetted the names realized—of the seven women, six were killed and one injured. There should have been far more injured than dead, just as there were more men who were injured than killed. That oddity should have cast even more doubt on the accuracy of the list.

Phillips was dismissive.

"I didn't consider going and digging to look at the ratio between women that were killed and injured and stretch this on and continue to have this elevated emotion throughout my province for a couple hundred bucks."

Panel president Porter asked, "Was continuing your mission more important than determining whether the right people were being paid?"

Phillips answered in COIN speak: "Saying you're sorry is not the same as accepting responsibility."

Afghans were being paid to lie—and the Afghans knew it. They knew the list of dead and injured was a fabrication. Instead of gaining their respect, paying *solatia* did the opposite. By buying into the corruption, American leaders such as Nicholson lost the respect of Afghans.

Not surprisingly, the number of alleged civilian casualties throughout the country spiraled upwards after the well-publicized May 2007 *solatia* ceremony.

Using figures reported by the media without any independent corroboration, and inflating them with their own battle dead, the Taliban could incite citizens to lash out against us. That anger diverted the Afghan public's attention away from the fact that insurgents often launched attacks while surrounded by civilians, willfully endangering the lives of innocent men, women, and children, and that their suicide bombings killed and injured their own countrymen.

Waple asked Pihana, "How likely do you think it is that thirty hard men are going to go out there, most of them combat vets, led by two seasoned Marine Corps officers, that they are going to engage in a complete breakdown in fire discipline and unfold?"

On average, each of the turret gunners had been on two previous combat deployments and three overseas deployments and spent more than six years in the Marines. None had ever before had an issue regarding a breakdown in fire discipline.

"I don't believe that thirty hard men had a complete breakdown of fire discipline," answered Pihana. "I believe that a couple of Marines had a complete breakdown of fire discipline."

Yet, in nearly the next breath, he praised our training.

"You could tell they had been, at least in my impression, well trained on how they were supposed to react in all of those different scenarios," he said. "So overall impressions were that they knew their jobs well. They knew what they were trained to do."

Col. Don Hill, the officer in charge of MARSOC's Special Missions Training Branch, who oversaw our work-up, echoed that praise. He wrote in an earlier evaluation:

"I attribute the training and discipline to the high quality of leadership that has been evident since my arrival, beginning at the platoon level. I am equally impressed with the caliber of character throughout the entire unit. The MSOC-F unit has demonstrated a sound professional approach in all avenues of their mission as I have personally witnessed the execution of their daily operations for a number of weeks. In the conduct of these operations, they have demonstrated a professional, focused, mission oriented posture with a no-nonsense businesslike attitude."

Hill testified at the COI that any inkling that a Marine might go off the rails, particularly when firing a weapon, would have caused that Marine to be retrained or reassigned.

"That's not what we teach or certify," he said, "and we sniff that stuff out." If any of his Marines did not qualify to the highest standard, they would not be allowed downrange.

Klein, in his statement to Pihana, said: "My life and the lives of the Marines in the convoy were at risk when we were ambushed... Everyone I fired at I positively identified firing at the convoy with a gun."

"I personally was behind my gun and I wasn't squeezing," said Ruiz, the gunner in Vehicle Three, who did not fire his weapon on March 4. "Just because a Marine is behind that gun, the Afghani out there on the side of the road, he might think these guys are just spraying... In his mind we are shooting at everything that moves, and really we weren't."

When Jack asked Harley, our attack controller who was also in Vehicle Two, if there were Afghans killed during the incident, he said there were— "the ones who were shooting at us, sir."

Nunnally pointed a finger at Pihana.

"You told each and every Marine that you talked to that if you ever found anything that you felt that they did wrong, that you would read them their rights?"

"Yes," said Pihana. "If at some point in time you suspect someone of a criminal act, you would have to stop the interview and read them their rights."

"To this day," Nunnally asked in exasperation, "you have never read any Marine his rights?"

"That is correct," Pihana replied. "I found out as I went along...even as I was gathering information, that I wasn't going...to really determine if a criminal act had occurred, unless someone, you know, just happened to blurt out in one of their statements, 'You know, on the way back or whatever, I just saw this guy and didn't like him and stopped and got out and shot him.'"

I thought Nunnally had once again scored a knockout.

But Pihana got up from the canvas and took a wild swing in an effort to go the distance: He insinuated that we had cooked up a conspiracy to cover up our misdeeds.

Pihana suggested that, before we returned to Jalalabad Airfield, we may have fired at our own vehicles to make it appear we had taken incoming fire!

That was a bizarre shot across the bow borne out of desperation. There was neither a time nor a place for any such collusion before we were safely behind the wire. Members of the platoon would also have had to huddle up before the debrief and agree to concoct a tale about being fired at.

But there were no winks and nods in the debrief as the men recited what they saw and experienced that day, or when they talked to Marines, such as Big Dave, who were not on the patrol.

"You know when a guy is lying to you or not lying to you," Big Dave told the court, dressed in civilian clothes after having retired from the

Corps. "And as a senior man, you know when young guys know that you're around, to look over their shoulder if it's not something you're supposed to be hearing. There was nothing contrived. I talked to the men when they got back from the patrol…and at no time…did I detect any kind of subtleties, you know, 'Hey, look, Top's (the highest-ranking NCO) is coming, keep your mouth shut' or nothing like that."

There was no reason to lie, no reason to conjure up a phony story. We had done nothing wrong.

The inconsistencies in the statements of my Marines, over hours of interrogations, had an unexpected plus for us.

"Is it more likely than not," Waple proposed to Pihana, "that because there are inconsistencies that the Marines did not get together and make the story up to make it all the same? They saw different things at different times."

"If everybody came in and said the same thing," Pihana admitted, "that would throw up a red flag."

The differences in testimony could be attributed not only to the "fog of war" but also to point of view—where someone was sitting in the six vehicles and when each vehicle passed a certain spot on Hell's Highway. Panel member Morgan agreed: "In my mind, everyone saw something different. If *you* looked at it a second after *he* saw it, it was different."

Panel member Daniels, the former enlisted Marine court reporter who had been present at innumerable trials, was suspicious about why the prosecution had asked DiVicenzo and NCIS to develop a list of inconsistencies for the Marines but not one for the Afghans.

"When you receive a case," he asked DiVicenzo sharply, "do you automatically think that the person is guilty?"

"Well, the case was investigated by the preliminary investigator and it would not be referred to us if someone was innocent," DiVicenzo said with startling candor.

So NCIS handled the Afghan witnesses with kid gloves, their word taken at face value, little critical scrutiny applied, and no tough questions asked. I scoured the Afghan interviews on my own and put together a list of statements illustrating their contradictions—but it was ignored by NCIS (see Appendix III). Only the Marines were treated with suspicion.

Ironically, the one person who could best refute Pihana's conspiracy accusation was an Afghan.

Our interpreter Ali was the only other person in the convoy besides Milton and Klein who was not at the debrief. He would be an ideal witness—he wouldn't have been part of any alleged conspiracy and he wouldn't have been influenced by whatever was said at the debrief.

But Ali was still nowhere to be found. Neither was his written statement, nor its audio recording we believe he'd made to Pihana, but which Pihana didn't remember.

All were MIA.

The prosecution, however, did have an eyewitness who was available and could give compelling testimony—a tribal elder, someone continually quoted in newspapers about March 4, someone considered reliable and trustworthy—Qomandan, the driver of the Prado.

The Headless Corpse

he last time I'd seen Qomandan, he had been firing at us with an AK-47.

When he appeared on the video screen to give his testimony, I was furious. I couldn't understand why he had been brought onto an American base without being in handcuffs for having tried to kill us.

Then again, the prosecutors believed his story, not mine.

But there was something strange about Qomandan's story.

He told reporters right after the ambush that three people were in his car—his father, an uncle, and a nephew. Yet in his COI testimony, he said he was driving only his father and his nephew Farid Gul, his sister's son. He made no mention of his uncle, Haji Shin Makhe who, according to the *solatia* list and Qomandan himself when he talked to *The New York Times*, had also died in the Prado.

Why did he not mention the loss of his own uncle? Another eyewitness swore that he saw three men dead in the Prado—Qomandan's father, a man named Haji Shin Gul, and an unidentified man. Yet Haji Shin Gul was not named as a deceased in either the Afghan commission's report or on the *solatia* list.

And what about the headless corpse, which was later brought to Qomandan's house? Who was he?

When Gabel was asked if she would be surprised if the headless corpse had been the man in the front seat of Qomandan's SUV, she replied: "Sir, it wouldn't surprise me given that .50 cals were used at the site that an individual could potentially be decapitated."

But Qomandan insisted he didn't know the man.

"I never said that he was in my vehicle, but I said, you know, for whatever reason his head was cut off. And if nobody recognizes who he was, that is why they brought his dead body to my house... When his relatives saw his shoes, then they recognize that this is him."

It was apparent, at least to me, that Qomandan was deliberately hiding the identity of one of the Prado's passengers. Why?

Three days prior to our arrival at Camp Torkham, Gabel and the MPs received intelligence from the Afghan Border Police that thirteen Taliban and eleven Al-Qaeda had recently come to the area, but she did not communicate that to us. At the COI, she excused her careless omission by saying the intelligence was not noteworthy because she always had such reports about Bati Kot.

Bati Kot was no Mayberry. Bati Kot was a bad place filled with very bad people, despite Qomandan's protest to the contrary. His contention that he didn't own any weapons because the area was very safe was preposterous. The criminal element of the poppy trade was everywhere, as were the gun-wielding, bomb making folks of Al-Qaeda and the Taliban.

If Qomandan's mysterious passenger was found to be one of those militants, his *solatia* payment and those for his father and nephew, a substantial sum in total, would be revoked. But we could discover nothing about the man.

Waple asked Qomandan: "Do you agree that someone was trying to kill Americans on 4 March of last year?"

But Qomandan would not even concede that.

"No, I do not agree with that, sir. Not at all." He shook his head. "Nobody was trying to kill American."

Well, other than the suicide bomber.

Jack asked him, "Isn't it true that when the Americans talked to you about your alleged injuries, you could provide no evidence of injuries?"

Qomandan had said my Marines shot him in his shoulder and lower back. If he had been shot in the back twice by a machine gun, the only type of weapons we fired, he would not be sitting months later at an American base in Afghanistan. He would be dead.

"I did not give them any proof," he said, because "the doctors were coming to my house, and he was putting bandages on my injured part of my body, and because I was busy with the funeral(s) for two months." He was preoccupied for months with funerals for burials that were completed within hours of the ambush?

"When I went back to the coalition base in Torkham," he continued, "I showed them my back and took some picture of it."

The MPs who saw the scars and photographs said they were obviously old ones, from a previous skirmish, perhaps from the war with the Soviets.

Jack rephrased his question: "To this day, you have provided no one any evidence of medical records, clothing with blood on it, any evidence of that kind: correct?"

Qomandan raised the white flag.

"That's correct, sir."

Jack moved on.

"And, sir, you are still looking to receive money from the United States for the loss of your Prado?"

"I refused to take, you know, what I was offered for my vehicle damage," Qomandan said with a smile. "But after the governor told me that we have some guests and it is not very polite to refuse that money in front of them, and he says that he would speak with the coalition to help me in the future again."

And that wasn't all he wanted. He also asked to be reimbursed for the cash, the 500,000 Afghanis, he allegedly left behind in the Prado's dashboard glove compartment.

"I hope the government of the United States of America will compensate me for my loss," he testified, "because I deserve it... I want that money. It is more than expectation. It is not just 500,000 Afghanis. I want this plus the damages that I got because of my vehicle."

"And what happened to the 500,000 Afghanis?" Jack asked. "Where did it go?"

"I do not know," he said, shrugging his shoulders. "The money might be destroyed there in small pieces because some people found little pieces of the Afghani notes... It was as result of that incident that my cash was destroyed along with my vehicle."

Whether the money existed at all, and whether it was ripped to shreds, was uncertain. What was certain, however, was that the Prado was *not* destroyed. Under tough questioning, Qomandan admitted that he subsequently sold it, 200-plus bullet holes and all, for 30,000 Afghanis.

But it was disheartening to watch as none of his contradictions stuck to him. When he was caught saying something starkly different at the COI than he had in a newspaper interview, Qomandan scampered away with a ready explanation.

"I have been giving a lot of interviews since last year," he said. "So I do not remember that... I can't even remember what I did yesterday."

With nothing left in our playbook, Jack threw the Hail Mary pass we had planned if all else failed.

He looked up at the Afghan on the video screen.

"Sir, do you know any member of Al-Qaeda?"

"No," Qomandan answered solidly, "I do not know any Al-Qaeda member and I am not involved in politics."

Interesting, because a shop owner in the Mar Koh bazaar said Qomandan had told him about intending to visit a man named Haji Ghalib on March 4.

I had my intelligence sources research Haji Ghalib. Who was he?

An "enemy combatant" recently released from the detention center in Guantanamo Bay, Cuba.

Formerly a resident of Nangarhar Province, Ghalib had been the Taliban's commander of security in Shinwar. He was implicated as a bomb maker after American forces discovered an IED production facility in a compound located next to the courthouse where he worked. He was taken into custody in February 2003. While not an official member of Al-Qaeda, Ghalib was considered close enough, and was transferred to Guantanamo in October 2005. Though U.S. authorities feared he would return to the battlefield if he were freed, he was released on February 8, 2007.

The suicide bomber of March 4 did not work alone. Suicide bombers never did. They needed to be supplied and their action needed planning. The follow-on attack also required supplies and planning as well as the willingness of fighters to fight.

Was it a coincidence that Ghalib had returned to Afghanistan on February 28, only days before the ambush? Was it a coincidence that Qomandan had recently purchased a large amount of gasoline and fertilizer (common ingredients for making IEDs) and there was fertilizer in his vehicle that morning of March 4? Not to me.

Waple asked Pihana if he thought Qomandan's actions that day were those of a retired *mujahideen* or one still fighting a war, this time against Americans:

"Just the facts that you remember, what the Marines told you about that Prado, the placement of that Prado, the IED blast, the fact that he was able to hit, roll, and get on the ground and survive, and now you got to look at him eyes on, didn't you find that very odd with that gentleman?"

"No, actually I didn't," said the antagonized Pihana. "When the IED blast happened, if he's driving along and that IED happens right there… and when the firing starts, especially if it's coming his way, he said he instinctively reacted, dove out on the ground… I thought that was reasonable and logical."

Qomandan could not have been part of the attack, Pihana said.

"I discounted that based on the fact, again, that if this was a *mujahideen* commander who had fought against the Soviets…it would be a great leap of faith now, in the open with small arms, (to) fire on an armed convoy…. To position a vehicle in the open… twenty five to fifty meters away from an armed convoy in a thinly skinned vehicle, and open up on a convoy from there, in my opinion, is either a very bad decision, a tactical decision, or suicide. And I just did not get the impression from the gentleman when I interviewed him that he wanted to commit suicide."

You did not have to be a genius to connect the dots. Sitting in that courtroom, I too realized that he had no intention to commit suicide.

Because Qomandan did not expect the Americans to shoot back!

I motioned Waple to my chair and whispered in his ear. He turned back to Pihana and asked:

"Did you ever consider the possibility that the people in the blue Prado...that their thoughts were that the Marines were going to do what the Army had done?"

Our attackers had made a mistake, a terrible mistake. We were not their intended victims. They had been waiting for the Army MP patrol they had seen staging.

When we rolled down Hell's Highway, they assumed we were the MPs. Following the IED blast designed to stop that patrol in its tracks, they were prepped to fire on the convoy, confident they could frighten the soldiers into ducking and running, and likely never stopping in their village ever again. Perhaps those soldiers might even foolishly exit their vehicles, in which case they could mow them down. Either way, the unmistakable message would be sent by the Taliban: Stay out!

But we reacted in a way they didn't expect. We fought back.

Pihana was speechless.

So too were the prosecutors after my intelligence sources scoured classified lists of known terrorists and a familiar name popped up:

Haji Liwani Qomandan.

Trust No One

Nicholson said the *solatia* list had been vetted to ensure no terrorists would be paid, and yet there was Qomandan, labeled a terrorist in data files, being paid for his injuries and the damage to his Prado.

Another familiar name was on both the terrorist and *solatia* lists—Farid Gul, his nephew, who curiously Qomandan referred to as a "martyr."

The prosecutors had been so supremely confident of Qomandan's veracity that they willingly put him on the stand. It reminded me of the prosecutors giving O.J. Simpson a pair of gloves to try on, certain they would seal a conviction—and discovering much to their chagrin that they did not fit.

I looked at Sanger and saw his face redden and his jaw tighten. Sanchez balled up his fists. They were so angry when they left the courtroom that they accosted the Marine intelligence NCOs who were my sources and accused them of planting false information.

"We know Galvin put you up to producing this intelligence report," they charged. "Tell us how he did it."

They actually thought I would create a false report and present it as evidence to a panel that included Morgan, deputy assistant chief of staff intelligence at Marine Forces Command, a three star general's command of all forces from east of the Mississippi to Europe. That would be a very serious breach of national security.

Both NCOs told them: "Gentlemen, you walk across the base to the 2nd Intelligence Battalion and have that report number pulled up using their system. It will pop right up on their classified computer exactly as it was shown in the courtroom."

Neither of the NCOs heard from the prosecutors again about their allegation.

Piecing together the information we obtained, I believe Qomandan meant to bloody the nose of American troops to discourage us from snoopin' and poopin' around Bati Kot. The Taliban, Al-Qaeda and HIG had established a staging ground there to facilitate the movement of jihadists to Kabul and Kandahar and elsewhere. Using suicide bombers and ambushes, they hoped to keep us out of the area.

Fox Company was their first target, but not their last, as the following months proved.

Some attacks were undoubtedly prevented when, on April 28, seven weeks after we were ambushed, coalition forces raided a bombmaking factory in the "peaceful" enclave of, that is correct, Bati Kot. The action took place after intelligence pinpointed the compound as a staging site for suicide attacks such as the one we suffered. Troops found AK-47s, shotguns, ammunition, and material suitable for constructing IEDs. Whether any of that had been used against us on March 4 was unknown, but likely.

During the April 28th assault, the special operations troops came under small arms fire and, in the gun battle that ensued, four militants were killed. So too were a woman and a teenage boy. The Afghan police claimed all of the deceased were civilians. Afterwards, of course, there were the usual protests by hundreds of villagers, a blockade of Hell's Highway, and cries of "Death to America!"

Then, on September 27, Reuters reported an incident eerily similar to the March 4 ambush, also in Bati Kot:

U.S. fire scatters crowd after Afghan bomb: witness

```
BATI KOT, Afghanistan - At least one U.S.
soldier opened fire to scatter a crowd of
civilians and police on Thursday after failed
```

suicide bomb attacks on a U.S. military convoy, the U.S. military and witnesses said.

A car bomb targeting a U.S. convoy in the
village of Bati Kot, fifteen km (nine miles)
east of Jalalabad, killed the driver, two
passengers and a nearby civilian, but none
of the soldiers was hurt, the U.S. military
said in a statement.

Afghan police securing the site in eastern Afghanistan were then attacked by an
insurgent dressed in police uniform. He was
killed by the police and coalition troops
before he could detonate his suicide vest,
the statement said.

To add to the confusion, a fire brigade
vehicle speeding to the scene rammed into
the U.S. and Afghan vehicles.

"I saw the fire brigade vehicle rushing
to the area at top speed. Somehow its brakes
failed and hit one police vehicle and coalition vehicles, then the Americans started
firing," said Reuters correspondent Noor
Mohammad Sherzai.

A spokesman for U.S.-led coalition
forces said only one soldier had opened
fire. "A U.S. serviceman fired two shots
and those shots were away from the crowd and
not directed toward the crowd," said Major
Joe Klopple.

The shots were fired to disperse the
crowd out of concern for their safety because
of what was thought to be another approaching suicide bomber, the U.S. statement said...

"A bullet hit the ground between my legs
while I was running," said Takiullah Taki, a
cameraman for private Afghan channel Tolo TV....

The Taliban claimed responsibility for
the suicide attack.

There were numerous other instances of enemy activity in the Bati Kot area in the two years after Fox Company left Afghanistan (see Appendix IV), during which time six American servicemen were killed.

Waple asked Qomandan if he had heard about the April raid.

"I do not know about those things that you are talking about," he said with disdain. "In Afghanistan every day thousands of people are dying and some of them are dying because of bombs or because of shooting, and I cannot keep record of all of them."

Waple glanced at his notes.

"Sir, if that is true then, why did you give an interview to the news media that the people killed in that incident were all civilians?"

"Same thing that incident," Qomandan said. "Everyone killed, you know, were all civilians. There was children, woman, shepherds, just regular people, and poor people."

Little of what he said, including about March 4, was true. Yet Qomandan began his testimony with a holy oath: "I swear by the name of Allah and I swear to the Koran that whatever I say is going to be the one hundred percent truth."

Unlike the Christian Bible, which commands unequivocally, "Thou shalt not lie," the Koran left some wiggle room when dealing with the infidel, such as Christians or anyone from a Western culture, according to an Islamic religious tenet known as *taqiyya*.

The basis for *taqiyya* was in Sura 3:28: "Let not the believers take the unbelievers for protectors rather than believers; and whoever does this, he shall have nothing of (the guardianship of) Allah, but you should guard yourselves against them, guarding carefully."

An Islamic scholar, Ibn Kathir, has elaborated that Muslims ought to tell the truth "except those believers who in some areas or times fear for their safety from the disbelievers. In this case, such believers are allowed to show friendship to the disbelievers outwardly, but never inwardly." In other words, as Mohammad's companion Abu Ad-Darda' said, "We smile in the face of some people although our hearts curse them."

Of course, not all Muslims accept lying to non-believers. But among radical Muslims, such as Qomandan, lying to the infidel was a matter of survival as well as culture *and* religion.

Statements made by Afghan witnesses were "politicized and may be false," cautioned an UNAMA aide during the ANP investigation. Pihana too reported that "we had some information where some of the Afghan witnesses lied to some of the NCIS investigators."

Rampant lying was further confirmed when Navy Capt. Dave Gallagher sent a letter to the court expressing his "uneasiness of the handling of the case by the US side." An advisor on police reform, he had been with the ANP's Lt. Gen. Mirza Mohammad Yarmand on March 10 when they discussed the investigation.

Though he was unaware of any testimony at the COI, Gallagher repeated that local elders told Yarmand the U.S. staged the explosion, with Marines tossing grenades. However, the ANP official explained to Gallagher that the elders were not always genuine. Without the elders, the village could not function but, at the same time, they were corrupt. Their truthfulness could be bought, and they were often paid off by drug traffickers or terrorists.

Even if some Afghans wanted to tell the truth, they found it difficult to do so.

Gallagher quoted Yarmand as telling him: "If I say the coalition forces were fired upon, then people will be pissed at me."

The political pressure in Afghanistan was too strong for anyone, even someone as well-placed as Yarmand, to buck. For the ANP leader to come out publicly and say the Marines were attacked after the bombing was unthinkable if not treasonous.

Among the villagers, there was peer pressure too. The mob mentality was powerful. None would say Fox Company was fired upon. They would be ostracized or, worse, suffer some very nasty consequences courtesy of the Taliban.

Nevertheless, DiVicenzo insisted in court that NCIS had used all due diligence in the gathering of evidence and the interviewing of witnesses.

"We try to corroborate what they tell us through any type of evidence that we can," he said. "I don't trust anybody. I'm trained to not trust anybody."

He certainly didn't trust my Marines, even though seven were granted immunity from punishment regarding March 4.

Along with Ruiz, the gunner in Vehicle Three, and Ortega, the driver of Vehicle Two, they were Khan (Vehicle Four), Davenport (the driver of Vehicle One), Reece (Vehicle One), Harley (Vehicle Two), and Staff Sergeant Chris Todd (the company's EOD leader in Vehicle Six).

They all provided sworn statements or testified without fear of prosecution. They could have reported anything we had done wrong or any conspiracy to cover up anything we had done wrong. None of them did.

Yet, perhaps they were simply being loyal to their brothers-in-arms. If only there was an eyewitness who was not a Marine or an Afghan civilian who could testify objectively to what happened on March 4.

Then one day, after I settled into the stuffy courtroom, I turned back toward the door and who walked in but Ali!

Harangued by our constant requests, the prosecutors had finally found him in the U.S. But no one, not the prosecution or defense, had time to do a pre-interview. No one knew what he was about to say.

Born and raised in Kabul, Ali moved to Islamabad in Pakistan before emigrating to the U.S. in 1990, when he was in his early twenties. Living in New York state, he became a U.S. citizen, married and had three kids. He still had aunts, uncles, and cousins living in Afghanistan, and since 2005 had been going back and forth to his native country on interpreter assignments as a civilian contract employee for the military. He was not a Marine, not a brother-in-arms.

In February 2007, he was assigned to MSOC-F. But our interpreters had a separate billeting area and a different security clearance. We weren't chummy with each other. As I saw Ali enter the courtroom, I too had no idea what his testimony might be.

Ali told the court that on March 4 he was in East's Vehicle Three, sitting behind Hackett the driver.

"When the explosion happened, what was your immediate reaction?" asked court advisor Lecce.

"Suddenly, I got very scared and, you know, shocked," he said softly. "A big, huge fireball right in front."

"What happened immediately after the explosion?"

"Our vehicle stopped...(and) I kind of ducked down," he said with some embarrassment. "I was frightened."

"What did you do next?"

"Sgt. Milton was sitting next to me to the right and he asked me if I was okay and he said everybody is okay. I heard Capt. East on the radio saying we are in contact." He continued, without prompting, "As soon as the vehicle stopped, I heard small arms fire."

That was music to my ears.

"What did it sound like?" Lecce asked.

"It sounds like a Kalashnikov, AK-47."

"Can you describe that sound?"

Ali hesitated, not sure what to say, until finally, "It is like single shots, you know, *dat, dat, dat, dat*, like that."

Lecce tried to help.

"Let the record reflect that I'm going to hit the table as fast as I can three times."

Tap-tap-tap.

"That is number one," he said. "And number two, I'm going to hit the table with a little bit of pause in between three times."

Tap...tap...tap.

"Which did it sound more like if you recall?" he asked Ali. "Number one?"

"Yeah," Ali answered.

"What did you hear next?"

"I heard bigger shots were fired," he said. "And it looked like Humvee Number Two was shooting."

"How fast did that come after the *tap-tap-tap*?"

"It was fast," Ali recalled. "It was like *brrrrrrr*."

"Hold on," said Lecce. "I'm sorry. I just got to explain this."

He walked to the court reporter and told her, "It is like a 'b' with a rolling 'r' afterwards, imitating machine gun fire."

He stepped toward Ali.

"At what point did you start going forward again?"

"After a couple of minutes that we were on halt... Still the shooting was going on... Capt. East said, 'Move, let's move out of here'... Vehicle Number Two, I believe, was shooting."

"Why do you believe that?" Lecce asked.

"Because I saw through the window as we were moving...that the turret was turning, actually was turning to the left side and then it turned to the right side. I saw a little smoke and heard the gunshot fire."

"You heard Vehicle Two shooting?"

"Yes," Ali said, adding with emphasis, "I heard *and* I saw."

Lecce had a final question, hoping Ali would yet reveal a chink in our defense.

"Did you ever see any cars with bullet holes in it after you passed the SUV?"

Ali answered strongly, "No, sir."

Disappointed, Lecce sat down and panel member Daniels took over the questioning: "Did you see or know of any Afghanis that were killed or injured?"

"The SUV vehicle that I saw," Ali said. "I believe there was people in there. That is the only one that I saw. I didn't see any oncoming traffic being shot."

"So when you heard the media reports of nineteen or fifty Afghanis killed, what did you think?"

Ali raised his eyebrows. "I would say it is a false report."

Morgan interjected. "Do you think that the Marines overreacted?" he asked. "Do you think they used too much force that day?"

Without a pause, Ali said, "I don't think so from what I saw, sir."

I smiled from ear to ear, probably for the first time in months.

Waple stood and posed another question to him: "Is it correct for this court to understand that the only investigator who spoke to you about what we just talked about came from the Navy, Naval Criminal Investigative Service?"

"No," Ali said, surprised.

I was not. I already knew NCIS had not interviewed him—but someone else had.

"Do you ever remember being asked any questions by an Air Force colonel in a U.S. Army uniform by the name of Col. Pihana?" Waple asked.

Ali nodded. "That is the investigator that came in and talked to me."

"Do you remember providing any statement to him?"

"Yes," Ali said. So he had in fact made a statement to Pihana, and Pihana had not included it in his report.

Waple had made his point: Pihana had cherry-picked evidence in an attempt to railroad Fox Company.

Nunnally summed it up bluntly to the panel: "The court could easily rule that the (Pihana) investigation into the shootout that followed the attack on the Marines convoy is so flawed that it should not be relied on as evidence."

Jack then found a "smoking gun" that questioned the motives of the COI's first witness, Milton.

Buried in the large NCIS investigation folders, we uncovered an email from his military account, in which he wrote excitedly, "It's going to be three hots and a cot. We are going back to the ship!" He was ecstatic that we were being kicked out of Afghanistan. Why?

"Your personal philosophy," Jack asked Milton, "was that you didn't believe that Americans had any business in the war in Afghanistan?"

"My sentiment started to grow more towards, 'What are we fighting this war for?'" Milton said, acknowledging that he had tried to get out of the assignment before we disembarked from the *Bataan*.

He testified that we had not been fired on, but we provided the panel an email we discovered that he'd sent immediately after returning from the patrol which said in part: "Yes, it was indeed a complex ambush. We were shot at from both sides of the road."

No longer a high-minded whistleblower, Milton now came off as a disgruntled Marine, one who might twist the facts to suit his opinion about the war.

Porter, frustrated by the conflicting accounts of what had actually happened on March 4, asked DiVicenzo: "We're not sure of anything, are we?"

"No," the NCIS agent replied, "because we weren't there."

From *Deet, Deet, Deet*
to *Tat, Tat, Tat*

"Here's the challenge we're all facing," said Waple to Pihana. "The Marines of that MSOC-F convoy are really our best of the best, both in terms of being (able) to observe (the) enemy and also in terms of their fire discipline. And your conclusions are... completely opposite of many of the elite Marines who were on that convoy, many of whom you spoke to, and many of whom gave you statements...."

"What my question is, sir, is 'why?'"

The answer, as I saw it, was that our military leaders were determined that COIN would succeed; which meant the best response to an incident Afghans and the international press labeled a war crime was to sacrifice us on the altar of world opinion. For Petraeus and those who marched behind him, we undermined everything represented by COIN. The two senior officers of Fox Company needed to take the fall.

We were not the first to be made examples of.

Only six months before March 4, Kearney had faced a decision about what to do with a Green Beret team in Afghanistan who'd killed a known terrorist.

The Green Berets watched from a hill 100 meters away as the ANP and border patrol called the Afghan, who had been vetted as an enemy combatant who could be legally killed, out of his house. After he twice identified himself, the Afghan police gave a prearranged hand signal to the Americans—and the Green Beret commander ordered his sniper to shoot. He killed the man with one shot to the head.

Kearney ordered Pihana to conduct a preliminary investigation. Pihana suggested there was misconduct and recommended that the case advance, in that instance, to the Army's Criminal Investigation Division.

The Green Berets were charged with homicide but were cleared of wrongdoing in each of two investigations. Kearney then demanded a third, and the soldiers were cleared again. It was a colossal waste of time and effort. But the affair served to portray Kearney as a COIN hero to those above him.

I knew all about that case, and Kearney's orchestration of the prosecution, because Waple had been the lawyer for the Green Beret leader.

Kearney took the same tack in our case. Again, he appointed Pihana as the investigating officer, for only the second time in his career. Again, Pihana delivered a damning report and a recommendation to pursue criminal charges.

The pressure from Kearney and others from the very beginning to pin a conviction on Fox Company was felt, overtly or not, up and down the command structure, from generals to their executive officers, such as Pihana and Ukeiley, to the NCIS agents and prosecutors. Not one general broke rank to stand behind Fox Company, and most of their subordinates fell into formation. If you were an officer looking to advance your career, it behooved you to "cooperate and graduate."

Pihana dutifully complied: His report was kicked upstairs to Mattis at MARCENT on April 8, five days *after* Hejlik told Fox Company in Kuwait that "I've seen the report and it doesn't look good."

NCIS complied by using Pihana's shoddy work as the basis for its own investigation.

And the prosecution complied by doing everything possible to send us to prison.

Nevertheless, more than two dozen senior Marine officers were bold enough to testify or write statements praising my performance and character. Smith, who recommended me to MARSOC, was one of them.

He spoke plainly of my relentless work ethic that helped ensure there was not a single combat death during our deployments from 2001 to 2006. He also recalled the Iraqi raid in which one of my Marines wounded another member of the platoon in a case of friendly fire. He remembered that I did not hesitate to tell him the truth, no matter the potential consequences to my career. Asked about my integrity, Smith used the word "uncompromising." He sounded like a proud older brother, and I was touched by his words.

Another character witness, Col. Brian Beaudreault, made an impressive entrance into the courtroom. The ribbons on his service Bravo uniform spoke of years of overseas service and combat campaigns, numbers that few Marine officers could match. One of four current or former MEU commanders who testified on my behalf, the lean, muscular, gray haired Beaudreault was now the CO of the 15th MEU. He'd been on three overseas deployments with me when I was a Force Recon platoon commander. He spoke of my meticulous mission planning and constant commitment to my Marines, and concluded by saying he would eagerly serve with me again.

Petronzio, who had moved on from MARSOC to become the CO of the 24th MEU, said the same, ending his testimony by declaring that if he could "make one decision again regarding who to pick to be the first MSOC commanding officer, I would pick Maj. Galvin fifty times."

I looked around the courtroom.

There were no members of the media present.

What Smith, Petronzio, and Beaudreault had to say was not heard by any news reporter. The same was true of other testimony that shined a favorable light on us, including Ali's.

With the court simultaneously examining the intelligence gathering mission East oversaw the night of March 9, it was easy to pull the wool over the eyes of the press.

That mission was classified, in fact, above Top Secret. So several times when a defense witness was about to provide positive testimony, Lecce would halt the proceedings. Though no classified or sensitive information was expected to be disclosed, he claimed that "we can't talk about that in open session" because it referred to March 9. Press liaison Gibson would then shepherd the media to a room above Andy's Cheesesteaks, a fast-food restaurant down the street, and court would continue in a closed session.

With Gibson and Lecce as the gatekeepers, nothing sympathetic to us could make its way out of the courtroom. Instead, the media heard only the juicy narrative of a mass murder at the hands of mad Marines.

They may not have even understood there was a March 9 incident. When the prosecutors purposefully referenced Marines being instructed to not tell the truth, the media did not realize they were talking about March 9. Instead, they were led to believe the Marines had tried to cook up a story about March 4.

The media buried us and, as Ukeiley walked to the stand, I figured he would carry the final shovelful of dirt.

"Oh, and congratulations for your recent selection to lieutenant colonel," prosecutor Sanchez said loud enough for the panel to hear.

Ukeiley responded with a huge smile and a "thank you."

He then detailed his job as our liaison. But the longer Ukeiley spoke, I could tell his self-serving testimony was not sitting well with the panel members.

They began to ask questions about *his* actions on March 4.

"How were you notified of the ambush?" Morgan asked.

"By phone," Ukeiley said, no doubt hoping his short answer would bring an end to the line of questioning.

But Morgan probed deeper.

"Where were you when you were notified?"

"I was in the CJSOTF-A JOC's break room."

Morgan looked surprised.

"How did they know to contact you in a break room? Did Fox Company know the phone number in there?"

"No," Ukeiley explained, "they called me on my cell phone."

Porter and Daniels were dumbfounded.

Morgan continued, excruciatingly slowly: "You had your cell phone in the Combined Joint Special Operations Task Force's Joint Operations Center?"

"Yes," Ukeiley said, swallowing hard. As a career intelligence officer and one appointed by Montanus as the security officer for the 2nd MSOB, he was well aware that he was admitting to a grievous breach of security.

There was worse to come.

Morgan wondered why Ukeiley was in the break room instead of the operations room while Fox Company was on a patrol.

"What you're telling me is that you left your post?"

I could see Porter and Daniels begin to seethe.

"No, sir, I'm not saying that."

"Well," Morgan snorted, "that's what it sounds like to me."

Ukeiley fumbled for an excuse.

"I never understood the expectation of 'your post is right here at this desk.'"

Daniels, his blood boiling, jumped in.

"How can you understand anything else when you have troops in contact?"

"Yes, sir, once it's 'troops in contact.'"

Ukeiley claimed the break room was close enough to his desk that if there was a problem, such as "troops in contact," he would be there in an instant.

But the panel members were having none of that. Being at your post is being at your post, not nearby.

"You have Marines, Americans in uniform, outside the wire," said a visibly upset Morgan, who had experienced an ambush and lost men. "You don't know when 'troops in contact' is going to happen!"

Because Ukeiley was not at his Bagram desk and eventually had to be informed via his personal cell phone to check his secure email messages. There was a delay of between twenty to forty minutes before he relayed that information to Haas. To cover his ass, Ukeiley quickly pulled together with Green Beret officers, those who had been causing us grief since we arrived, a PowerPoint brief titled "The Failures of MSOC-F," which was sent to Haas, his staff, and across the MARSOC and SOCOM community.

Among the list of our "failures," Ukeiley charged that we did not use our satellite radios to report being in contact and that Haas had to find out from the media about what had happened.

But Johansson, who maintained his office inside our operations center in Jalalabad, told NCIS that he heard voice radio reports and saw data message transmissions from the convoy within two minutes after the attack. Even Ukeiley was forced to admit on the stand that he heard a TIC announced in the operations center before he departed for the break room. He just did not think it had anything to do with us.

Ukeiley had depicted Fox Company as unresponsive about reporting and me as disobedient for going on a patrol without Nicholson's blessing. That was why Nicholson was angry when he heard about the ambush, understandably if that had been the situation. But the truth was that we promptly reported "troops in contact" and the patrol was approved by the CJSOTF-A staff in Bagram.

Ukeiley's duplicity touched a nerve with the panel members and they reacted with a vengeance.

Daniels pointed to a peculiarity about the fitness report, required for Ukeiley's promotion to lieutenant colonel, that had been filed by his commanders.

"You stated that they told you to ghost write your fitness report?" he asked.

"Yes, sir."

"What kind of a fitness report do you have as a Marine LNO to CJSOTF-A?" Daniels inquired, seemingly innocently.

Ukeiley was matter of fact.

"It was a very positive fitness report, sir."

"So what is inconsistent," asked Daniels, suddenly sharp, "the fitness report or your actual performance?"

Ukeiley thought for a second, then sighed.

"From March 4th," he said, "the fitness report would be inconsistent."

At least he manned up to his own incompetence. But Daniels was not finished with him.

"So I want to make sure I understand this, you have testified here that you have a fitness report that went before the board for lieutenant colonel that is not accurate; is that true?"

"I don't know if I would characterize it that way, sir," Ukeiley said with a hem and a haw.

"Well," Daniels offered, "you tell me how you would characterize it."

"I didn't sign the fitness report, sir."

I guess he thought writing the report but having his superior sign it would let him off the hook.

Daniels was incredulous.

"Nobody signs (their own) fitness report, do they?"

Ukeiley sighed again. "No, sir."

Porter looked at Daniels and, out of the side of his mouth, said: "When they write it, they do."

I smiled, just a little.

They also found that Ukeiley had written his own citation for a combat award for the three months he was on the headquarters staff in Afghanistan.

"What type of an award was it?" Morgan asked.

"A Bronze Star," Ukeiley replied.

Morgan threw up his hands. "You wrote yourself up for your own Bronze Star?"

"Yes," Ukeiley confessed. He looked shaken, perhaps finally realizing that his testimony was not going very well.

A disgusted Morgan had heard enough.

"Do you know what a '10-day letter' is?" he asked sternly.

The beleaguered Ukeiley responded, "No."

A 10-day letter would be sent to a Marine whose promotion was withheld because of concerns about his fitness expressed by a senior officer. The Marine had ten days to respond as to why he or she should be promoted despite those concerns. Being asked about a 10-day letter was not a good sign for Ukeiley.

When he walked out of the courtroom, Ukeiley was in shambles. Nunnally told me that never in forty years of practicing law had he ever seen a man torn down on the stand as much as Ukeiley that day.

But the trial was barreling to a conclusion and I worried all of our efforts might not be enough.

The media was unrelenting. A story appearing in the *New York Daily News* on January 23, based on information from an unnamed source, began: "A Marine special operations outfit in Afghanistan was trying to help the CIA wage a secret war against Al Qaeda infiltrators along the Pakistan border last year when they mowed down 19 civilians."

I worried that the public and political pressure would be too strong for the panel members to buck. To appease the Afghans, the U.S. needed to pay them, apologize to them, and offer a scapegoat. Absolving us would spark outrage on the streets of Afghanistan.

The prosecutors called their final witness.

I heard the voice of a woman with a European accent via a live audio feed from Afghanistan. I didn't know who she was, had never seen or heard her before, and our attorneys had never interviewed her.

Alice Pfluger was a development consultant from Switzerland who had been in Afghanistan overseeing aid projects, including the construction of schools and clinics, for many years. In her early forties, she had worked in some pretty tough places, such as the Sudan, Ethiopia, and Kosovo. She agreed to testify only with the assurance that she could be anonymous, since she was continuing to work in Afghanistan.

On the morning of March 4, she explained, she was visiting two of her projects near Spin Pul, reinforcing a canal in the riverbed north of the bridge and conducting a community basket weaving project under the bridge at its foot.

Pfluger said that, despite her wish not to be surrounded by armed guards, the engineering firm that employed her insisted two security men carrying AK-47s accompany her. So much for Qomandan's claim that the area was "very safe and secure and there is nothing happen wrong."

She was also certain there was no bulldozer present that day, again contradicting Qomandan, who said he stopped his Prado to let pass a bulldozer which had pulled out in front of him. Pfluger testified that sometimes a bulldozer was used on the canal project, but not that day or in the two weeks prior to March 4.

She was taking photos, as she usually did to document the progress of her projects, when the car bomb went off.

Image of the suicide car bomber's smoke plume taken by NGO worker immediately upon detonation (Courtesy of Galvin's Defense Counsel)

"I felt the earth move," she remembered.

Turning around, she instinctively snapped a photo of the enormous dark cloud of smoke that rose in the sky. That photo, the only one that existed of the explosion, was displayed on a screen in the courtroom.

"Ma'am, after the explosion, what did you do?" Waple asked.

"I looked at my engineer and he looked at me and said, 'Are you afraid?' I said, 'No, I'm not. It didn't hit us (our workers in the riverbed), did it?' And he said, 'Shall we just continue to walk away from it to the other projects?' We agreed that would be the best thing to do."

"How many, approximately, workers were there in the riverbed that you saw that day?"

"It is a bit of a variable on the number of people day-by-day," she said. "But I think it was about forty." She added that there were another twenty workers at the basket project half a mile away.

Waple asked, "Did you hear any shooting at any time?"

"Yeah, quite quickly after the explosion there was quite intense firing," she recalled, "and quite quickly it start spreading. And actually, it spread so far that I look back at the river to...see if everyone is all right."

Waple saw the opening and took it.

Bringing to mind Ali's testimony about the sound of the gunfire, he asked, "Were you hearing any single pops as opposed to the *tat, tat, tat* of a machine gun?"

"I can give you the sounds that I heard at first," Pfluger suggested, "and then the sounds how it started spreading."

"Sure, do that," Waple said.

Sanger and Sanchez looked suddenly distressed.

"It started *deet, deet, deet, deet, deet, deet.*"

Her description was very much like that of Ali, who said the first shots he heard was automatic fire from AK-47s.

She continued: "And then later on it was *tat, tat, tat, tat, tat, tat.*"

"Did it sound to you like there were different types of weapons being fired," Waple asked, "or was it all one type of weapon being fired?"

"The intense fire was the first sound I gave you," she explained, "and later on it started spreading through the area with the second sound."

She said the shooting of the second kind, our machine guns, continued over a span of only some five minutes, as we confronted the Prado, other vehicles and the assembled mob driving away from the blast site.

Waple asked her: "At any time did you believe or feel like the firing that you heard was being directed at you?"

"No," she said, "never."

"Could you observe any impacts of any rounds in the area in which you were located?"

"No, I did not," she said. "Otherwise, I would have probably ducked. I did not feel threatened at any time."

Waple conveyed his next question slowly.

"With regard to the workers who were in the riverbed, were any of those workers injured?"

The prosecutors leaned forward.

She was talking about her workers. Her answer would be the definitive word on the subject.

"No, definitely not," she said. "They ran away actually. The moment the bomb went off, my hard labor, they all fled away and ducked under."

Within just a few minutes of testimony, she had confirmed that there was an IED, that we were fired on first and thus were victims of a complex ambush, that there were no injuries among workers at the riverbed, and that we did not continue firing for several miles down the road.

Hallelujah!

I felt like standing up and cheering, and I prayed that her impartiality—she had nothing to gain by telling falsehoods—would hold great sway with the panel.

When the shooting ended, Pfluger said she traveled to the basket weaving project, where apparently unconcerned villagers joined her, and then went with them to their compound to drink *chai*.

Before she finished her testimony, panel member Porter gave her a piece of advice: "The next time a car explodes, please, take cover."

"That is what somebody else told me as well," Pfluger said with a laugh. "I will."

Prosecution: Closing Statement

T he longest war crimes trial in Marine Corps history, three and a half weeks, came to an end on Tuesday, January 29, 2008.

Sanchez presented the prosecution's "impartial and unbiased" closing statement.

"Gentlemen, we've had over forty witnesses testify over three weeks, delivered 5,000 pages of documentation, both classified and unclassified, as part of the record. When we finish here today, you're going to have to wade through all of that (and) try as you might, facts will not fit together neatly. I'm not talking about discrepancies that would naturally flow from the fog of war. Instead you will be forced to decide whether certain individuals are lying to you."

Using a rather peculiar analogy, Sanchez referenced the 1967 tragedy of Apollo 1, whose anniversary occurred two days earlier. Three astronauts were killed during training in a fire some say was the product of "go fever," a desire to move ahead on a mission despite the lack of proper safeguards.

In the incident of March 4, Sanchez charged, "chillingly and very similarly the ravages of 'go fever' are very glaringly apparent.... Once the timeline to build the Marine Corps' capability was compressed...in an initiative driven by SOCOM, 'go fever' permeated the process," he said. "This fever, this burning desire to achieve the mission produced a false sense of urgency. They were out the door first. They were the best equipped. They were the first MSOC. They needed to prove themselves. And they weren't going to let anybody get in the way. Not the lack of logistics. Not the lack of support. Not the wrong mission. Not the wrong AO. None of them was going to stop them from proving that they were a world-class DA (direct action) force....

"Gentlemen, most of them didn't have the dust of Afghanistan on them and they're already worried about whether they can kill somebody there. 'Do we have enough time? Because if we don't do Level Twos, well, then we're not doing what we're supposed to be doing'.... They were there in February. They knew they had to redeploy in May and retrograde had to start in April. That gives them, basically, two months, sixty-day window, to achieve and prove that concept. They trained too hard to not be able to prove themselves... They were forced to achieve success quickly, but that was self-imposed, gentlemen....

"You couple that with this: The 'can't fail' mindset. 'We're the best-ever trained in the Marine Corps. No one has had DA training better than we have. We can't fail. We can't be wrong.' That's the reason why MSOC-F has taken no responsibility for any decision or any operation that they did... 'I can't be wrong. Everybody else must be. It's the world against MSOC-F. We did everything perfectly. We did everything right. Everybody else is hosed up'.... And that forced them to compromise their integrity and shows an absence of moral courage when confronted with the possibility of having made a mistake....

"Gentlemen, we started this on 7 January. Today is the 29th. We've been at this for twenty-two days. We've spent as much time analyzing MSOC-F and looking into it as they did operating in Afghanistan."

Neither the Army or SOCOM conspired to torpedo Fox Company, he said, and neither our lack of logistics or the inexperience of Ukeiley had anything to do with what happened on March 4. Fox Company alone, and me in particular, was responsible not only for all our failures but for causing a strategic setback in Afghanistan for all coalition forces.

"The commander is responsible for everything his unit does or fails to do," he said, staring at me. "As Marines, this is a fundamental tenet of leadership—absolutely rock core, ingrained in us from the first day, either when our feet hit the yellow footprints or we stand in line for OCS."

He spun around to address the panel and tried to put a positive spin on any outcome of the trial.

"Now, if you turn your attention back for a moment to the failed Apollo 1 training mission…. The subsequent investigation enabled critical self-examination, which ultimately guaranteed that the astronauts of Apollo 11 would reach and walk on the moon. In the same way, the failed deployment of MSOC-F and the recommendations that will flow from this Court of Inquiry will actually guarantee the future of MARSOC, and the success of other MSOC missions and deployments. Thank you, gentlemen."

Sanchez's scathing indictment of my leadership was ironic, given the job I *still* had in the Marines. Throughout the COI, I was training the entire force of 2,650 Marines in MARSOC.

An officer facing an inquiry into negligent homicide and dereliction of duty was the training officer running the whole show for Marine special ops.

The prosecution did not see the hypocrisy.

Defense: Closing Statement

Nunnally offered the first closing statement for the defense, ending powerfully by saying:

"Ask yourself this when you go back and consider what happened on 4 March," he told the panel members. "If instead of MSOC-F returning from that convoy with...minimal damage (and) one slightly wounded Marine, if instead they had been burying body bags that contained the lifeless bodies of those Marines in Vehicle Two or any of those other gunners on Vehicles One through Six, would we still be asking the same questions today?"

With that somber question hanging in the air, Waple followed.

"I want to tell you sincerely that I consider this to be an honor and privilege to be here...representing one of the finest officers in the American military that I have certainly seen in over thirty-plus years."

He then quickly trashed Sanchez's accusation of "go fever."

"I would suggest to you in response that if there was a 'go fever,' it was largely the result and the responsibility of higher commands, specifically, MARSOC and MARCENT...(and I) would suggest that there has been, established by a preponderance of the evidence, a circle more of reluctance, a circle of resistance, and an unwillingness to accept MSOC-Fox by CJSOTF-A and its staff which...in part has contributed to why we are here today."

Waple said the answers to six questions should determine the panel's verdict.

One...

"Did the MSOC Marines experience a complex attack?"

The answer, he said, was yes.

Two...

"Did the MSOC Marines make up a story that they had come under a complex attack?"

The answer, he said, was no.

"It has to do with spontaneity," he explained, referring to the immediate communications within and from the patrol, including my text message that we were receiving small arms fire. "These spontaneous descriptions of receiving and seeing evidence of small arms fire are what we call...'excited utterances'... Statements made during a startling event or while under the stress of excitement possess inherent reliability...(because they) remove any opportunity for calculation... The Marines, as they are declaring over the radio what they are seeing and hearing, had no opportunity to...make up anything."

Keep in mind as well, he continued, that "Maj. Galvin's character for truthfulness, his character for honesty, and straightforwardness was absolutely impeccable."

Three...

"Did the civilian Afghans interviewed by NCIS in this case have any motive to exaggerate, fabricate or lie in the information they provided?"

The answer, he said, was yes. Political and peer pressure, and the promise of *solatia*, presented powerful, maybe impossible to resist, incentives to lie.

Four...

"Did the MSOC-Fox Marines exercise proportionate and discriminate fire?"

The answer, he said, was yes.

He pointed out that even if you accepted the inflated Afghan claims about the number of injuries, 80 percent of them were in oncoming vehicles. They were not pedestrians or bystanders. My Marines, in other words, did not shoot up the neighborhood. Nor did we shoot at every vehicle in our path. Afghans themselves testified that *after* the blast my Marines often used hand and arm signals to get vehicles to move off the road—hardly a sign of "juiced up" Marines engaging in a frenzy of excessive force.

Five...

"How thorough and reliable was the investigation conducted by Col. Pihana and what impact Col. Pihana's investigation had on the NCIS investigation?"

The answers, he said, were "not at all" and "a whole lot," respectively.

He reiterated that Pihana ignored any information that did not agree with his own erroneous analysis, and that analysis was the foundation for the NCIS investigation.

Six...

"Was there a disconnect between MSOC-Fox's deployment to Afghanistan with CJSOTF-A and (Nicholson's) Task Force Spartan?"

The answer again, he said, was yes.

"Neither Col. Nicholson or Col. Haas sat down with Maj. Galvin or his staff to clarify their mutual expectations of MSOC-Fox's mission," Waple reminded the panel. "MSOC-Fox was not trained, manned, or equipped to operate on an extended period of time away from the MEU, but they were asked to do so... MSOC-Fox was set up for failure, with the CJSOTF staff unable to supply minimal support."

Wrapping up, Waple spoke for me in saying that I "certainly regret the collateral injuries or deaths that may have been caused to some of the civilian Afghans as a result of the 4 March incident. But the principal responsibility for those collateral injuries and collateral deaths lies with the individuals responsible for the complex attack on the Marines on the morning of the 4th of March 2007."

I have never said this publicly before, but I am certain there were innocent civilians killed and injured on March 4. They may have been victims of the blast, enemy small arms fire, vehicle accidents near the site, or ricochets from return fire aimed at our attackers. Their deaths and injuries were unfortunate, a terrible consequence of a war in which terrorists regularly used civilians as sacrificial shields and political pawns.

In conclusion, Waple said, "I wanted to leave you with this thought: General Douglas MacArthur in his report to the General Chief of Staff to the United States Army made comments which are particularly appropriate in this particular case, and they deal with the military justice system and the need for fundamental fairness, which is all that we are asking in Maj. Galvin and Capt. East's case.

"(He said that) 'the unfailing formula for the production of morale is patriotism, self-respect, discipline and self- confidence within a military unit...' But here's the important point: '...joined with fair treatment. It will quickly wither and die if soldiers come to believe themselves victims of indifference or injustice on the part of their government or of ignorance, personal ambition, or ineptitude on the part of their military leaders.'"

Show Cause

I expected a verdict within days. But weeks and months went by and still there was no word. Holly and I had scheduled our wedding for mid-May, and we decided to push ahead with that date.

The ceremony at the Country Club Christian Church in Kansas City was beyond beautiful. Holly in a traditional wedding dress and I in my formal Marine blues walked beneath an arch of drawn swords held by our fellow Marines in their dress uniforms. It was a challenge to get as many of our colleagues there as we wanted, with many overseas and others in training, but the church filled with about 250 friends and family. Those who were there remember the occasion as *the* classic wedding of two Marines in love.

With the rest of my life on hold, we went on our honeymoon, an eight day Mediterranean cruise from Barcelona to Venice to Croatia. It was my first cruise on a ship that did not belong to the Navy, and I was amazed to discover that everything actually worked onboard, unlike that of a Navy ship!

We were having a wonderful time—until we pulled into the port of Dubrovnik in Croatia. Holly strolled into an internet café, went online and unearthed a press release announcing that, four months after the COI had recessed, a verdict had been reached.

The report of the COI had been completed in February and the panel members had briefed the convening authority, Helland, in mid-April. But the announcement wasn't made until late on May 24, the Friday before the Memorial Day weekend.

Why Helland waited more than two months to issue a very concise press release was curious to some. But not to me.

There would be little attention paid to a press release that dropped on a "news dump Friday." There would be even less thanks to the holiday weekend. Also, by having the information disseminated just as the command departed on a ninety-six hour weekend pass, there was a good excuse for being unable to respond to any reporter's questions.

Employing a tactic that senior military leaders often leaned on, Helland hoped to bury yet another sore subject.

In one short sentence, the press release said that Fox Company "acted appropriately and in accordance with the rules of engagement and tactics, techniques and procedures in place at the time in response to a complex attack."

There would be no court-martial, for me or any of the men of Fox Company.

I was certainly happy to hear that! But after what we'd been through for more than a year, I had hoped the wording would be stronger. I wished the press release had said we were "innocent." I wanted complete vindication.

The executive summary was far more detailed and decisive:

"The Court finds no failure or dereliction on the part of Maj. Galvin or Capt. East arising from the 4 March 2007 incident relative to the tactical conduct and fire discipline of the MSOC-F convoy....

"The Court found the statements and the testimony of the personnel in the MSOC-F convoy to be consistent, truthful, and credible....

"MSOC-F personnel applied the proper EOF procedures and ROE....

"These incidents do not evidence a pattern of the indiscriminate use of force, or the disproportional use of force...

"MSOC-F leadership properly reported and documented 4 March 2007 to CJSOTF-A...

"The incidents of 9 March 2007 are factually independent of the 4 March 2007 incident."

In conclusion, the court recommended "that no punitive and/ or adverse administrative action be taken against the personnel of the MSOC-F convoy with regards to the combat action on 4 March 2007." The court also ordered that the Combat Action Ribbon be awarded to all convoy personnel, Klein be awarded the Purple Heart for his injury, and any other pending awards be processed without delay.

One problem: The press never saw the executive summary.

That document was not made available to the media or the public, and the complete ninety-nine page final report remains classified to this day.

Several months after Helland's press release, I was finally authorized, holding my Top Secret security clearance, to review that report in Camp Lejeune, but only under the close observation of two military attorneys. I was permitted to read it, but I could not take notes or copy any part of it.

I was surprised to read that the panel pulled no punches in its criticism of senior officers—even Nicholson.

The report roundly scolded him for "inappropriately" requesting Fox Company's eviction from Afghanistan when he did not know all the facts about March 4 and took him to task for falsely accusing East and myself of conducting the March 4 and March 9 missions without approval.

The COI recommended that "no further action should be taken against Maj. Galvin" regarding the events of March 9 but added that "it was appropriate that Maj. Galvin was relieved of command and issued an adverse fitness report due to his loss of operational control of his unit."

That stung. An adverse fitness report follows an officer for the rest of his career and usually shortens that career.

Who instigated and signed that report?

Montanus.

He got in the last word after all.

East too was admonished for March 9, cited for submitting a false official statement, failure to obey a lawful order, and obstruction of justice. But, the summary continued, "given Capt. East's superior combat record and the mitigating action taken by him to correct his mistakes, Capt. East's case should be referred to COMMARSOC for appropriate disciplinary and/or administrative action" rather than sending him to a court-martial or demanding his separation from the service.

Being cleared of all potential charges by the COI, I felt as though the horrid experience was finally over. I had my life back.

So, I was stunned to discover that my ordeal wasn't over. I hadn't counted on the determination of the senior command to exact retribution for us winning in their court. I had the gall to fight back and they were determined to make me pay, one way or another, if not for March 4 then for March 9—and their first salvo was fired almost immediately.

That same Friday afternoon I learned about the verdict, Helland ordered Jack to notify me that I would face a Board of Inquiry (BOI) in Camp Lejeune within thirty days.

Helland directed his staff to take the COI's twelve thousand pages of evidence and testimony and conduct another investigation, this time aimed wholly at me for substandard performance of duty, misconduct, and moral or professional dereliction regarding March 9. I would have to justify my remaining in the Marines or else be involuntarily separated. Despite the COI's recommendations, they still wanted to kick me out!

But Jack didn't call me that day with the bad news.

"Fred, I wasn't going to call you and spoil your trip," he told me later. "They could court-martial me if they wanted to. But I knew you were coming back within thirty days anyway." I stayed blissfully ignorant until I returned to Camp Lejeune.

The thirty days came and went. Every time a hearing date was set, it would later be changed. Meanwhile, I was on a "legal hold," which meant I could not transfer to a different duty station. When my new bride Holly went off to her next posting, Okinawa, I was forced to stay behind in Camp Lejeune. Here we were newlyweds and again we were apart, far apart.

I requested a transfer to Okinawa in anticipation of the legal hold eventually being lifted. Because few people volunteered to go to the Rock, the assignment officer said he could put Holly and I together when I was free to go. I would be the operations officer for the Special Operations Training Group in Okinawa—assuming I was still in the Corps.

I waited and waited for the BOI hearing, from July to August to September. I think they were hoping to run me into the ground as the MARSOC training officer, which I continued to be after the COI, and that I would resign my commission in frustration. Not only was I overworked but my superiors found fault with what I was doing on a daily basis. Previous evaluations had always ranked me at the top of the pyramid. Not anymore.

When Jack asked about the possibility of resigning, I told him point blank, "No, I'm going to fight this."

The hearing date was finally set for a Monday morning in late November. By then, Holly and I had not been together for five very long months.

On the Friday before the three man Board of Inquiry was to convene, Jack flew to Camp Pendleton to pay the hard-nosed Helland a visit. He reminded the general that the COI had ruled there be no further administrative actions against me, whether for March 4 or March 9. Besides, he pointed out, the BOI would likely come to the same conclusion as the COI—no misconduct, no dereliction of duty. Plus, the media might find it unseemly that I was being put on trial yet again. Heck, it might appear Marine leadership was engaged in a personal vendetta.

Helland reluctantly agreed to postpone the hearing, but on one condition: He wanted to talk to me first.

He ordered me to meet with him when he was in Quantico in early December. I drove the five hours from Camp Lejeune and reported to him in an office he borrowed for the occasion.

As I stood at attention, he handed me a four page "non-punitive letter of caution" titled "Report of No Misconduct in the case of Maj. Galvin" which rattled off every "deficiency" I had exhibited regarding the incidents of March 9.

After I finished reading, Helland, sitting in his chair, berated me for the next thirty minutes, a one-on-one, first class, butt-chewing while I stood at attention. As the saying goes, rank has its privileges.

Helland demanded answers.

"Why did vehicles roll over?" he asked, his hostility apparent.

I calmly responded that the rollovers might have been prevented if any effort had been made by CJSOTF-A to provide our company with the proper supplies and qualified support personnel.

He looked at me with a sneer.

"Why did a patrol utilize an unauthorized route, a route you were not aware of?"

I told him that the plan had been concealed from me. The patrol did not contact any enemy forces and returned to base uneventfully. No harm, no foul.

That was not good enough for him.

He asked again, louder: "Why did a patrol utilize an unauthorized route, a route you were not aware of?"

I explained what happened, but Helland was no longer listening. I could tell he knew little about the facts of the case and cared even less about my side of the story. He was never going to accept anything I said that challenged what he had been told by the prosecutors, who probably wrote the letter of caution.

All he wanted to do was give me a good whipping.

And he did.

After he dismissed me, the hearing was canceled and I was informed that I was no longer on a legal hold. I immediately booked a plane ticket to Okinawa and landed there on Christmas Day.

I expected a deliriously happy reunion with Holly. But it was quickly clear that my absence had not made her heart grow fonder.

During the next two years, there were rocky times, and we grew further apart. One night, she walked into our bedroom and, a moment later, came out holding divorce papers.

I felt like I'd been kicked in the stomach.

I was a devout Marine, and my duties were all-consuming. That destroyed my first marriage. I was grateful that Holly, someone who was also in the Marines, understood the pressure a military life puts on a marriage. But not understood by either of us was that Holly was accustomed to being free and unattached, including months on ships where she was one of few women surrounded by twenty-six hundred men.

The commitment of marriage or not, Holly wanted to hold onto her status as the belle of the ball.

While the divorce was being finalized, I joined the 3rd Recon Battalion in Okinawa as the operations officer, which included being responsible for delivering surface fired rockets as well as aviation munitions, which was what I had taught in Yuma.

And I was soon headed back to Afghanistan.

Danger Close

Four years after the ambush, March 4 followed me to Afghanistan.

On Monday, June 6, 2011, 1st Platoon, Bravo Company, was embroiled in a hellish firefight in broad daylight in a village in the Sangin Valley in notoriously dangerous Helmand Province. Outnumbered, pinned down, and nearly enveloped by the enemy, they were slammed by RPGs, mortars, medium machine guns, and AK-47s.

It was a nasty scrap.

The battalion commander, Lt. Col. Travis Homiak, was an intelligence officer who had never previously been to Afghanistan, and never had rounds fired directly at him anywhere.

When he came into our operations tent, the Taliban were about four hundred meters from our men. At first, Homiak wanted to use a MK-19 automatic 40mm high explosive grenade launcher in the hands of Charlie Company, which was positioned on a mountain overlooking the site. But I advised him that those Marines had not been fully trained on lobbing ordnance from such a high elevation and had never test-fired that specific armament to prove its accuracy. Trying to hit the enemy by firing those grenades over the heads of 1st Platoon, there was a risk to our own forces and to civilians. The MK-19 was a powerful weapon. We had one when we were ambushed on March 4—and chose not to use it because the danger to civilians was so great.

Homiak agreed. We talked about a possible air strike and discussed the aviation assets above the battlefield—a Reaper drone armed with a laser-guided Hellfire missile with ten pounds of high explosives, a C-130 with a laser-guided Griffin missile carrying four pounds of high explosives, and two Harriers with 500-pound laser-guided bombs.

"I want to talk to the staff judge advocate," Homiak said.

He was lawyering up. He knew he would be lambasted if he went "bombs away" and inflicted casualties on Afghan civilians.

While he consulted with the JAG officer and his intelligence team, an excruciating fifty minutes went by.

The enemy drew closer, to two hundred meters. Our Marines were taking heavy fire.

Finally, he was assured there were no civilians in the immediate area.

"Sir, our guys are going to get killed," I said, trying to prod him into action.

Still uncertain, he brought in the battalion air officer.

"You have to make a decision," I urged.

The enemy had moved even closer, firing from a building just forty meters away.

It was now too late to drop the five hundred pound bombs, they would land too close to our men. Each bomb had 250 pounds of high explosives encased in 250 pounds of steel and was designed to propel hunks of shrapnel the size of your fist over a wide area. In Yuma, we were told to never drop a five hundred pounder when friendlies were within two hundred meters of the target. Our Marines were five times closer than that. With the experience of having called in more than 2,000 air strikes, I recommended that we use either the ten pound or four pound munitions—and as soon as possible.

Instead, Homiak requested another confirmation that there were no civilians in the area. He also wanted to know if Bravo Company still needed help. The answers were yes and yes!

Then, over my objection, he ordered a five hundred pounder let loose on that building.

When you order a drop at distances inside "danger close," we say you "buy" that bomb, and you must physically put your initials on that order. That is how serious that is taken.

Homiak signed "TLH."

Of course, by the time the Harrier dropped the bomb, the enemy had fled the building, which was destroyed.

But the pressure of the blast rocked the heads of the Marines. Having received multiple impacts from explosives, I knew about the potential damage, usually permanent, to the soft tissue in the brain. An impact that large at that close a range could also later trigger Post-traumatic Stress Disorder (PTSD).

One of the Marines on the ground later said: "We knew Maj. Galvin was there, and it was the only thing that gave the Marines some peace of mind—we knew we'd be OK if he was there. As soon as the GBU (Guided Bomb Unit) dropped, we all knew that something was wrong."

A corpsman in Bravo Company, trying to gather his wits while treating a casualty and engaging targets—our Marines were still pinned down—relayed that the platoon should be placed in a concussion protocol when they, hopefully, returned to base.

Homiak wanted to drop another five hundred pounder!

Fortunately for our Marines, the Harriers were no longer near the target, having had to break off to refuel.

Again I suggested that we use either the ten pound or four pound laser-guided munitions. They were designed to defeat threats by using overpressure rather than sending shrapnel everywhere for dozens of meters.

Again, Homiak rejected my recommendation. He had a different weapon in mind—a High Mobility Artillery Rocket System (HIMARS) battery of surface-fired rockets, each weighing 675 pounds when filled with high explosives that would detonate on impact.

Using the HIMARS in that situation was like performing surgery with a chainsaw instead of a scalpel. Those rockets were so destructive that the Probability of Incapacitation, the chance of a friendly casualty, was 1 in 1,000 if one landed 225 meters away; 1 in 100 if it landed 180 meters away.

If it might land within 135 meters of a friendly, there was a standing order that we not fire the weapon at all.

But Homiak ordered the firing of the HIMARS—not one rocket, but two simultaneously—at an enemy position only seventy meters from the Marines.

Worse, they were fired in "open sheaf" formation, thus spreading the shrapnel over a greater distance than if fired in "closed sheaf" formation.

The explosions were monstrous. Every Marine in the platoon should have been killed or injured.

Thankfully, undetected by our satellites and therefore unbeknownst to us at the operations center, the Marines were positioned in a canal. Being hunkered down below ground level saved their asses.

The firefight continued, lasting four grueling hours, and the platoon requested more support. Homiak refused.

"That commander isn't doing his job," he said angrily, losing control of his emotions. "He needs to break contact."

Apparently, and inexplicably, two fire support missions were Homiak's limit. He was leaving that unit out there on its own.

Anxious minutes ticked away—until we heard the platoon had successfully disengaged and withdrawn.

Once back behind the wire, the Marines expected Homiak to visit with them and conduct a debrief. But instead of talking with them and showing concern by pulling them off the line for a minimum twenty-four hour concussion observation period, he went to sleep in his bunk. I did the debrief.

The next morning, I met with Homiak.

"Sir, I have the information from the patrol about what went on. I'd also really like to talk to you about your intentions for fires so I know going forward what you expect me to do."

He was about to leave for a few days, and I would be in sole charge of the battalion's operations. I wanted to be certain, if there was a similar scenario as the day before, that we were on the same page, since obviously we had not been.

"Fred, I want to make something very clear to you," he said forcefully. "I am willing to sacrifice the lives of these Marines for the greater good. And I need to know right now if you are too."

I was surprised. I knew Homiak was a COIN enthusiast and had been quoted in a news report trumpeting "the concept of restraint" and "being nice to people" but I had no idea that his view only applied to Afghans and not to his own Marines.

"Sir, I was a Force Recon platoon commander," I answered. "I've walked through many explosive charges going into homes where people were firing at us. I understand that the lives of these Marines may be required."

I fixed my eyes on his.

"But yesterday the fires you ordered were danger close to our Marines, far less than the acceptable fratricide distance."

He repeated himself, more sternly, as if I did not hear him the first time.

"Fred, you need to understand that I'm willing to sacrifice the lives of these Marines for the greater good. And I need to make sure that you are too." He paused and sighed. "I expect on future occasions that you will do the same thing I did yesterday."

"Sir, I...I..." I stammered. I knew what I was going to say, what I had never said before, what I had to say, but I didn't know how to say it. Homiak was my superior officer and I needed to be respectful.

"What you've told me to do will needlessly injure and kill Americans," I said. "Needlessly. If that's what you're ordering me to do, sir, I can't do that in good conscience." I took a deep breath. "I have a duty to disobey an unethical and unlawful order."

He stared at me.

"Then effective immediately," he said, "you're relieved of your duties."

For the second time in my career, I had been relieved. But this time it was on my own terms.

Homiak tried to sweep the incident under the rug. While remaining the CO of 3rd Recon in Afghanistan and for six months afterwards in Okinawa, he prohibited the unit's medical staff from evaluating the June

6 Marines for traumatic brain injury. As a result, what happened that day was not included in their medical records.

Shipped back to Okinawa, back to the training sweatshop, I wrote letters to every member of the House and Senate Armed Services Committees, other senators and congressmen, and the inspector general within my chain of command, pleading with them to open an investigation.

Once more, Congressman Jones stepped up to the plate, officially requesting an inquiry. The response to him on December 11 by the deputy commandant for the Office of Legislative Affairs, on behalf of Gen. Amos, was that the affair had been investigated and it was determined that no punitive or administrative action would be taken against Homiak.

That was strange—because they had not assigned an investigating officer or interviewed anyone in the platoon that had been under fire. They never spoke with me either, and I was the operations officer. That was not an investigation, that was a whitewash.

On December 13, I asked Jones to request a copy of the alleged investigation.

That must have pissed someone off because on Sunday, December 25, the lieutenant general who was deputy commandant of Manpower and Reserve Affairs went to his office, during a 96, to sign a letter ordering me to a BOI with the intent to kick me out of the Marines—again.

The official reason given was that when the promotion board considering my elevation to lieutenant colonel saw two adverse fitness reports, one from Montanus and now one from Homiak, they wanted a BOI to determine if, given my "substandard performance," I should even be in the Marines.

The order was hand delivered.

Merry Christmas.

The BOI was scheduled for Camp Foster on Okinawa on March 8. I was represented by a military lawyer assigned by the Marines, square jawed Maj. Jason Durden. The prosecutor was supposed to be a female attorney and major. But the day before we went to court, she was replaced by Capt. Jeffrey Tharp—who had been one of the attorneys working with the prosecution at my COI!

The first witness was Montanus, who said "(Galvin) is one of the better tactical Marine officers that we have. (But) I would rather have Maj. Galvin separated rather than work with him again."

The feeling was mutual.

The second witness was Homiak, who saw me as difficult and troublesome, not a team player. He testified that he relieved me because he could not be certain that I would do as ordered. Why did he believe that? Because, he said, I did not agree with the COIN strategy. Belief in COIN, which was at the heart of why East and I were subjected to a COI, once again reared its ugly head.

Every other witness, however, expressed a very different view of my performance.

A lieutenant colonel I had served under said, "I have two boys; and if they were going into combat, I would hope that they would have a commander like Fred Galvin that would take their best interest and bring as many of them back as possible."

When another lieutenant colonel was asked if he believed an assessment of substandard performance, he replied, "No. I would categorically reject that. I would say (the)...words that come to mind are 'absurd,' 'preposterous'.... This is an outstanding officer and compared to his peers he's, in my book, he's in the top five percent of his peers across the board, mentally, physically, morally, work ethic.... My son is a corporal and if Maj. Galvin was his battalion commander I would be happy to have...my son under his charge."

As I took the stand, I recognized the irony that an officer who was once accused of being too aggressive was now being accused of not being aggressive enough.

Again, I had taken a polygraph, again administered by the esteemed O'Malley. I had the results in hand. The two relevant questions were:

"Did Lt. Col. Homiak say to me, 'I am willing to sacrifice the lives of these Marines for the greater good'"?

"Did he repeat to me that he was willing to sacrifice the lives of these Marines for the greater good?"

My answers to both were "yes" and the polygraph confirmed there was no deception.

I was prepared to be grilled about June 6. But Tharp ambushed me.

He regurgitated what Milton said at the COI about Fox Company killing civilians.

"Do you remember the name of that Marine that provided that testimony?" he asked.

I lost my cool.

"Do you remember the binder that I created on him," I shot back, "that had his emails in it?... He himself stated 'yes, it was a complex ambush.'"

"That's not what we're getting into," said the sly Tharp, "that's not what this is about."

Oh, yes it was, all over again. I had been carrying that heavy cross for going on five years. I was not about to let anyone crucify Fox Company another second.

I was mad, and I was fed up.

"Let's talk about Ali... Do you remember him? Do you remember when Ali sat in a booth like this after he was sworn in and said, 'I was on the patrol, I remember being shot at'? 'How do you remember?' 'Well, I'm Afghan, you know, I know the sound of AK-47 fire.'"

"I'm not talking about the combat ambush," Tharp argued. "I'm talking about the EOF..."

I jumped in before he could continue.

"Do I know my own case, inside, outside and upside down?"

"I'm not saying..."

"I know what happened!" I shouted. "I was an eyewitness, I was there that day... What are you trying to get at?"

"Well, sir, I'm just..."

He was flustered, and I was disgusted.

"You want to talk about the MARSOC 7, seven lives that were ruined?"

My pent-up anger erupted.

"You know what, where are we going with this?... I know what happened! Those Marines, I consider them *my* Marines. To this day, even though they are out, I take care of those Marines. Like Marine leaders should."

Tharp tried to pull himself together.

"The Court of Inquiry," he said, fumbling with the notes in his hands, "agreed with the adverse fitness rep because you lost operational control. I mean, do you think there's anything that you can look back and look at and say, 'Hey, I could have done that differently or I wouldn't have gotten relieved if I would have done that?'"

I sneered, I think for the first time in my life.

"I could have done a lot of things differently, everyone could have," I said. "We planned the mission, we briefed it, we executed it and, you know, can you do things different? Yeah... (But) we tried our very best, just like General Patton says...'A man gives his very best, what else is there?'"

Tharp nodded.

"Like I said, you were cleared of criminal charges."

And here I thought the COI had not been a prosecution but rather was about "fact-finding."

"Let's talk about loss of control," I said, sneering again. "Because you've been overseas. Have you been in a gun battle?"

Tharp was on his heels.

"Sir, this BOI isn't about me... It's about you."

"Well, let me talk about it..." I ignored him and plowed ahead. "War is not a noun, it's a verb. Things are very dynamic and you train and train... and you rehearse and rehearse as we did. But, you know, that day we got in an ambush...do I think that we should have done things different? I'll tell you, I did things as best I possibly could."

There was silence, as if all the air had been sucked out of the room.

Feeling the heat of my raw, emotional outburst, the three members of the board looked unsettled.

Tharp collected himself before he looked down at his notes—and changed the subject, asking about June 6.

Calming down, I explained to the panel about the potential consequences of dropping a five hundred pound bomb or firing HIMARS rockets danger close to friendly forces. If Homiak's decision had been made during a training exercise, he would have flunked the course. But this was not about training, this was about life and death. I found it morally and professionally reprehensible, I said, to order an action that might recklessly inflict casualties on Americans. If I had been in command, I could not and would not do that.

When Tharp snidely repeated Homiak's allegation that I was relieved because I did not understand the COIN effort, I lit into him again.

"(If) you don't think I understand COIN...think again... You know, I'm single for a reason. I study war (all the time)."

I did disagree with the leadership about COIN, and I would speak my mind in private. But when a decision was made in the field, even if I held a different opinion, I became an obedient servant, as I did on June 6. I was relieved not because of an opinion, but because I faced up to Homiak and he didn't like it.

In the end, the prosecution had two witnesses, Montanus and Homiak, on its side. Everyone else lined up on mine, whether in person or through letters, including one from COI panel member Morgan.

In his closing, my defense attorney Durden honed in on Montanus and Homiak.

"I'm not impugning Col. Montanus' integrity or anything like this," he said gingerly, "but there's obviously an issue he has with Maj. Galvin."

He also pointed out that Montanus, the CO of the 2nd MSOB, was not my boss while I was in Afghanistan in 2007. My boss there was Haas.

"He wasn't in control of Maj. Galvin with what this fitrep was written adversely for.... This was all passed through second hand information." Montanus had based my adverse fitness report on Pihana's preliminary investigation and what Ukeiley told him, and both of them had been discredited.

As for Homiak, Durden noted that he was at MARSOC during the time I was being tried in the COI. He could not have missed the negative light cast on me—I was the guy with the scarlet 'A,' for Ambush, burned into his forehead. Complicating our working relationship further, I was already the operations officer for 3rd Recon when Homiak took command. I was not chosen by him.

Durden framed my meeting with Homiak the day after the bombing and rocket launches as a discussion, not a confrontation.

"I thought that's what we do as a Marine, especially after combat operations, is try to talk about how we can make it better the next time. He walked in there and he wanted to see what the thinking was and what the guidance was.... To have a Marine die (needlessly)...that was unacceptable to Maj. Galvin and he let Col. Homiak know that...and, as soon as Col. Homiak has the opportunity to relieve him, he does."

Durden ended with a heartfelt personal statement.

"I don't get an opportunity to get up and argue for Marines like this very often as a defense counsel. And I get kind of passionate when I do get one... and I actually have some sort of evidence to put on in front of members to say I got a good Marine in front of you, we've got a good Marine—and he deserves to be able to stay in the Marine Corps."

The board recessed to deliberate. There was a minimum amount of time—forty-five minutes—mandated before a verdict could be announced in a BOI. The board reconvened after an hour and ten minutes. I was told they reached a verdict so quickly that they went to lunch for the remaining time.

The BOI ruled that the allegations of substandard performance were unsubstantiated and there was no finding of fact that warranted my separation.

Cut and dried. Case closed.

Unfortunately, over the next few years, my fears about the Marines in the blast area on June 6 proved true. Nearly every one of them was diagnosed with PTSD, including a young sergeant named Randall Stevenson Jr.

After his release from active duty, Steve-O, as his friends called him, began to suffer extreme mood swings and episodes of severe depression. He would frequently tell his mom and dad that something was "fucked up in my brain." He would threaten, "I'm going to blow my fucking brains out."

On the evening of Tuesday, April 5, 2016, three days after his 25th birthday, an anguished Steve-O hanged himself in his Baton Rouge, Louisiana apartment.

A Fragile Trust

The lack of detail in Helland's press release about the verdict left doubts in the minds of many Americans, doubts that have continued to this day about whether murderers had been let off easy. Some people hate the fact that we didn't go to prison for a war crime and will never forgive us for escaping punishment. Some claim that nothing happened to those Marines of Fox Company.

They are wrong. The ambush of March 4 continues to plague me and my Marines to this day.

When the public searches the internet, they do not find the classified COI final report, and the vast majority of the trial transcript remains locked in a safe at MARCENT in Tampa, protecting the careers and legacies of senior military officers.

What they see instead are news articles about a savage and ruthless Fox Company shooting to death more than a dozen innocent civilians. We are branded as killers who then fled the battlefield and attempted a conspiracy to cover up our crimes.

The *Marine Corps Times* published three articles, quoted earlier, which became the source of much of the misinformation. When those articles came out, in February 2008, we were under a gag order and unable to correct anything that was factually inaccurate, defamatory, or libelous. I never threatened to sue. I just wished the public could read the true story.

Other scurrilous pieces followed, including an article in the *Charleston Mercury* on December 29, 2009, headlined "What Happens when ROE are Ignored" by James Rembert: "They shot their way out of what they thought was an ambush, killing every Afghan they saw over a hurried ten-mile skedaddle from the IED site. They killed 19 civilians and injured dozens."

Soon after, the International Bar Association and Amnesty International tried unsuccessfully to resurrect the case, citing WikiLeaks reports that there was *prima facie* evidence that Fox Company killed Afghan civilians.

Their source? Qomandan!

On July 26, 2010, more than two years after the verdict, *The Guardian* in London, England published an especially inflammatory article by Declan Walsh.

Afghanistan war logs: How US marines sanitized record of bloodbath

```
It started with a suicide bomb. On 4 March
2007 a convoy of US marines, who arrived in
Afghanistan three weeks earlier, were hit
by an explosives-rigged minivan outside the
city of Jalalabad.

The marines made a frenzied escape, open-
ing fire with automatic weapons as they tore
down a six-mile stretch of highway, hitting
almost anyone in their way - teenage girls
in fields, motorists in their cars, old men
as they walked along the road.

Nineteen unarmed civilians were killed
and 50 wounded...

Two hours later Americans returned to the
scene of the bombing to conduct an "exploita-
tion of the blast site with pictures/grid
```

cords as well as debriefing ANP leadership on scene".

Journalists on the spot gave a more detailed account. They said angry marines tore their cameras from their hands, insisting they delete the pictures they had taken of bullet-pocked vehicles on the roadside.

Rahmat Gul, a freelance photographer working for the Associated Press, said two soldiers and a translator came up to him and asked: "Why are you taking pictures? You don't have permission."

Then they deleted his photographs.

Later, Gul said, one of the soldiers came up to him and raised his arm, as if to hit him. Taqi Ullah Taqi, a reporter for the private Tolo TV channel, said the Americans told him through a translator: "Delete them, or we will delete you"...

But there would be no punishment. The marines, angered by the criticism of their unit by an army commander, held their own inquiry into the shootings and issued their findings a year later. It exonerated the marines. The troops "acted appropriately and in accordance with the rules of engagement…in response to a complex attack," said Major General Samuel Helland, the commander of marine forces in the Middle East and Afghanistan…

The findings of the court of inquiry, which ran to 12,000 pages, were not released. No criminal charges were brought against any officer, although some did receive an "administrative reprimand".

The article was filled with shockingly egregious errors and oversights and exhibited an utter lack of corroboration. There was also one curiosity—Taqi Ullah Taqi was the same supposedly harassed reporter quoted in the Reuters story about the September 27 raid in Bati Kot!

But the narrative fit what some wanted to hear. Journalist Walsh, instead of being castigated for his poor work, was hired by *The New York Times* and made that paper's Pakistan bureau chief in 2012 and later its Cairo bureau chief.

Meanwhile, the Marines of Fox Company were branded with a stigma that has been with us every day since we last drove down Hell's Highway.

Nearly all of us have exhibited symptoms of PTSD—anger, anxiety, nightmares, feelings of helplessness—not from being in combat in Afghanistan but from what occurred afterwards in America.

These brave, confident men who were once vibrant and emotionally healthy became distrustful, even of those closest to them. Some became emotionally numb; others were unable to regulate their feelings, abruptly swinging from rage to tears.

Family life became difficult and relationships fractured. Of the four married Marines in the MARSOC 7, three divorced following the COI. Only Walker's marriage survived.

We anticipated and planned for what we would face from the enemy. Unexpectedly, we were more seriously scarred by what happened to us *after* the battle. We became victims of a different kind of friendly fire.

When Walker checked into his new MARSOC unit, his sergeant major got in his face: "I don't know anything about what happened but what I do know is that your unit embarrassed the Corps."

"Well, Sgt. Major," said Walker, "if you want me to tell you what happened, I can. I was there. I was behind the gun. I can tell you, if you care to know."

But, like many others, the sergeant major did not want the whole story. He had already heard the story he had been told to believe.

Walker persevered and remained in MARSOC, which returned to Afghanistan multiple times after Fox Company's ouster and, beginning in 2014, took the name Marine Raiders. Promoted to master sergeant, though slower than his peers, he served on multiple deployments. The youngest of us, he looked up to me and I was proud not only of what he accomplished in the field but at home, keeping his family together.

The easygoing Pratt also heard the snickers and accusations, but he too took them in stride. After finishing another tour in MARSOC, he joined an interagency partner. Like the majority of the MARSOC 7, his sense of duty was so strong that he continued to serve his country long after the COI.

I was knocked for a loop when I saw how difficult a time Gunny Clarke, the toughest guy on the block, had dealing with the harassment. Fox Company was held over his head every day—"you guys got kicked out!" The humiliation that weighed on him from the endless ridicule made him miserable, and the once-unyielding gladiator withdrew into a cocoon.

Gunny was not drummed out of the Corps but he was forced to take medical retirement due to his diabetes, the onset of which I lay at the doorstep of the COI. Still, he could not completely let go of MARSOC and soon signed on to serve as a civilian instructor. Ultimately, however, he was hustled out the door.

The road ahead of Klein also proved difficult. Joining MARSOC's India Company, where he was happily joined by several others from Fox Company, including Ruiz, Ortega, Harley, Khan, and Todd, he was tortured by the belief that other Marines were always looking down on him. Whenever something negative happened, such as being passed over for a promotion, he was convinced it was because of March 4. More troubling, Klein was tormented by nightmares in which NCIS agents showed up at his house, demanded entry, handcuffed him, and hauled him off to prison.

After a while, he left the Marines, went home to Mississippi and, despite earning a college degree in political science from Ole Miss, became a farmer. But the nightmares continued. Before long, he was battling substance abuse problems, escalating from alcohol to drugs, and sank into a deep and frightening state of depression.

I knew he needed help. Fulfilling my obligation to the men who had been under my command was important to me. I did not want him to suffer the same feeling of abandonment I had experienced as a kid from my father.

I invited Klein to stay with me in Okinawa for ten days over a Christmas holiday. We talked about what he was going through and I did my best to reassure him that all was well.

"It's over," I told him. "You have nothing to worry about."

He believed me, and we had a great time hanging out together, but in the depths of the night his fears would flood back and overwhelm him.

Betrayed by our leaders, each of us had suffered a wound to our soul, and that is the sort of wound that does not easily heal. For Klein, it was far more painful than the shrapnel he took on March 4.

As for East and me, we sure as hell were not going to give in and let the machine chase us out.

After the COI's decision was announced, East was ordered to Camp Pendleton to account for his actions on March 9 directly to Helland.

Because it dealt with an intelligence mission, East's BOI was classified. The result, however, became public: Helland banned East from any future operational assignments with MARSOC. For all intents and purposes, he was kicked out of special operations.

Being cut down like that was a cruel blow and he took it hard. Also battling cancer, he was weakened by the radiation and surgery. But East being East, he refused to accept defeat on either front. Not only did he conquer his cancer but amazingly he returned to combat!

In the Marines, one of the highest accolades for an officer is for his men to say that they would "pick up a rifle and follow." That is how the men of Fox Company felt about East.

"He strikes me," said Todd at the COI, "as one to be more concerned with his Marines and the troops under him than himself." Reece too had made no bones about his feelings toward Fox Company's officers: "I'd follow them to the end of the world."

After recovering his health, East returned to the infantry and was selected as a company commander in the 2nd Battalion, 2nd Marine Regiment. He returned to Afghanistan too, to vicious fighting in Helmand

Province, in late 2009. After exiting active service, he joined the Marine Corps Reserve and has since kept on serving his country in a civilian role.

The MARSOC 7 were nearly crushed beneath the weight of a bureaucracy infested with careerism and the abuse of power by senior officers. Instead of rewarding subordinates for being willing to stand up, commanders rewarded them for how well they bowed down. The result was a generation of followers, not leaders. They offered leadership from the rear, leadership by email.

Fox Company was "failed by a perfect storm of dirty officers," Morgan charged in a press interview. "It's like some sort of cancer is afflicting the officer corps of the United States Armed Forces. General Amos disgraced himself (numerous charges of unlawful command influence, with two cases overturned as a result)... Gen. Petraeus disgraced himself (an extramarital affair, breach of security, and lying to investigators).

"The COI clearly implicated Kearney, Nicholson and Pihana as being at best incompetent and at worst culpable of criminality. Yet, no action was taken against any of these.

Incompetence was rewarded instead of punished."

Haas was soon moved to Special Operations Command Africa, promoted to major general and then appointed Director of Force Management and Development, Special Operations Command. Before Haas retired, he was named deputy chief of staff of the Resolute Support Mission, whose commanding general was none other than Nicholson.

Haas was never reprimanded for an incident in which he was caught lying, under oath, at the COI.

When he was sworn in, Haas was asked if there was anyone else in the room with him, for security purposes. He replied, "No." But as he fielded questions via live video from the Bagram headquarters of CJSOTF-A, Woodard, East's military attorney, noticed him frequently look to his right before he responded. When Woodard brought the awkward off-camera glances to the attention of Lecce, the panel members were apprised of the situation.

Panel president Porter asked Haas to stop his testimony and Lecce again asked him if he was alone. This time, Haas acknowledged that his staff judge advocate, essentially his lawyer, was present. Haas was consulting with him while testifying and had lied about it to the panel.

Then there was Montanus, who nabbed multiple red carpet assignments, from carrying the "football" (the briefcase with the nuclear launch codes) for President George W. Bush to serving as the commanding officer of the oldest post in the Corps, the Marine Barracks in Washington, DC. A highly coveted assignment, he was responsible for the ceremonial Silent Drill Unit which performed at notable military funerals as well as countless parades and events attended by the President, lawmakers, and other dignitaries.

The commandant who selected Montanus for that post?

Amos.

Finally, I understood the reason for the oddly distant reaction I received from Amos at the Officers' Club. Looking at the name tape on my uniform, he realized that I was the officer set to command the first Marine special ops company. Montanus, one of his boys, had objected to my assignment—and therefore Amos was not happy either.

If Montanus could not bury Fox Company, Amos sure could. As revealed during the COI, an unnamed general had ordered Fox Company to be stripped of all support during our training. I was now certain that general was Amos.

With Montanus at the Marine Barracks, Amos continued to play the protective godfather. In 2012, Amos traveled to all major Marine commands across the globe to impress upon each of them that he would not tolerate sexual assault. A lawsuit had recently been filed by eight female Marines, both enlisted and officer, alleging they'd been raped at the Marine Barracks. On the heels of tremendous pressure from Congress to address the issue in the military, the commandant pledged he would hold lieutenant colonels and colonels "accountable for acts of sexual misconduct inside their commands."

Yet, somehow, Montanus escaped unscathed. He later was appointed the Director of Humanities and senior Marine at the Naval Academy before retiring after a sunset tour with the European Command in Stuttgart, Germany.

Col. Montanus and Gen. Amos entertain Secretary of Defense Leon Panetta

Nicholson became a media darling. He basked in the spotlight when he returned to Afghanistan in 2008 and NBC's *Nightly News* dubbed him "Mr. Fix-it," the superhero Army officer who would win the war once and for all. Ascending to the rank of major general and then pinned with a fourth star, he took command of all coalition forces in Afghanistan.

In 2012, Nicholson invited *New York Times* reporter Carlotta Gall, who penned that paper's articles about the ambush of Fox Company, into his chambers at the Pentagon for an interview she requested for a book. In *The Wrong Enemy*, which would be published in 2014, Nicholson and Gall once again took aim at Fox Company.

Gall lauded Nicholson's "strong sense of right and wrong. That stood out with his public reaction to calamity on March 4, 2007, when a U.S. Marine Special Operations Company ran amok along a busy main highway... In the panic and confusion after the bomb, the Marines reacted ferociously, blasting through the supposed ambush, firing indiscriminately at passing cars, pedestrians, and even people working in the fields. Along a ten-mile stretch of road, they killed as many as nineteen people and wounded fifty others."

Shockingly, despite the findings of the COI, Nicholson did not disagree, and told her that the fault was in our "training, leadership, and discipline, there were lapses in all three."

Gall wrote that "when I asked him later why he reacted to the shooting so strongly, his answer showed a deep sympathy and affinity for the Afghans. Nicholson said, 'These people, they have lives of such hardship and endure such deprivation that if you take away their respect, if you show disrespect to them, you have offended them much more deeply than say a Westerner can be offended by similar actions... It is inconceivable how damaging it is to show disrespect to these people.'"

The self-aggrandizing Nicholson had no such qualms about disrespecting Americans under his command. He never retracted or apologized for his comments condemning Fox Company prior to the completion of a formal investigation, despite Congressman Jones' official written request.

In 2016, Nicholson boldly told the Senate Armed Services Committee that "since 9/11, the U.S. campaign in Afghanistan has largely defined my service." I guess he considered that a badge of honor instead of what it actually was—a sign of abject failure.

Four years after bombs were dropped on Pearl Harbor, our enemy surrendered unconditionally. Yet our great nation could not win a war against people wearing flip-flops, building homemade explosives, and using weapons designed in the 1940s.

The war in Afghanistan became the longest war in American history. There was something wrong—and the blame starts at the top. Our military leadership failed our country and the men and women who do the fighting.

The COIN strategy developed by Petraeus found mixed success in Iraq but was an unmitigated disaster in Afghanistan. The two countries are not the same, not even in their driving habits, as Fox Company discovered.

Because of aggressive operations in Afghanistan from 2001-2005, Al-Qaeda and Taliban forces were routed. Then, in 2006, the COIN doctrine was applied to Afghanistan—and violence sharply escalated. In 2007, more foreign fighters entered Afghanistan than in any previous year, and the U.S. death toll (100) was the highest of any previous year. In 2008, that ignominious record was broken, with 113 deaths.

With the situation growing ever more perilous—Adm. Mike Mullen, Chairman of the Joint Chiefs of Staff, called it "precarious and urgent"—Afghanistan received a surge in troops, just as Iraq had. But the COIN doctrine continued, and the surge failed. Once the defensive mindset of COIN took hold, there was little chance we would ever win the war in Afghanistan. As gamblers say, "You can't win it unless you're in it."

In 2014, the U.S. began to pull back its troops. The withdrawal was celebrated by Islamic extremists, earning their cause more recruits around the globe. While our remaining troops were only there to "advise and assist" the Afghan military, the war went on and Americans continued to die—fifty-six service members and 101 civilian contractors in 2014. In December of that year, the coalition officially ended combat operations in the country—and not surprisingly, the Taliban made a major comeback, joined by a new militant force, the Islamic State of Iraq and the Levant (ISIL) aka ISIS. On February 9, 2017, Nicholson, by then a general, told Congress that coalition forces in Afghanistan were facing a "stalemate."

Ten years after Fox Company was kicked out of Afghanistan, the strategy promoted by Petraeus, Mattis, Nicholson, and others, was wholly discredited. Putting the final stake in COIN was the announcement in October 2017 that Mattis had approved a change in the ROE—no longer did U.S. troops have to be in contact with enemy forces before opening fire.

Yet not a single general was held accountable for the failure of the COIN doctrine. Some were so fearful for their careers should the American public become aware of their folly that they were willing to destroy the lives of innocent servicemen, the men of Fox Company.

Kearney, who like Hejlik never dared to step foot into or testify at the COI, pinned on a third star after the trial and became the deputy commander of SOCOM later in 2008.

That September, Acting Defense Department Inspector General Gordon Heddell announced that Kearney did not abuse his authority or exert undue command influence in removing us from Afghanistan.

Curiously, Heddell's decision was almost completely based on the result of Pihana's investigation and the initial opinion of Nicholson—despite the COI concluding that Pihana's investigation was fatally flawed and Nicholson later admitting that he should not have recommended our removal.

Secretary of Defense Mattis meets with Gen. John Nicholson, ISAF Commander, Kabul, Afghanistan (Courtesy of ISAF Public Affairs Officer)

The decision, dated July 10, was made while the Inspector General of the Department of Defense was Army Lt. Gen. Claude Kicklighter, who previously served as Chief of Staff, Department of Veterans Affairs, under Jim Nicholson, Gen. Nicholson's uncle. Kicklighter departed his post on July 13.

Kearney served at SOCOM until 2010. He retired in 2012. By then, he had gifted Pihana with a Distinguished Service medal. Pihana was also given one of only a handful of colonel level command assignments within the Air Force Special Operations Command. He retired in 2017.

Kearney has since said that the MARSOC 7 incident and aftermath "destroyed my career" because he never received his fourth star. In 2015, showing no remorse for negatively impacting our lives, he maintained that expelling Fox Company from Afghanistan "was the easiest decision

I've ever made...with the toughest blowback that I've ever had in my military career."

Even Hejlik distanced himself from Kearney.

Only months after condemning us and standing next to me as I announced I was being relieved of command of Fox Company, Hejlik told the AP: "Obviously, it was not my decision to bring the company out of theater.... I will never second guess the commander on the ground. I will say, I did not agree with it. To this day, I do not agree with it."

Hejlik was subsequently awarded a third star and promoted to lieutenant general. He succeeded Amos as commanding general of the II Marine Expeditionary Force before being named commanding general of Marine Forces Command, controlling all Marines in the eastern half of the U.S. and throughout Africa. He retired in 2012.

A few weeks after the COI, I came face-to-face with Lecce while on line at a Camp Lejeune chow hall. He tried to be chummy, as if nothing had happened between us. But when I spoke to him, probably a little louder than a major should when addressing a colonel about his unlawful interrogations with NCIS, he suddenly became nervous.

He took me by the elbow and walked us outside, where we could speak in private.

"I was just part of the process," he grunted.

"I know what your role was, sir," I said, "but you crossed the line when you harassed and threatened my Marines."

He offered no excuse, no explanation.

Lecce was subsequently promoted to major general directly from the rank of colonel, leapfrogging brigadier general, and was appointed staff judge advocate to the Commandant of the Marine Corps in 2018, becoming the highest ranking legal advisor in the Corps. The announcement was made by then-Secretary of Defense Mattis, who had ordered the COI.

Even Ukeiley was able to dodge serious repercussions for his improper conduct. When the COI released its recommendations, the final one was that Ukeiley "be charged with dereliction of duty (Article 92 UCMJ) for his performance as MARSOC LNO, but specifically for his actions and inactions on 4 March 2007." But he was not charged. A panel member did issue a ten-day letter on him, preventing his promotion to lieutenant colonel. But Ukeiley was allowed to continue his service until he retired as the CO of the Marine Corps Intelligence School.

Only one person received an honor he deserved.

On a sunny Tuesday morning, July 8, 2008, behind the 2nd MSOB headquarters building at Camp Lejeune, a small group of Fox Company Marines stood in formation—and I pinned a Purple Heart on Klein's chest.

He had faced the impact of a van full of explosives detonating a mere ten feet in front of him, wounding him and knocking him to the floor of his Humvee. To protect his fellow Marines, he courageously stood back up and engaged the enemy in a Taliban controlled town.

Klein was a hero.

I told him we were brothers and we would be in this battle together until it ended, until every member of Fox Company was free of any stain from March 4.

As I read aloud the award's citation, the big man fought back a wave of emotion. He almost cried.

So did I.

Epilogue
Always Faithful

"I am concerned for the security of our great nation; not so much because of any threat from without, but because of the insidious forces working from within."
—*Gen. Douglas MacArthur*

Major Fred Galvin

As for Filthy Fred, I had no intention of leaving the Corps. As my tour of duty on the Rock neared its end, I requested an assignment on the west coast where I'd first put on a Marine uniform.

Instead, I was sent to a Navy base in Virginia.

In the summer of 2012, I checked into a Marine Corps Security Force Regiment in Norfolk, Virginia, to command a unit called 1st FAST (Fleet

Anti-terrorism Security Teams). There are three FAST companies; 1st FAST was tasked with Europe and Africa. They are the SWAT teams of the Marines, designed to protect vital national assets from embassies to nuclear facilities at naval bases. When needed, FAST responds, well, fast.

The first time my 1st FAST company readied for action was after an attack by Islamic extremists made international headlines.

Christopher Stevens, the U.S. ambassador to Libya, sensed a crisis coming and sent numerous communiques requesting the State Department beef up security at our embassy in the capital of Tripoli and the diplomatic compound in Benghazi. Those requests were ignored or denied. As the situation deteriorated, two platoons of 1st FAST were pre-positioned in Rota, Spain. They were sitting on gear, ready to go, with our C-40 cargo planes waiting on the runway.

But the order to deploy never came.

On the 11th anniversary of the terrorist attacks of September 11, the facility in Benghazi was stormed and torched. Two Americans died, including Stevens; two others were killed at an annex nearby. The next morning, as I coordinated the deployment from Norfolk, FAST's 6th Platoon was on the ground in Tripoli taking control of the embassy. FAST secured the building for the next ninety days, until a unit of Marine infantry arrived.

After commanding nine more 1st FAST deployments over nearly two years, I retired from the Marines.

It was not by choice.

I was only forty-three years old. I had served for twenty-seven of those years, active and reserve. Despite everything that had happened, the Marines were still my family. I enjoyed being part of something special, where you had the opportunity to do extraordinary things and become a part of history. I loved the Marines and wanted to continue to serve.

But because I had not been selected for promotion to lieutenant colonel, thanks to March 4, I had reached a dead end. An officer either moves up or out. I was given a retirement date, April 1, 2014. It seemed only appropriate that it was April Fools' Day.

I told my commander I didn't want a ceremony. But he ordered me to submit to an official farewell. It was informal though, attended during a Tuesday morning breakfast by a few friends at a golf course restaurant in Norfolk.

Cajoled into saying a few parting words, I got choked up and managed to put together only a couple of sentences. I can't remember what I said but I know what I thought: Being a Marine was why I was born. Being a Marine was who I was.

Now that part of my life was over.

Returning to hometown Kansas City as a civilian, I was thrown into an unfamiliar world. I applied for more than 700 jobs—and could not land one. All a potential employer had to do was a quick internet search to find press reports about killing innocent men, women, and children, and being put on trial by the Marine Corps. No one would hire me.

Out of desperation, I started my own business, coordinating the sales and installation of drive-up ATM machines. Among my duties was transporting cash to and from ATMs in the worst sections of the city. Believe me, carrying around $100,000 at one in the morning in some of those areas, all by myself, was as dangerous as anything I did in a foreign combat zone.

During those nights I could hardly keep myself from laughing as I recalled Qomandan saying he had all that Afghani money in his Prado but did not need to carry a weapon. He and his money wouldn't have lasted ten minutes in the Prospect Avenue or Van Brunt neighborhoods of Kansas City!

I also continued my mission for Fox Company—to do everything I possibly could to clear the reputations of my Marines.

The Corps didn't make my task easy.

When I again requested copies of the NCIS audio and video tapes, MARCENT responded that they had been destroyed, a convenient outcome for them. When I filed a Freedom of Information Act (FOIA) request in 2011 for the release of documents from the COI, the Marines stonewalled. They did the same to Morgan, who repeatedly came to our defense in public, when he submitted several FOIA requests.

Only after I hired an attorney to push the matter in 2015 did we begin to receive thousands of pages of documents. Telling the true story of Fox

Company here would not have been possible without those documents, many of them newly declassified.

That same year, we urged the new Marine Commandant, Gen. Joseph Dunford, who succeeded Amos, to issue a public apology to the men of Fox Company. He responded in a letter that "no Marines from MSOC-F faced judicial or adverse administrative action for the events on March 4, 2007, nor is there any adverse information in their military records associated with this incident."

In other words, nothing happened to them, so get over it. It was hardly the apology I had hoped for.

Congressman Jones tried a different approach. On January 3, 2017, he introduced House Resolution 21:

RESOLUTION

Expressing the sense of the House of Representatives regarding the firefight that occurred on March 4, 2007, between members of the United States Marine Corps and enemy forces in Bati Kot District, Nangarhar Province, Afghanistan.

Whereas during the morning of March 4, 2007, 30 Marines of Fox Company, Marine Special Operations Command, on patrol in Bati Kot District, Nangarhar Province, Afghanistan, were attacked in a complex ambush by enemy forces;

Whereas the Marines of Fox Company responded to the attack with proportionate defensive fire in accordance with the existing Rules of Engagement;

Whereas, in their response to the ambush, the Marines of Fox Company did not engage in the intentional or indiscriminate killing of any civilians;

Whereas, as commander of Theater Special Operations forces, Lieutenant General Frank Kearney prematurely decided to expel the entire Marine Special Operations Company from Afghanistan notwithstanding their appropriate response to an attack by the enemy;

> Whereas General Kearney skewed public perception regarding the incident with his statements, which led to an Inspector General investigation into his actions;
>
> Whereas, not only was the response by General Kearney unprecedented, but none of the investigations that have been completed would warrant such action, and General Kearney's decision damaged the development of the Marine Special Operations Command and the personal livelihood of these Marines; and
>
> Whereas the Marines conduct during the complex ambush was exemplary and reflected the high standards to which they were trained: Now, therefore, be it
>
> Resolved, That it is the sense of the House of Representatives that the Commandant of the United States Marine Corps should issue a public document certifying that members of Fox Company of the Marine Special Operations Command were not at fault in the firefight that occurred on March 4, 2007, between members of Fox Company and enemy forces in Bati Kot District, Nangarhar Province, Afghanistan, and the Marines of Fox Company involved in this incident deserve to have their names cleared.

The resolution was never voted upon. Perhaps it was a coincidence that Mattis had just been nominated for, and was soon to be confirmed as, Secretary of Defense. Perhaps. (See Appendix V for a similar 2018 Congressional Record entry from Congressman Rohrabacher.)

But I was grateful for Jones' effort. He stood up for us when few others did and I wanted to thank him in a special way. So I gave him a paddle.

Each World War II Raider was issued a small wooden paddle which they used to row their rubber rafts during amphibious operations. They would keep that paddle throughout their career—and a paddle became a cherished symbol of the Raiders. That tradition was continued by Recon

Marines who, along with the dreaded sling rope, carry a paddle throughout training, whether on land, sea or air.

When a Recon Marine leaves active duty or is killed in action, his brothers-in-arms take his paddle, polish it, and garnish it with adornments that have personal meaning for that Marine as well as the history of Recon Marines. He or his next of kin is then presented the paddle as a cherished symbol of his service.

For Jones, I created a paddle that symbolized his significant impact on the lives of the MARSOC 7 and all of Fox Company, dressed it up in parachute cord, and presented it to him at his office in Greenville, North Carolina as a token of our appreciation.

Congressman Walter Jones stands next to the paddle made by Major Galvin for his support in the MARSOC 7's exoneration

On January 2, 2019, the first business day after Mattis officially departed as Secretary of Defense, the Department of the Navy's Board for

Correction of Naval Records announced the following decision, which had been made May 24, 2018 but was not revealed until seven months later:

"The Board, after noting Petitioner was exonerated by the COI for the response to the 4 March 2007 ambush, concluded this event corrupted the judgment of the RS [Reviewing Senior, who was Montanus] and ultimately resulted in Petitioner being removed from theater. The Board determined the enemy information operation and responses of senior leaders were the proximate cause of the MSOC-F redeployment and actions taken against Petitioner were 'collateral damage.' The Board determined the events of 4 March 2007 set in motion events that contributed to the unsuccessful operations of 9 March 2007 and the perception Petitioner lost operation control... The Board also noted the March 2012 BOI did not find Petitioner's performance during the March 2007 incidents was substandard."

Almost twelve years after the ambush, Task Force Violent, the MARSOC 7 and Fox Company were finally vindicated—and so was I.

The report continued: "For the period 1 June 2011 to 7 June 2011... (the Board) found Petitioner rightfully took a moral stand when he challenged Lt. Col H's [Homiak's] decision to needlessly expose Marines and Afghan civilians to injury and death... The Board concluded the adverse fitness report was Lt. Col H's unprofessional and unjustifiable response to being challenged about his tactical decisions which placed Marine lives at great risk on 6 June 2011."

The board wiped my slate clean.

"Upon the removal of the adverse fitness reports...an SSB (Special Selection Board) shall be convened to consider Petitioner for selection to promotion to Lt. Col."

But it wasn't to be.

Despite being cleared, despite having twice the number of commendation awards, more than twice the number of combat deployments, more than twice the number of overseas deployments, more than twice the amount of time as a commanding officer, executive officer or operations officer, and more than twice the amount of time serving on an operations staff than any other major during the evaluation period, I was informed on July 17 that the board had declined to select me for promotion.

None of the MARSOC 7 has received the Marine Special Operator Insignia each deserves for his service in Afghanistan in early 2007—and Fox Company is still waiting for an apology from the Marine Corps.

What happened to the Marines of Fox Company should never happen again. If, by telling our story, I can spark a desire to prevent the abuse of authority that victimized us, I will have done my duty.

Rarely is making your mark in the military about jumping on a grenade or taking a two thousand yard sniper shot. Most of the time, it is simply about trying to do everything you can for the men beside you. They are my brothers, and I love them like brothers.

I never lost a man.

Semper Fidelis - Always Faithful
—Marine Corps motto

Appendices

THE UNITED STATES OF AMERICA

THIS IS TO CERTIFY THAT
THE PRESIDENT OF THE UNITED STATES OF AMERICA
HAS AWARDED THE

BRONZE STAR MEDAL
(WITH COMBAT DISTINGUISHING DEVICE)
TO
CAPTAIN FRED C. GALVIN, UNITED STATES MARINE CORPS

FOR

HEROIC ACHIEVEMENT FROM 15 FEBRUARY TO 1 AUGUST 2005

GIVEN THIS 8TH DAY OF NOVEMBER 2005

LIEUTENANT GENERAL, U.S. MARINE CORPS
COMMANDER, U.S. MARINE CORPS FORCES
CENTRAL COMMAND

COMMANDER, US MARINE CORPS FORCES, CENTRAL COMMAND

The President of the United States takes pleasure in presenting the
BRONZE STAR MEDAL to

CAPTAIN FRED C. GALVIN
UNITED STATES MARINE CORPS

for service as set forth in the following

CITATION:

For heroic achievement in connection with combat operations against the enemy as 4th Platoon Commander, 1st Force Reconnaissance Company, Regimental Combat Team 2, 2d Marine Division, II Marine Expeditionary Force (Forward) in support of Operation IRAQI FREEDOM 04-06 from February 2005 to August 2005. Captain Galvin led his platoon on 41 complex raids throughout his area of operations. His courageous leadership directly contributed to the capture or killing of 147 members of various insurgent cells, to include 29 enemies classified as High Value Individuals. On 15 March, Captain Galvin led his platoon on an eight kilometer dismounted infiltration into the northern Jazirah Desert resulting in the capture of 12 insurgents, to include a high-level weapons dealer who had been sourcing insurgents from Husaybah to Mosul. Later that month, he led his platoon on a time sensitive, 11-hour helicopter borne interdiction mission against insurgents detected crossing into Iraq that culminated in the capture of 11 foreign fighters. On 8 July, Captain Galvin conducted a platoon pre-dawn dismounted raid across a pontoon bridge onto Jubbah Island, which resulted in the capture of 4 insurgents and the discovery of a significant weapons cache. By his zealous initiative, courageous actions, and exceptional dedication to duty, Captain Galvin reflected great credit upon himself and upheld the highest traditions of the Marine Corps and the United States Naval Service.

The Combat Distinguishing Device is authorized.

For the President,

J. F. SATTLER
LIEUTENANT GENERAL, U. S. MARINE CORPS
COMMANDER, U. S. MARINE CORPS FORCES, CENTRAL COMMAND

Summary of Action

Captain Galvin was in receipt of Imminent Danger Pay during this period. The Combat Distinguishing Device is authorized.

Captain Fred C. Galvin is enthusiastically recommended for the Bronze Star Medal while serving as 4th Platoon Commander, 1st Force Reconnaissance Company, Regimental Combat Team-2 (RCT-2), 2d Marine Division, II Marine Expeditionary Force (Forward) in support of Operation IRAQI FREEDOM 04-06 from 15 February to 1 August 2005.

During this period, Captain Galvin aggressively led his platoon on 41 highly complex and dangerous raids throughout the 30,000 square mile Regimental Combat Team 2 Area of Operations (AO) to capture high-level insurgent leaders and facilitators. Operating almost exclusively in periods of low lunar illumination, Captain Galvin expertly utilized a wide-range of raid insertion techniques to constantly keep Anti-Iraqi Elements off balance, ranging from helicopter inserts squarely within the target area, off-set helicopter inserts followed by long-range dismounted infiltrations, motorized infiltrations utilizing both High Mobility Multi-purpose Wheeled Vehicles (HMMWV) and Light Armored Reconnaissance Vehicles (LAR), and an amphibious infiltration employing small craft on the Euphrates River. His courageous leadership and sterling example directly contributed to the capture of 126 members of various insurgent cells operating throughout AO Denver, to include 29 targeted cell leaders and facilitators. Coincident with these captures was the discovery of numerous weapons caches throughout the target locations. In concert, these captures and cache discoveries greatly disrupted the ability of insurgent groups to adversely influence the strategically vital areas of Ramadi, Fallujah, and Baghdad. Among the over 40 superbly executed raid missions, a number stand out in bold relief:

On 15 March, Captain Galvin led his platoon on a daring raid deep into the northern Jazirah Desert in the vicinity of Bayji to strike a known insurgent safe haven and arms smuggling waypoint that, due to its remoteness, had seen little Coalition presence throughout Operation IRAQI FREEDOM. Conducting a heliborne off-set insert followed by an eight kilometer dismounted infiltration throughout a moonless night, Captain Galvin's platoon achieved complete surprise by breaching multiple targets simultaneously at the prescribed time-on-target, resulting in the capture of a high-level weapons smuggler whose influence extended throughout AO Denver, as well as 11 other insurgents. He skillfully integrated members of the Iraqi Freedom Guard, which facilitated the rapid exploitation of the target sites. This textbook raid was a result of Captain Galvin's flawless detailed planning, preparations, and execution and served to signal insurgent cells that there were no true safe havens, even in the most remote stretches of AO Denver.

Captain Galvin again demonstrated his cool leadership on 25-26 March when he was tasked with interdicting an unknown number of foreign fighters that had been detected, through multiple intelligence collections assets, crossing the Jordanian border into Iraq. With very little time and information with which to prepare, Captain Galvin quickly task organized his platoon and seamlessly integrated members of a highly specialized Iraqi strike force supported by members of another U.S. government agency and launched in two CH-53E helicopters to interdict the foreign fighters at a pre-determined point along Main Supply Route (MSR) Mobile in the southern portion of AO Denver. Over the next 11 hours, Captain Galvin led his platoon in the establishment of multiple snap heliborne vehicle checkpoints along MSR Mobile. Several times throughout the night, he was forced to re-embark his platoon on the helicopters to re-establish checkpoints at new locations farther east based on updated intelligence. When the targets had finally stopped at a truck stop at the 160 kilometer marker of MSR Mobile at 0230 on 26 March, Captain Galvin led his platoon in an unsupported raid in an area well outside the range of any Coalition Force reinforcement and captured 11 foreign fighters destined for the greater Ramadi area. His relentless pursuit in accomplishing this mission in an area that was well known as being a haven for transiting insurgents, while knowing there was little chance of timely reinforcement, was a testament to his courage and unbending resolve and that of the Marines and sailors in his charge.

On 16 April, 1st Force Reconnaissance Company (-) conducted a raid in northeast Husaybah to seize an empty mansion to establish a base of operations to support future raids against insurgent cells in the greater Al Qaim region. While enroute to the objective, the Company came under an intense 1,300 meter long complex ambush in Karabilah consisting of Improvised Explosive Devices (IEDs) combined with machine gun and rocket-propelled grenade fires. Captain Galvin led the lead element of the Company convoy through the ambush, directing the fires of his Marines while concurrently coordinating with convoy elements to his rear and with his Joint Tactical Air Controller (JTAC) to obtain immediate air support. Reaching the targeted building, Captain Galvin led his platoon in the rapid seizure of the objective despite meeting enemy small arms fire. Additionally, he quickly coordinated the establishment of a medevac landing zone and was instrumental in the rapid evacuation of three wounded Marines to Camp Al Qaim for medical treatment.

On 20 April, 1st Force Reconnaissance Company (-) led a clearing operation of the 440-Housing Area in southwest Husaybah astride the Syrian border in an effort to relieve some pressure against Company I, 3d Battalion, 2d Marines at Camp Gannon after a series of Suicide Vehicle-borne Explosive Device (SVBIED) attacks against the embattled compound. In a display of controlled aggressiveness, Captain Galvin led his platoon in the clearing of over 60 structures within this known launching point for insurgent attacks against Company I, providing a security buffer for Camp Gannon while sending a clear signal that further attacks emanating from this area would be met with a significant Marine response.

On 27 May, Captain Galvin was instrumental in the capture of 15 known insurgents associated with a cell in the Dulab area just south of Baghdadi. That cell had been responsible for numerous rocket attacks against Al Asad Air Base over the previous six months. In another flawless performance, he led his platoon on a long dismounted infiltration to separate target sites. His platoon achieved absolute surprise, resulting in the capture of the cell leader who was the technical expert behind all of the rocket attacks, as well as other members of the insurgent cell.

On 18 June, Captain Galvin led his platoon as part of a larger company-sized operation to conduct a Tactical Recovery of Aircraft and Personnel (TRAP) of a U.S. Special Operations Command MH-53J helicopter that had sustained significant damage during an operation along the Syrian border north of Husaybah. Flying to the scene within hours of notification, he quickly assessed the situation and established his sector of security while concurrently setting over watch on the dominating escarpment to the north of the crash site. Over the ensuing two days, Captain Galvin's leadership contributed greatly to the ultimate recovery of the highly sensitive aircraft.

Utilizing yet another insertion technique to perfection in the early morning of 25 June, Captain Galvin led his Marines in a heliborne assault of a known insurgent safe haven in Abu Wherda on the north side of the Euphrates to capture a tribal sheik that was responsible for numerous attacks against Coalition Forces in the Hit-Hadithah corridor. Landing virtually in the middle of a group of target buildings in two CH-53E helicopters under low lunar illumination, Captain Galvin led his platoon in the rapid clearing of six separate target sites, resulting in the capture of the targeted sheik and eight other members of his insurgent cell.

After just concluding his platoon's post-operations maintenance and debriefs from the aforementioned 25 June raid, Captain Galvin's platoon was tasked with a short-fused raid to exploit a weapons cache located in an area of dense palm groves just south of the city of Hit that had just recently been discovered by an aerial collections platform. Again embarking on CH-53E helicopters with little information, he rapidly coordinated a scheme of maneuver and launched into an area known to be a hotbed of insurgent activity. Over the next 18 hours, Captain Galvin led his platoon in the discovery of a significant weapons cache that, if left undiscovered, could have had a significant negative impact on the planned Operation SWORD in Hit scheduled to commence the next day. While staged for heliborne extract in the late morning of 26 June, Captain Galvin's platoon interdicted a car full of insurgents moving through their area enroute to Hit. The ensuing firefight resulted in four enemy killed, to include a known insurgent leader that had been on the RCT-2 list of high value insurgent leaders and facilitators. Over the course of this 36-hour period, Captain Galvin's platoon dramatically impacted the ability of Anti-Iraqi Elements to conduct operations in the Hit-Hadithah corridor.

In the early morning hours of 8 July, as the opening gambit of a larger Task Force cordon and search of the village of Jubbah that straddles the Euphrates River north of Baghdadi, Captain Galvin led his reinforced platoon of over 100 Marines and sailors on a bold foot-mobile assault across a pontoon bridge onto the island of Jubbah. Jubbah Island housed insurgent leaders who had recently fled from the greater Hit area as a result of RCT-2's Operation SWORD. His aggressive spirit set the stage for the rapid clearing of the island and both the southern and northern portions of Jubbah village, contributing to the capture of 11 known insurgents, 8 of which had previously been classified as high value individuals. Additionally, his platoon uncovered a significant weapons and munitions cache on the island and nearly $50,000 in U.S. currency.

Captain Galvin also led his platoon on six separate multi-day ambush missions throughout the Hit-Hadithah corridor and in the greater Rutbah area to kill IED and mine emplacers who had consistently targeted Coalition vehicles on the primary MSRs and ASRs. Over the course of these missions, Captain Galvin's platoon killed 18 insurgents attempting to emplace IEDs and mines along regular convoy and resupply routes throughout AO Denver. His regular success rate on these missions was due largely to the detailed pattern analysis of IED and mine attacks and discoveries and his corresponding expert positioning of his ambush locations to leverage that analysis.

His platoon was also instrumental in larger-scale operations in AO Denver. During RCT-2's Operation MATADOR from 8-14 May, Captain Galvin led his Marines in essentially cutting off the line of withdrawal to Syria for foreign fighters by providing four days of over watch of a key chokepoint from positions on top of the escarpment just north of the RCT's primary objectives in Ramana.

Throughout this period of consistently high-tempo combat operations, Captain Galvin demonstrated tremendous courage, highly advanced technical and tactical skills, and superb leadership in the successful accomplishment of over 50 dangerous and complex Force Reconnaissance missions. He routinely operated with his small force in known high-threat areas and, with the exception of the Karabilah ambush, achieved complete surprise on every raid while conducting surreptitious infiltrations and rapidly dominating the different target sites. He has led from the front in over 40 motorized movements that covered thousands of kilometers across AO Denver while routinely traversing some of the most dangerous roads and trail networks in order to successfully accomplish his assigned missions. His small-scale tactical actions clearly achieved operational-level results in supporting 2d Marine Division's larger disruption effort throughout the RCT-2 Area of Operations.

As highlighted above, Captain Galvin is enthusiastically recommended for the Bronze Star Medal.

II

Hejlik's Submission to the COI

Maj. Gen. Hejlik provided a written submission dated December 19, 2007 to the COI titled "Interrogatories for Commander, U. S. Marine Corps Forces Special Operations Command." Pertinent questions and answers were:

> Q. What were Maj. Galvin's responsibilities while under your observation/command?
>
> A. The training of MSOC-F in Direct Action and Special Reconnaissance.
>
> Q. Why was Maj. Galvin selected to be the first MSOC commanding officer?
>
> A. I personally interviewed him and found him to be the most qualified candidate based upon his previous experience with reconnaissance units.
>
> Q. What were the selection criteria?

A. 1. Leadership, 2. Maturity, 3. Flexibility, 4. Experience, and 5. Joint Special Operations Forces Experience.

Q. What were the challenges for MSOC-F when they were directed to go to Afghanistan vice Iraq?

A. There were many challenges faced by Fox Company as a result of the decision to send them to Afghanistan vice Iraq. The company was unable to focus their training on the specific theater in which they were going to operate, and had to focus on conducting generic DASR techniques, tactics and procedures. Additionally, the Company had very little experience in Afghanistan operations, as most were Operation Iraqi Freedom veterans. While there are differences in the operating environments between Iraq and Afghanistan, both geographically and philosophically, MSOC-F would have faced similar challenges integrating with either CJSOTF-A or CJSOTF-AP (Arabian Peninsula, aka Iraq) given they were a new unit with unknown capabilities.

Q. What changes in training/preparation were made to prepare them for Afghanistan?

A. Any last-minute changes were minor and were primarily implemented onboard ship during transit. These changes included sending a robust ADVON (advanced echelon) forward to establish a footprint and send information on operational overviews back to the MSOC command element on the Marine Expeditionary Unit, including CJSOTF-A Rules of Engagement, briefings, and bringing in an Afghan cultural expert to teach them about Afghanistan and cultural norms while on ship.

Q. Was MSOC-F supposed to be self-supporting or fit into another command's support structure?

A. MSOC-F was designed to be able to support itself tactically with enablers, but the assumption of reliance on support infrastructure (either service common or joint) for additional combat support and combat service support functions for sustainment and maintenance.

Q. What was your impression of the causes of conflicts between Col. Haas and Maj. Galvin?

A. A lack of knowledge and understanding on the interoperability and integration of MSOC-F with CJSOTF-A.

III

Additional Afghan Witness Information

Compiled from statements made to NCIS investigators:

1. Niaz Mohammed declared that none of the workers in the dry riverbed were injured or struck by bullets.
2. Mubarez, a laborer, stated he was in the ditch and could see bullets hitting the ground but none of the workers were struck by bullets.
3. Shakir, the aid project supervisor, stated his personnel never fired their weapons and that the workers in the riverbed were not shot by the Marines.
4. Mohammad Khan, told to come in by his village elder, stated that five minutes after the explosion the ANA arrived. He also stated his cow was shot twice in the neck and died one month later. Upon further questioning, Khan stated his cow had been inside his house, there were no bullet holes in his house, and he did not report its death.
5. Zarab Gul stated he did not see any injured people or damaged vehicles.
6. Sher Pao, team leader for the day laborers, said none of them was injured.

7. Ali Pur stated the Marines stayed on the Spin Pul Bridge for two hours.

8. Nasir heard sporadic, fully automatic machine gun fire and single-round gunfire.

9. Khan Wali stated that even though all three vehicles fired at the laborers, they were not hurt.

10. Khan, a taxi driver, said nobody from the Marines dismounted.

11. Adbul Qadir said several elders encouraged him to report false information to receive financial compensation.

12. Zahidullah Hohistani stated that elders instructed him to claim he was fired upon by coalition forces in order to receive financial compensation.

13. Tahsel stated that Vehicle One opened fire from about one hundred meters and the bullets shattered his front windshield, injuring his eyes and face, and grazing the right side of his head. Shaswar, a passenger, received eye injuries from the windshield fragmentation.

14. Sedaqat, a taxi driver, stated his car was shot multiple times but that he had replaced all the damage (headlight, battery, and engine). He had no proof of any damage and said it had been completely repaired.

15. Hussein stated that either Vehicle Two or Three fired on his car and the taxi ahead of him, but nobody was injured in either vehicle. His vehicle was shot from fifty meters in the headlight and hood area. He had since then sold his car and had no proof of any damage.

16. Mati Ullah, driving a van next to the SVBIED when it exploded, saw the Americans waving at cars to move but never saw the blast or the Americans shooting. He later came in to say he saw the Americans shooting.

17. Qand said the gunners fired at the workers in the dry riverbed, but none were struck.

18. Khan advised that the turret gunners were doing all the shooting.